LEARNING TO TEACH

8

Also available from Continuum:

Helen Nicholson (ed.): *Teaching Drama 11–18*

Martin Blocksidge (ed.): *Teaching Literature 11–18*

Angela Thody, Barbara Gray and Derek Bowden: *Teacher's Survival Guide*

Sue Cowley: *Starting Teaching*

John Beck and Mary Earl (eds): *Key Issues in Secondary Education*

Learning to Teach Drama 11–18

Andy Kempe and Helen Nicholson

CONTINUUM

London and New York

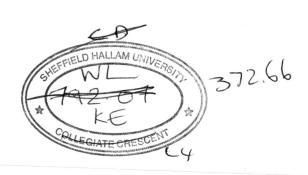

Continuum

The Tower Building   370 Lexington Avenue
11 York Road   New York
Waterloo SE1 7NX   NY 10017-6503

First published 2001

British Library Cataloguing-in-Publication Data
A catalogue record for this book is available from the British Library.

ISBN 0-8264-4841-0

Designed and typeset by Ben Cracknell Studios

Printed and bound in Great Britain by Biddles Ltd, *www.biddles.co.uk*

Contents

Acknowledgements

As this book reflects our experiences in initial teacher training, there are inevitably many people to thank. Student-teachers in the Universities of Cambridge and Reading have taught us a lot about teaching drama. We would particularly like to acknowledge advice and contributions from Barbara Foskett, Bruce Foskett, Hamish Fyfe, June Hurst, Alix Izzard, Jan MacDonald, Sarah Patterson, Kate Tapper and Tom Winskill. As she has now moved on, Helen would like to pay tribute to her former colleagues Gabrielle Cliff Hodges and Mike Younger at Homerton College, Cambridge. Lastly, it has been a pleasure for us to collaborate on this book, giving us the opportunity to acknowledge and celebrate the creativity and skills of drama teachers.

Abbreviations

ACCAC	Awdurdod Cymwysterau Cwricwlwm ac Asesu Cymru (Qualifications, Curriculum and Assessment Authority for Wales)
ACGB	Arts Council of Great Britain
AQA	Assessment and Qualifications Alliance (examinations syndicate)
AT	attainment target
CCEA	Council for the Curriculum, Examinations and Assessment (Northern Ireland)
CEP	Career Entry Profile
DfEE	Department for Education and Employment
Edexcel	examinations syndicate
DENI	Department of Education, Northern Ireland
GCE	General Certificate of Education. (There are two tiers to this qualification: the one-year AS (Advanced Subsidiary) and the two-year A (Advanced))
GCSE	General Certificate of Secondary Education
GNVQ	General National Vocational Qualification
GTCS	General Teaching Council of Scotland
GTP	Graduate Teaching Programme (a school-based training route)
HEI	higher education institution
ICT	Information Communications Technology
IEP	individual education plan (drawn up for pupils with special educational needs)
INSET	In-Service Education of Teachers
ITT	initial teacher training
KS	Key Stage (in secondary schools, pupils are deemed to be in KS3 up to age 14, KS4 between 14–16 and thereafter at KS5)
LEA	local education authority
LMS	local management of schools
NATD	National Association of Teachers of Drama
NATE	National Association of Teachers of English
NC	National Curriculum
NCLN	National Centre for Literacy and Numeracy

ND	National Drama
NLS	National Literacy Strategy
NQT	newly qualified teacher
OCR	Oxford, Cambridge and RSA Examinations (examinations syndicate)
OFSTED	Office for Standards in Education
PGCE	Postgraduate Certificate of Education
QCA	Qualification and Curriculum Authority
QTS	Qualified Teacher Status
RALIC	Reading and Language Information Centre
SAT	standard attainment test
SCITT	school-centred initial teacher training
SEN	special educational needs
SENCO	special educational needs co-ordinator
SQA	Scottish Qualifications Authority
TTA	Teacher Training Agency
WJEC	Welsh Joint Education Committee

x
_____

Beginning Training

Learning to teach drama?

Take a moment to consider the vastness of the concept of drama. We all experience plenty of dramas in our own lives. We do not need to be taught about these kinds of dramas – they just happen to us or because of what we do. Taking another sense of the word, drama is often associated with play, especially play that involves pretending to be someone or something else. Play is an important element of children's learning, and although it may be enhanced by teachers, most children do not have to be taught to play. However, drama also has an aesthetic dimension, is associated with artistic practices and has significance in a diversity of cultural contexts.

This book is about teaching drama in the context of secondary education. Because drama is such a complex subject, with such a wide range of practices, it requires those teaching the subject to undertake a rigorous process in learning how to teach it. Drama education involves exploring and gaining insights into the nature of real life dramas. It is playful in that it draws on and develops young people's aptitude for learning about themselves and the world around them by pretending to be other people in other situations. As a curriculum subject, it gives pupils a practical knowledge of how drama works as an art form and encourages them to recognize how drama is integral to cultures in different times and places.[1]

It is all too easy to take the meaning of a word that is used in so many different ways as self-evident. The consequence of this might well be that, because it figures so large in our language, it is seen as being something simple and that 'teaching' it must therefore be pretty straightforward. Although nothing could be further from the truth, those who wish to teach drama are rarely put off by realizing its complexity. In fact, it is often the very richness of practices that may be included in drama and what may be learned through it that appeals to those who teach it.

Perhaps in some ways the title of this book is misleading. Although it is primarily intended for those who are undertaking initial training as drama teachers, learning to teach drama is a continual process. Drama teachers are always learning, as new practices emerge, as new theatre forms develop, as educational research and policies become integrated into the drama curriculum. When they start on the process of learning to teach drama, people will, inevitably, have many different reasons for wanting to become drama teachers. Some will be able to articulate very precise reasons, others will hold less concrete ideas but may nonetheless have positive views of how the subject has engaged them and how it might contribute to the education of others. The aim of this book is to help those who would like to teach drama to explore the complexities and practicalities of the subject.

Applying for initial teacher training (ITT)

There is an increasingly wide range of routes into teaching and, in times of teacher shortage, new government initiatives intended to attract entrants to the profession emerge. However, there are, broadly speaking, two main ways for graduates to train to be teachers. One is to follow one of the small number of school-centred courses where training is undertaken 'on the job', and the other is to follow a full-time course which is run by a university or higher education institution in partnership with local schools. The second route usually leads to a Postgraduate Certificate in Education (PGCE) with qualified teacher status (QTS), whereas school-based routes usually simply confer qualified teacher status.

There is no doubt that the PGCE is the most popular graduate route into teaching. On these courses, student-teachers have the opportunity to share experiences and expertise with others in the group. This has major advantages, particularly as these courses are designed to integrate educational theory and classroom practice. Subject-lecturers in both drama and education studies encourage student-teachers to read widely, to reflect on their teaching experiences and to extend their understanding of how pupils learn. School-based training routes often have the advantage of providing training in good local schools, and this route may suit those who are tied to a specific region. The disadvantage of such training programmes is that, whilst student-teachers may receive individual attention from senior staff, they may find their work isolating, particularly if there are no other drama specialists in the school.

Finding out about schools

Before applying for an ITT training course, it is sensible to spend a little time in a state secondary school finding out about the realities of teaching. Most schools will accept visitors, and prospective applicants are well advised to write to the headteacher explaining why they wish to visit, what kind of things they hope to be able to see and offering a choice of dates. This will usually be passed to the head of drama, who may well agree to be shadowed for a day. All teachers, and perhaps particularly drama teachers, are extremely busy, so it is important to prepare economical questions in advance. There is a need to keep a sense of proportion when making such visits – some more experienced members of staff may delight in telling horror stories!

Visiting schools: asking questions

Consider carefully what you wish to find out. Remember that you are not making judgements about individual schools or teachers, but finding out about the job of a drama teacher. Questions you may wish to consider are:

- What kinds of drama activities and practices do the younger pupils engage in?
- How has drama teaching changed in the last few years?
- What areas of drama practice are explored at examination level?
- What are the best things about teaching drama? The worst?
- What responsibilities does the teacher have apart from teaching drama?
- Which books would the drama teacher recommend you to read?

Finding out about courses

Applicants may decide to apply for School-Centred Initial Teacher Training courses (SCITT) or Graduate Teaching Programmes (GTP). The majority of applicants, however, will wish to apply for a university-run PGCE course. Details of how to make applications can be found on regional government websites. However, it is important to consider not only the location of courses, but also their particular values and qualities. For PGCE courses, the prospectus will provide details of the overall structure and course content. However, applicants may well wish to undertake more detailed research before making a decision about where to apply.

Some PGCE courses specialize in drama, whereas others offer training in both English and drama. Applicants who are interested in training in both subjects should check the proportion of time spent in each as they vary considerably. They will also need to ensure that their degree course has given them adequate subject-knowledge in both subjects. Other information about PGCE courses can be gleaned from OFSTED reports, which are published on the

Internet and, perhaps most usefully, from teachers in local schools or former students who know about the course. It may also be useful to look for books or articles written by course tutors in order to get an idea of the kind of educational values they espouse. It is also a good idea to find out about the range of placement schools in the partnership; some people will wish to spend some time in middle schools and sixth-form colleges as well as 11–18 schools.

Application forms

For PGCE courses there are standard application forms. Whilst they vary according to region, applicants are usually asked to complete a personal statement in which they outline their reasons for wanting to train as a teacher. These are quite difficult to complete well, and need to be drafted. It is useful to interviewers if they contain information about previous experience with young people, about work in drama and theatre, and identify broad educational values. It is better to be factual rather than whimsical, and to show that the decision to apply for initial teacher training has been made carefully and with some understanding of what teaching involves.

Applicants are asked to supply names and addresses of two referees. In practice, it is unlikely that the second referee will be required to write a reference, but out of courtesy both should be asked before they are named on the form. The first referee will usually be a lecturer on the applicant's undergraduate degree course. If the degree was completed a long time ago, however, it may be more relevant to cite a referee with more recent professional knowledge of the applicant.

Preparing for interview

The purpose of the interview is to consider applicants' potential as teachers, and to assess their suitability for the particular course to which they have applied. The emphasis is very much on potential; candidates are not expected to be able to recite the National Curriculum, although having a basic knowledge of what it entails and where drama fits into it is useful. Nor is it necessary to have a clear view about every educational issue introduced into the conversation. What is expected is an open mind, an ability to think ideas through in discussion and to have some informed ideas about the role of teachers in general and drama teachers in particular. This requires careful preparation.

In order to acquire some up-to-date knowledge about education issues, it is very useful to read the education press. Weekly newspapers written for an audience of teachers and educators, particularly *The Times Educational Supplement*, are more likely to give a clear and accurate account of debates in education, without the sensationalism which sometimes accompanies education stories in other newspapers. Look in particular for articles about drama, English and arts education but also try to discover which major education issues are under discussion.

Many applicants find that evaluating their own experiences as pupils and students of drama is an important part of the preparation process. Consider, for example, what qualities your teachers possessed, what approaches to teaching and learning you found satisfying and successful, and what memories you have about school which are less positive. Reading books about drama education can help candidates compare their own experiences as pupils with contemporary classroom practice. It is wise to go to a major bookshop and scan the shelves for recent drama education books and ask drama teachers for recommendations. In addition, it is very useful to find out about suitable plays for young people and to learn about the education programmes given by different theatre companies.

Although it is likely that the interview will focus in particular on the teaching of drama, it will undoubtedly include questions about the general role of teachers in schools. Drama teachers obviously work as part of a larger team, and many drama teachers are instrumental in the creation of the school community. There is also the pastoral role of the teacher to consider, the role of drama in the life of the school, and issues about literacy, citizenship and other whole-school learning policies. No interviewers will expect applicants to ITT courses to be fully versed with all these issues but they should be prepared to consider them carefully and thoughtfully when asked.

The interview

Many institutions regard the interview process as the first stage of the learning process in initial teacher training, and will have carefully constructed programmes which encourage applicants to think about different aspects of teaching. The nature of interviews varies, and each institution will have evolved ways of working which suit their purposes. The style and form of the interview will reflect the approaches to learning on the course, so it is worthwhile paying attention to them. For PGCE courses, candidates will usually be interviewed by one of the subject-lecturers and a teacher in a local school. Interviews often involve group discussions with other candidates, as well as a brief individual interview. Questions and topics for discussion are likely to be open ended, and will focus on drama education and other general education issues.

Good presentation at interview is important. Candidates for ITT courses must realize that they are applying for a professional training programme and that they will be judged in this light. First impressions are important; if the interview is taking place in a school or in a university candidates will need to arrive on time, with any documentation requested, and be appropriately dressed. The interviewers will also notice how candidates behave towards each other. Interviews for ITT places are unlikely to be competitive as candidates are rarely called if there are insufficient places on the course. In group discussion, therefore, candidates can afford to support each other and offer suggestions which build on the ideas of others. These are, in themselves, important teaching skills which experienced interviewers will notice.

In the individual interview, candidates may be asked to explain aspects of the personal statement from their application form. Interviewers may wish to probe areas of weakness or significant gaps in candidates' subject-knowledge. By the end of the interview, if they have listened carefully, candidates should have a clear idea about what they need to work on before the course begins. It is worthwhile anticipating this process, and many interviewers are impressed by candidates who seem to know their own areas for development and have some idea how to address them. These may or may not be particularly appealing! It may be that candidates have little knowledge about children's literature which is useful to drama teachers and a pleasure to read on holiday, but weaknesses in spelling are serious for teachers; extra work in this area is essential but less exciting. It is better to be honest about any gaps or difficulties – trying to cover them up is always a mistake. Interviewers may need to know if candidates drive or have special reasons why they need to be located in a particular district. This is to aid placement in schools and is not a criteria for acceptance or rejection of the candidate's application to the course.

The interview is a two-way process, and candidates will wish to find out about the course. Interviewers should talk through the structure of the course and point out the relationship between the training programme and practical teaching experience. Candidates may wish to find out about assessment procedures, the kind of workload to expect and how they will be supported in schools. It is helpful if candidates arrive with such questions and leave with realistic expectations about the course. Although most student-teachers really enjoy the year, initial teacher training courses are very hard work.

Interview procedures

Read through these interview questions and procedures, and consider how you would respond.

- Group discussion about the aims and values of a drama department: why should a school include drama in the curriculum?
- How do pupils get better at drama?
- Describe a teacher you admire. What qualities did he or she possess?

- Choose a play you think would be suitable for 11–14 year olds to read which challenges their ideas of drama in performance. How would you teach it?
- What might be the issues for teaching drama in a multi-faith, multi-cultural school?
- Group discussion based on a video extract of a drama lesson: what are pupils learning?
- Describe a Year 7 drama lesson you would like to teach.
- What qualities do you think a pastoral tutor should possess?
- Role play or discussion about responding to challenging behaviour in the classroom.
- Group discussion about a newspaper article on a general educational issue.

Preparing for the training programme

Once candidates have been accepted on a training programme, they will need to consider how to prepare for the course. Individual student-teachers may wish, following interview, to seek advice and begin to address gaps in their own subject-knowledge. To prepare for the ITT course, all student-teachers will need to begin to consider two interrelated elements of drama education: theory and practice. Understanding how theory and practice are related to each other is one of the most important conceptual challenges of the initial teacher training year. In order to address this, it is extremely helpful to undertake some observation in school and focused reading.

For some courses, a period of observation in a primary school is a specific requirement. The purpose of this observation is to focus on the experiences of children in education at different ages. Primary school visits enable student-teachers to understand how children progress, and to observe at first hand how the National Curriculum works at Key Stages 1 and 2. It is therefore helpful to spend time with children of different ages, looking at the structure of the day and how the teacher facilitates learning in different ways and at different times. In preparing for the course, many student-teachers will also arrange to undertake a period of observation in secondary schools. Specific advice about observation is given in the next section, 'Beginning the training programme'. In preparatory visits to schools there is much to learn from spending time in different areas of the school rather than just staying in the drama area.

No creative student-teacher in drama will be satisfied by simply copying the work of experienced teachers. In order to develop their own ways of thinking and working, student-teachers will need to support their ideas with careful reading. There are three different forms of reading which need to be undertaken both before and during the course. These include educational theory, theory and practice of teaching and learning in drama, and research in drama and theatre which might extend student-teachers' own practice and be suitable for pupils in secondary schools. Many training programmes will suggest pre-course reading. It is difficult to digest some of this material without knowledge of the classroom context, but it is important to try and gain an overview of what is available so that specific issues can be revisited later in the course in the light of experience and with new insights.

Beginning the training programme

First visits to school

It is helpful, on entering a new school environment, for student-teachers to review the place as a micro-cosmic community which has its own codes of conduct. It is not easy to understand these codes instantly because this requires knowledge of the wider context in which the school operates. Student-teachers' placement schools may be very different from the ones they attended as pupils or visited prior to joining the training programme. The way drama is taught in the school may also be very different. Equally, making assumptions about schools on the grounds of their names or locations risks subscribing to popular mythologies which can be misleading. Similarly, dismissing out of hand the content of the drama curriculum or the way drama is taught would be unlikely to endear a student-teacher to the staff. It is more sensible, of greater educational value, and certainly more professional, to consider the situation roundly and allow members of the school staff to explain their ethos and ways of working.

When they first visit their placement schools, student-teachers will be introduced to members of staff in school who have particular responsibilities for their professional development. Professional tutors are likely to oversee all the student-teachers in the school, and will have overall responsibility in the school for constructing the school-based elements of the training and induction programme and for assessment of practical teaching competence. Student-teachers will also meet their 'mentors', usually the head of drama, who will work very closely with them and guide them through a structured programme throughout their placement. Both professional tutors and mentors will have undergone training for the role, and many work with university colleagues year after year in what is called a 'partnership' scheme.

Learning through observation

What will help me move on? It would be me observing other teachers. It would be me getting help from other teachers by them coming to observe me.

You need to be observed otherwise you can't take a short cut. If you really want to improve your teaching methods, to take a short cut, you need to have someone there to watch you. I believe that if you want to progress with the way you teach you also have to develop observation skills. Stop looking at yourself and observe. That's why it's so energy-consuming because you've got to observe, observe, observe.

These two quotations taken from interviews held with newly qualified teachers reviewing their own development clearly signal the value of observing both other teachers at work and being observed by experienced practitioners. Student-teachers, whether they are on a PGCE course or taking a different route through their training, can expect to have their classroom practice scrutinized by a number of different people. Whilst part of the purpose of this is to assess their ability to teach, an experienced observer will be able to make a tremendous contribution to the development of effective practice. Conversely, learning how to observe others at work will also play an important role in coming to understand what makes teachers effective.

Observing the staffroom

There are a number of fairly obvious points to bear in mind when visiting schools. For example, before initial visits are made it is important to know what time student-teachers are expected to arrive. Procedures regarding dress and movement around the school need to be checked at the earliest opportunity as making the wrong assumptions can be awkward. No one expects student-teachers to be timid wallflowers. Rather, colleagues will expect them to want to fit in and demonstrate an interest in what is going on. On the other hand, student-teachers who slump uninvited into the comfiest chair in the staffroom, help themselves to the coffee, and light up, are likely to alienate themselves from the people they need to help them.

Staffrooms are fascinating places. Visitors can learn a great deal by watching and listening as staff come and go. A great deal of educational 'business' is conducted through hundreds of short exchanges as teachers ask or tell each other about individual pupils, resources and activities. The staffroom will reflect much of the culture of the school. In some schools, the staffroom is rarely used as teachers gather in faculty or department rooms. In others, the staffroom is a place where teachers from different disciplines mix together and share information and views. Without being intrusive, it is worth noting what sort of notices are displayed and what sort of publications are around. Attending staff briefings will also provide a sense of how the school is managed and what is considered valuable enough to be communicated to the whole staff. It is also useful to listen to how the language of education is used in daily interactions.

Whether in the main staffroom or the faculty/department room, teachers will be found to be constantly reflecting on what has happened in lessons and how they have dealt with particular situations. Initial appearances though can be very deceptive. The teacher who rushes in claiming to have just taught the worst lesson of her life may not in fact be a weak teacher at all but one whose busy mind is processing what has just happened. Teachers who always look cool and rarely talk about their lessons may have stopped thinking about ways of developing their practice. What teachers say about their own teaching in the informal setting of the staffroom can also offer insights into the way they deal with the pressures and pleasures of the job. Contrasting these observations with what they actually do in the classroom and how they analyse their practice provides student-teachers with a rich canvas to consider.

Task: observing staffrooms

How is drama represented in the staff/faculty room? Are there posters or photographs of recent productions? What information about extracurricular drama is shared with the staff? What does the head of drama value about the staff/faculty room? Compare your findings with student-teachers placed in other schools.

Initial observations of lessons

Observing experienced drama teachers at work is a real privilege. But simply sitting in on lessons can become very dull and give student-teachers little to reflect on or evaluate. The problem is that if observers do not know what to look at they are unlikely to see anything at all. It is therefore much more productive to have a specific agenda for observations. There are many ways of observing lessons and it is worth applying a range of techniques during any period of initial observation. Whatever method of observation is used it is always important to remember that the purpose of observing is to raise questions that will help build an understanding of *why* teachers are doing what they are doing.

Student-teachers can fall into the trap of being judgemental about what they observe. This is of little value and can make teachers defensive and resentful. Certainly, it is likely that the student-teacher will see some lessons that do not appear to work very well and they may see some teachers who are struggling with a particular class or subject. It is not their role however to criticize teachers or pupils about whom they probably know very little. While student-teachers may well want to make a note of things to guard against in their own classroom work, what can most usefully be learnt from such an experience comes from trying to understand the context and dynamic of the lesson. Trying to analyse what decisions the teacher made and what their effect was is more useful than concluding, 'I'd never have done it like that!'.

The most productive way of going about observing in the initial stages is to either ask the class teacher if there is anything in particular that she thinks is worth observing in the lesson to come, or sharing with her the agenda for the observation. Working to an agenda makes it much easier to formulate specific questions about what has been observed. Ideally, the observer will have the chance to pose these questions to the teacher soon after the lesson. But teachers are busy people and may only have a few minutes to talk before rushing off to another class. Presenting a list of dozens of questions is unlikely to get much of a meaningful response; better to pick up on just two or three points in the lesson that were particularly interesting or thought-provoking.

Writing up observations clearly, so that they will make sense later on, is essential if student-teachers are to move towards reflecting on their own practice. Making notes in lessons is invaluable but there is a need for discretion. Writing large exclamations of disgust at what the teacher is doing, then leaving the notes lying around, will undoubtedly lead to trouble! As with evaluations of lessons taught, attempting to write up on Saturday afternoon what was observed on Tuesday morning is a fruitless exercise in paperwork. Looking back over observations as the training period progresses will remind student-teachers that they are involved in a complex process in which their own attitudes and beliefs are likely to undergo considerable changes. Student-teachers should therefore continue to observe teachers at work throughout the school experience. As they become more experienced in the classroom themselves, their insights into the practice of colleagues will deepen.

Using a nudge sheet

'Nudge sheets' offer a bank of elements that might be used to select a particular focus for a classroom observation. It is clearly impossible to focus on all of the questions suggested here in any one lesson but it can be very interesting to use the same set of questions under a particular heading in two contrasting lessons.

Nudge sheet for classroom observation

The classroom environment

1. What is the procedure for entering and leaving the classroom?
2. How is the room set out?
3. Are stimuli and working materials organized and laid out ready for use?
4. Do pupils know where to go and what to do at the start of the lesson?
5. What evidence of pupils' work is on display in the room?
6. What other material for supporting learning is readily apparent (e.g. word walls, reference books/computer, etc.)?

The working atmosphere

1. How much noise and movement is there and what is its nature?
2. What is the balance between pupils working alone, in groups or as a whole class?
3. To what extent are pupils co-operating with each other and the teacher?
4. How interested and enthusiastic are the pupils about the work?
5. How is the lesson brought to a close and the pupils dismissed?

Communication

1. What different sorts of communication are apparent, e.g. instruction, discussion, reprimand, questions?
2. How does the teacher ensure that the pupils understand the language he or she is using?
3. How is the pupils' use of language supported and developed?
4. What sort of questions does the teacher use and how do the pupils respond?
5. How does the teacher use his or her voice to excite, clarify or maintain order?

Teacher actions

1. What is the teacher's manner towards the pupils?
2. How does the teacher initially engage the class?
3. How do they introduce new activities?
4. What techniques do they use to group pupils?
5. How do they intervene to keep a productive working atmosphere?
6. How do they support individuals and groups when they are working on a task?
7. How do they deal with interruptions, e.g. people coming into the classroom or unexpected incidents?
8. How does the teacher use praise and sanctions?

The lesson overall

1. Are the objectives of the lesson clear to the pupils?
2. What sort of stimulus and support material is used?
3. How is the lesson structured?
4. What different teaching methods are employed?
5. To what extent are pupils' ideas and contributions used to develop the lesson?
6. How does the lesson provide for pupils' progression?
7. How are the different abilities of individual pupils catered for through differentiated activities?

In reflection

1. What surprises were there in the lesson?
2. What new questions arise from the experience?
3. What would it be useful to focus on next?

Chronological description

This technique involves simply noting down the main events and incidents of the lesson in the order they happen. For example:

9.05   Bell rings for start of lesson.
9.06   Pupils begin to line up in corridor outside studio.
9.10   Teacher starts to take register. Engages in conversation with pupil regarding absence in previous week.
9.12   Teacher introduces first task: make a tableau of key moment from last week's work. Picks four 'volunteers' to demonstrate an example, drawing on ideas from rest of class.
9.18   Teacher allows pupils to get themselves into groups. They do this quickly and start working.
9.25   Teacher starts moving around checking groups are ready to show.

Using this method of noting the events of a lesson throws into relief the way the teacher uses the time available, how much of the lesson is given over to teacher-talk and how long the pupils spend on a task. Logging the events of a lesson in this way also helps pinpoint moments when the teacher takes the decision to intervene.

Shadowing the teacher

The focus here is entirely on the teacher: what she says, does, how and where she moves, and so on. For example:

- Recap on last week's session. Simple description of what was done. Business-like voice.
- Change of voice. Lowers the tone and leans forward in her chair. Mysterious atmosphere. Asks if they've heard about *bodysnatchers* . . .
- Sits back. Waits for excitement to wane. Nods. Says, 'Hmmm!'.
- Picks up book. Opens it purposefully, stands in very upright posture. Waits. Starts to read report on Burke and Hare in loud, grave (ha, ha!) voice.
- Quick change of voice and posture. Sense of urgency as she sets task – create the courtroom for Burke and Hare's trial.
- Hurries from group to group, encouraging, asking questions, sometimes in role of court usher (?), sometimes as herself, checking the pupils have understood the task.

This method is helpful as a basis for discussing with the teacher how the lesson was structured and what guided decisions about when and how to do things, for example changes in tone or vocal register.

Shadowing a pupil

This works, essentially, in the same way as above but allows the observer more time to pose questions about why a pupil is behaving or reacting in a certain way. For example:

- Listening to other group members. Difficult to tell how engaged he is – no particular facial expression.
- Suggests something very new (that they do the scene in mime). Group seems a bit stunned by this! He tries to explain why. It seems that he's on the verge of hitting on an exciting thing here but can't articulate it.
- Runs out of steam! He looks frustrated. The group almost immediately continue to babble on with their original idea. He really needed help here to form the idea . . .

This sort of observation can lead to fruitful discussion on the way teachers differentiate between pupils and assess them in context.

In each of these cases, the observations made in the lesson need to be discussed afterwards. If it is not possible to talk through the observations with the class teacher, it may be possible to discuss them in seminar groups or informally with colleagues.

Observation tasks

- Aim to write a detailed account of at least one observation each day in the early stages of school placement. This can be reduced later as your own planning and teaching begins to take up more time, but it really is worth disciplining yourself in order to quickly formulate a sound grasp of the way teachers work.
- You will find it helpful to look for different aspects of classroom practice. Try to ensure that you vary the focus of the observation.

The context of drama lessons

Student-teachers will of course want to observe a wide range of lessons in their own subject specialisms. It is, however, extremely valuable to observe other teachers at work and consider the different methods used in other subjects and various types of classroom environments. With specific reference to the work of the drama department, student-teachers should ensure that they ask lots of questions in order to understand the background to individual lesson observations made in drama. Examples of useful questions are:

- Does the department have a specific policy and syllabus?
- How many members of staff teach drama and what experience and background do they have?
- What is the relationship between the drama department and other departments in the school?

14

- In what ways does the drama department contribute to the delivery of the National Curriculum?
- What examination syllabus does the department use and how many candidates are there usually?
- How does the department assess and report on pupils' progress in drama?
- Is homework set in drama? If so, what form does it take?
- What philosophy of drama does the department favour? What are the ultimate aims for drama in the school and what methodology is preferred?
- What contact do the pupils have with professional theatre and practitioners?
- What opportunities and special provisions does the department make for pupils with special educational needs?

It can be very tempting to join in with sessions even in the early stages of school placement and this can, of course, give fresh insights into the way teachers and pupils work. However, becoming actively engaged in this way can make it more difficult to consider the decisions the drama teacher is making, so it is best to balance this sort of experience with the sort of approaches to observation outlined above.

Observing in the primary school

The transition from primary to secondary education is an important milestone in many children's lives. For some it is a traumatic event and heralds a downturn in achievement and motivation. Research shows that a significant number of young people (boys in particular) do less well in the first year of secondary school than they did in primary school. Many primary teachers justifiably complain that their colleagues in the secondary school are not well informed of the content and methods employed in the first six years of children's formal education. In some regions the transition is less marked at the age of 11, as there is a system of middle-school education which children leave at 14. What is certainly true, unfortunately, is that few teachers have the time to share their ideas and experiences across phases.

Making a visit to a primary school, possibly one of the network schools for the main practice school, gives student-teachers the chance to begin to consider issues and problems of transition. In addition to exploring the different environment and methods used generally, it is particularly useful to consider the following questions about drama.

Children's play

- How do children play in the playground? Consider the way they organize their own games, the way they use playground equipment, the way they play on their own, the different roles they seem to adopt.

- Are there elements of play in the classroom? Listen to the way they talk or use role-play in the context of the work. Note also any subversive play that is going on and consider why it has occurred.
- Does the teacher utilize their play in any way? Has the room a play or home corner which is used effectively?

Drama

- Drama is a formal part of the National Curriculum for English and the National Literacy Strategy. In what ways does the school address this?
- How else does drama manifest itself in the school?
- What is the head's attitude towards drama? Is there a whole-school policy towards it? What do other teachers think is the place of drama in the primary school?
- Is drama taught as a separate subject or used as a method in the teaching of other subjects? Does it usually happen in the hall or the classroom?
- To what extent does drama reflect the cultural backgrounds of the school's intake?

Task: reflecting on primary education

Write a reflective report on your primary school experience. Formulate a number of questions to discuss with your mentor in your secondary school looking at, for example:

- primary/secondary transfer arrangements;
- use of test data;
- planning for progression from Key Stage 2 in drama;
- how knowledge of the Key Stage 2 National Curriculum and National Literacy Strategy informs planning of Year 7 drama curriculum.

Getting organized

The training process for initial teacher training is intense, and requires student-teachers to work in a number of different contexts. In addition, student-teachers are expected to document and keep evidence of their progress, and meet deadlines set in school and by the training institution. This means that all student-teachers have to be very organized about their work. Many drama students are used to juggling rehearsals with academic work and have learnt how to organize themselves. However, anyone who knows they are disorganized will need to learn fast!

The teaching file

Student-teachers will be expected to keep a teaching file. This will become a complete and coherent record of all work undertaken in school. The teaching file is likely to include:

- lesson observation notes made by student-teachers;
- lesson plans made by student-teachers;
- evaluations of lessons taught;
- mentor's observations of student-teachers' lessons;
- records of meetings with drama mentors;
- details of drama department's syllabuses and units of work;
- information about departmental policies such as special needs provision, discipline procedures, sanctions and rewards, drama resources and facilities.

It is important to keep this file well ordered because, by the end of the year, it will contain a huge amount of material. It may also be read by examiners, mentors, subject-lecturers and OFSTED inspectors. It is sensible to divide it into clear sections, with a section for each class observed and taught. In this way, it will be possible to see the relationship between teaching and the pupils' learning. Other sections may focus more explicitly on the student-teachers' progression and targets set and achieved on the school placement. For more details about target setting and mentor meetings, see pages 188–90 in Chapter 7.

Course handbooks, deadlines and assignments

Because the initial teacher training programme contains so many different elements, course leaders usually provide handbooks which give full details of the process. It is very important for everyone involved in the training programme to read these carefully. Handbooks are likely to contain the following information:

- course content, key dates and timetables;
- details of school placements;
- requirements for written assignments;
- reading lists;
- assessment criteria for QTS (Qualified Teacher Status).

In particular, student-teachers should note any deadlines for written assignments. These assignments will be used to assess their understanding of the relationship between teaching and learning. The nature of the assignments will vary from course to course, and they will be spread over the training period in order to show progression. Student-teachers obviously need to keep up to date with these formal assignments and should ensure that they are aware of all deadlines. There may be also less formal tasks which student-teachers are expected to complete. Anticipating all deadlines lessens potential stress levels considerably.

Student-teachers' progression towards QTS

During the course of initial teacher training, student-teachers will be expected to become increasingly aware of their own progression. In order to progress, they will need to understand how they are getting on, negotiate targets for their own professional development and find ways of meeting them. To achieve this, student-teachers are helped when they recognize their own skills, values and areas of expertise. By the end of the training programme, their knowledge, skills and understanding will be measured against a series of predetermined 'standards' in areas of subject-knowledge, classroom management, planning, assessment and other professional issues. These standards, prescribed in detail by government teacher training agencies, identify the competence required for qualified teacher status.

Opening Position Statements

An Opening Position Statement is a useful way for student-teachers to consider their aspirations and identify their aims at the beginning of the training programme. At the end of their training they will be required to complete a Career Entry Profile (CEP) in which they will identify the strengths and areas for development in their practice. The CEP gives student-teachers the opportunity to set targets for the first year of teaching and serve as an agenda for induction into teaching; the Opening Position Statement serves as a useful precursor to this exit requirement. It is very helpful to share this statement with fellow student-teachers, subject lecturers and mentors.

Compiling an Opening Position Statement

Consider the following questions, and write notes or a brief paragraph on each.

- What knowledge and expertise am I bringing with me to the training programme that will be relevant to teaching?
- What opportunities do I expect there to be on the course to utilize and develop my existing knowledge and expertise?
- What personal qualities do I already have that will help me in the training programme?
- What areas of subject-knowledge do I feel I need to develop in order to prepare for a career in teaching?
- What action do I intend to take by way of preparing myself for the training year?
- What targets do I intend to set myself for the year to come?
- What are my current expectations of, attitudes towards and feelings about the forthcoming training year?

Evidence, assessment and QT Status

In order to qualify as teachers, student-teachers will have to fulfil specific areas of competence. These competences, which vary according to the different regions in the UK, are described precisely. It is therefore useful for student-teachers to refer to them at regular intervals during the course, ensuring that they recognize how they are progressing. However, it must be stressed that that these descriptors of competence are quite mechanistic and, taken at face value, represent a fairly impoverished version of teaching. Teaching drama is far more creative and intellectually stimulating than the competences for achieving QTS suggest.

Evidence of having achieved the required standards is gathered from a range of different sources, and student-teachers have some responsibility for keeping records which demonstrate their abilities as teachers. Sources of evidence for student-teachers' competence may include:

- observation of classroom practice;
- written observation notes;
- lesson plans and evaluations (in the teaching file);
- regular formal, written reports on classroom practice;
- records of targets set and achieved;
- written assignments.

Assessors will want to see evidence of progression, as well as evidence of having addressed a particular standard. It is therefore very important that student-teachers keep records right from the beginning of the training programme. This kind of portfolio or log also provides student-teachers with valuable insights into their progress and learning.

The next six chapters in this book are designed to follow different areas of competence prescribed by teacher training agencies in the UK, against which student-teachers will be assessed. However, in writing this book, we have assumed that readers will wish to become more than merely competent as drama teachers. We hope we have included ideas which will challenge and support those learning to teach drama, and whose aim is to become informed, creative and reflective practitioners.

NOTE

1   In most schools, young people are referred to as 'students'. However in this book we will use the rather more old-fashioned term 'pupils', in order to avoid confusion with 'student-teacher' . OFSTED refer to student-teachers as 'trainees' in official documentation, but to us this sounds rather mechanistic and implies a simple model of learning how to teach rather than the more rewarding and productive notion of developing an effective praxis.

Subject-knowledge and Understanding

Subject-knowledge

Student-teachers arrive on their training programmes with considerable knowledge and experience of their specialist subject. Those learning to become drama teachers will probably have degrees in drama, theatre studies or cognate disciplines. Some may have worked in the theatre, media, the arts or education in various capacities. Some may have higher degrees or hold relevant professional qualifications from other careers. Others may already be qualified teachers, undertaking an in-service course in order to learn to teach drama. Whatever the breadth and depth of their knowledge, student-teachers usually appreciate that effective teaching involves more than transferring a body of knowledge possessed by the teacher to the pupils. Teaching drama is far more complex and interesting than that. It entails both practical and theoretical knowledge of drama, an understanding of how young people learn and, at its most exciting, the creative exploration and communication of new feelings and insights. In fact, student-teachers of drama often report that it is exactly this eschewing of dry, 'traditional' models of education in favour of a more dialectical and experiential approach that attracted them to drama as pupils and led them to want to teach it themselves.

However, rejecting the value of existing knowledge on the grounds that the only really useful knowledge is acquired through experience has never been a sound argument (must children get burnt to learn that playing with fire is dangerous?). If pupils are to benefit from the knowledge teachers possess *and* develop their own ability to think and act independently, a subtle balance must be struck. On the one hand, young people will need to appreciate and understand the world from a range of cultural reference points if they are to participate as citizens in a pluralist society.[1] On the other hand, they will also need to develop skills as critics and interpreters in order to make independent judgements about information they receive. This involves greater critical awareness than is usually afforded by an induction into traditional, canonical forms of knowledge.

Drama teachers thus need to find ways of encouraging pupils to participate in drama as an art form, with all the implications for personal and emotional involvement this entails, as well as ensuring that they are provided with the knowledge, skills and understanding necessary to understand and contribute to a rapidly changing world. For student-teachers, learning how to achieve such a balance requires coming to understand *pedagogy* (the theory and practice of teaching) and how drama as a curriculum subject contributes to the education of young people. In broad terms, teaching drama rests on three different, but related, forms of subject-knowledge:

- knowledge of drama as an art form, as practice and as a field of academic study;
- knowledge of different approaches to drama education as a practical pedagogy;
- knowledge of how drama relates to broader educational contexts which influence and sometimes prescribe how it is taught in schools.

This chapter addresses these three aspects of subject-knowledge and identifies the increasing role of information and communication technology to them.

Subject-knowledge in drama

To assume that all new drama teachers share a core of knowledge about their subject would be wildly off the mark. Degree courses in drama and theatre vary considerably and graduates will have chosen options within their courses which reflect their own interests and skills. Consequently, while some student-teachers may have studied bookshelves of plays or dived deep into theories of theatre production and reception, others will have spent much of their time devising new work or specializing in particular skills or genres. Recognizing and celebrating the diversity of experience and specialist knowledge which student-teachers bring to their training programmes can only be beneficial to the long-term health of drama education. Drama is, after all, a very broad subject and good drama teachers, however experienced, are always developing their own knowledge and extending their skills as drama practitioners and as teachers.

In order to work productively in schools, student-teachers will also need to know and understand how Information and Communications Technology (ICT) relates to drama teaching, and this may necessitate extending their own ICT skills. The drama curriculum needs to acknowledge and reflect the impact of technical innovations on the art form, and the management of drama in the classroom can benefit enormously from the imaginative use of audio-visual and specialist stage technologies. More generally, lesson planning, administration and recording pupils' progress may all be positively enhanced by the efficient use of ICT.

Knowledge of drama education

Developing a clear, well-informed rationale for the teaching of drama is one of the most important elements of the training programme. To achieve this, student-teachers will need to understand how to select, reformulate and repackage their own subject-knowledge in ways that suit the pupils they teach and the contexts within which they are teaching.[2] By the end of the training period, student-teachers should have a good knowledge of different approaches to drama education and the philosophies on which they are built. PGCE courses in particular emphasize this form of subject-knowledge on the grounds that, without a clear rationale for teaching drama, there is a risk that as newly qualified teachers they will quickly lose their sense of purpose and direction.

Over the last forty years or so, the theory and practice of drama education has developed a significant corpus of knowledge. Writers in the field of drama education draw not only on drama practice and theatre studies in their work, but are also influenced by related disciplines such as cultural studies, social psychology and aesthetic theory. If student-teachers are to be able to make robust and informed contributions to drama education, they will need to be able to analyse critically how different theoretical perspectives influence and inform day-to-day practice in drama classrooms.

Contextual knowledge

Drama teachers do not, of course, work in isolation. There are both local and national influences on the ways in which drama is taught in schools and student-teachers need to acquire a knowledge of the contexts in which they are working. Despite increased centralization in recent years in education, there is still considerable autonomy over how drama is taught in the local contexts of schools. Many drama teachers have developed complex curriculum frameworks and approaches to teaching drama which reflect their own educational principles and interests in drama whilst also assimilating a plethora of new government initiatives.

Drama education is particularly closely allied to other arts subjects and to English teaching. It also has a long history of contributing to whole-school learning policies and practices. The nature of these contributions has changed over the years, but drama teachers are often involved in developing and supporting innovative approaches to literacy learning, ICT and interactive teaching methods. In many schools, drama education is highly valued for the contribution it makes to pupils' moral and cultural education, and to an education in and for citizenship. This approach to education accepts that there are key skills which inform pupils' learning, and it is designed to provide pupils with coherent educational experiences in a curriculum which is compartmentalized by subject disciplines.

Auditing subject-knowledge

The variety of background knowledge and experiences student-teachers bring to teacher training courses reflects the multi-faceted nature of an art form which includes writers, directors, performers and designers. Student-teachers will need a breadth of knowledge and skills which encompasses all these areas, although they do not need to be particular experts in any specific aspect of drama. As a subject, drama is vast and constantly changing and it is impossible to be familiar with all dramatic practices and forms. However, it is reasonable to expect new teachers to have a robust general knowledge of drama in addition to an in-depth knowledge of some particular areas; in the classroom, teachers need to be able to cope with subject-specific questions pupils ask.

The bottom line?

What sort of things do you think are essential for drama teachers to know and be able to do?

Talk to other drama students and teachers about this. It is also useful to find out what a wider range of teachers, parents and young people think specialist drama teachers should know. Make a note of any expectations with which you agree yet do not feel you could currently meet.

Start with your strengths

Rather than panicking about the myriad things you don't know or can't do, make a list of your existing strengths in subject-knowledge. What particular areas of expertise do you already have? You may have specialized skills such as stage fighting or mask work or perhaps you have talents as a writer, director or designer. Are there periods of theatre history, particular playwrights or genres, that you have studied in depth?

Consider your broader experience: plays you have performed in, professional or voluntary work associated with drama? You may have knowledge and experience of theatre other than that found in mainstream Western culture.

The trouble with canons

Are there certain plays, playwrights, practitioners and genres that all drama teachers should definitely know? What does the term 'know' actually imply? There is clearly a big difference, for example, between knowing Shakespeare's plays in depth as practitioners or critics and simply knowing which plays he wrote and being able to summarize a few plots. Furthermore, it is possible to have a theoretical knowledge of dramatic forms, but not have the ability to realize them as practitioners (or vice versa).

Critics of liberal humanism have shown that the study of 'great' plays was initially introduced into education as a means of cultivating the 'right' moral values.[3] This was based on the assumption that some plays (particularly those of Shakespeare) revealed 'universal truths' which, it was hoped, would inspire and elevate young people's imagination. As a result, a canon of suitable texts was recommended which, in practice, was almost exclusively confined to the work of dead white men. More recently, critical theorists have argued that legitimating certain works of art at the expense of others is not only socially divisive, but also ignores the active and political role of the interpreter.[4] As a result, there have been significant moves to include critical and dramatic practices from a range of social perspectives and cultural fields, and many new graduates have experience and knowledge of a range of dramatic forms outside the traditional canon.

In terms of drama education, an awareness of different critical perspectives and the active role of the interpreter has led drama teachers to find ways of working practically with texts which encourage a dialogue between existing knowledge and the pupils' own critical faculties.[5] Nevertheless, debates continue to surround the justification and wisdom of including any kind of list of writers and their works in National Curricula and examination syllabuses. Even if such lists are presented as examples of the sort of writers and works that might be studied at any given level (rather than advocated for their supposedly morally uplifting qualities), there is always controversy around the criteria for inclusion or exclusion from such a list. In considering their own subject-knowledge in drama, student-teachers may wish to consider the following questions:

- What rationale appears to lie behind the choice of texts and practitioners studied at different levels?
- What contrasting or additional resource material might be used to enrich a critical appreciation of such texts and practice?
- To what extent does a knowledge of the broader cultural and historical context within which plays, practitioners and genres developed and were received contribute to an understanding and appreciation of them?

Check your knowledge

Look at the 'How much do you know about . . . ?' and 'How much working knowledge do you have of . . . ?' check-lists. What aspects of dramatic practice do you know well? Which elements would you wish to know more about? What other genres, practitioners or theatre companies would you include? What criteria do you think have been applied in compiling this list?

How much do you know about . . .?

Genres/periods	Practitioners	Contemporary companies
Agit-prop	Mike Alfreds	Charabanc
Ancient Greek theatre	Antonin Artaud	Clean Break
Ancient Roman theatre	Bobby Baker	DV 8
British realist theatre	Eugenio Barba	Forced Entertainment
Chinese classical theatre	Pina Bausch	Forkbeard Fantasy
Commedia dell'arte	Augusto Boal	Frantic Assembly
Community theatre	Bertolt Brecht	IOU
Documentary theatre	Peter Brook	Joint Stock
Elizabethan theatre	Edward Gordon Craig	Paines Plough
Epic theatre	Rose English	Red Ladder
Farce	Tim Etchells	Shared Experience
Film genres	Dario Fo	Split Britches
German Expressionism	Jerzy Grotowski	Tara Arts
Improvisation	Kathryn Hunter	Tawala Theatre
Indonesian puppet theatre	Keith Johnstone	Theatre de Complicite
Jacobean theatre	Mike Leigh	Trestle Theatre
Kabuki	Robert Lepage	V TOL
Kathakali	Joan Littlewood	Welfare State International
Kuttiyattam	Simon McBurney	
Live art	Vsevolod Meyerhold	
Mask work	Arianne Mnouchkine	
Masques	Erwin Piscator	
Melodrama	Richard Schechner	
Mime	Max Stafford-Clark	
Mummers and folk plays	Konstantin Stanislavsky	
Music theatre	Lee Strasberg	
Mysteries and moralities	Jatinder Verma	
Naturalism		
Noh theatre		
Pantomime		
Performance art		
Physical theatre		
Political theatre		
Radio drama		
Restoration comedy		
Revenge tragedy		
Roman theatre		
Symbolist theatre		
TV drama		
Theatre for development		
Theatre of the Absurd		
Theatre in education		
Verse drama		
Well-made play		

How much working knowledge do you have of . . . ?

Directing	Choreographing movement
Script writing	Stage management
Devising	Stage fighting
Acting	Making and using masks
Designing and operating stage lighting	Designing and operating sound systems
Stage management	Constructing analytical essays
Designing sets	Writing reviews
Designing and making costumes	Making and using puppets and marionettes
Video equipment	Theatre administration

Lists such as these can look rather daunting (just imagine what a list of culturally significant plays and playwrights might look like!), but it is important to remember that subject-knowledge audits, whatever their form, are not ends in themselves. Rather, they should be part of an ongoing and dynamic process of learning. On the other hand, many student-teachers find that check-lists like these are a helpful way of recognizing subject-knowledge they already possess, identifying relevant gaps and moving towards addressing them. In the first instance student-teachers will want to ensure that they have the depth of knowledge necessary to fulfil their immediate obligations and responsibilities as classroom teachers; there is little point in making a major study of minor Restoration playwrights in the vague hope that it will one day be useful in school. Most training courses provide practical drama activities and assignments which are specifically designed to help student-teachers address significant omissions in their subject-knowledge, and school-based mentors often offer invaluable advice about how to prioritize this process.

Planning a study programme

Having identified areas that you think you need to know more about, plot a programme of study for the training year. One way to do this would be to list study areas in one column and note how to tackle them in another. This may include library-based study or Internet searches, and listing books and sites to read as the year proceeds. Consult with your drama mentor or university lecturer about what areas will be most useful for your teaching and set yourself a series of manageable targets. Be realistic about what you can achieve. You may find it particularly useful to share ideas, research and workshop practices with colleagues. Most importantly, try to see the work of interesting practitioners (the work of small experimental companies often provide the most stimulating ideas for teaching).

Applying the subject-knowledge audit to teaching drama: what is useful?

Auditing general subject-knowledge in drama by using the kind of check-lists on pages 26–7 is helpful in establishing independent study plans. There is also the need, in the context of a school placement, for student-teachers to consider whether or not they have sufficient knowledge and resources to allow them to start contributing actively to the drama curriculum. Notwithstanding their expertise, student-teachers often feel less than wholly confident in their subject-knowledge when they first face a class and begin to teach. Although many soon realize that they possess valuable skills hitherto unidentified, they may be helped by asking a series of broader questions which focus on the application of their subject-knowledge to teaching. The following chart is designed to aid this process.

Knowledge for teaching drama

Are you familiar with . . .

. . . the Shakespeare texts prescribed in the curriculum for English and the ways in which knowledge of these is tested (e.g. SATs, GCSE)?	. . . contemporary plays which would particularly enhance pupils' understanding of performance?
. . . plays recommended or prescribed on examination syllabuses in drama?	. . . critical texts which could be used to assist further study of plays for 16 + students?
. . . material to illustrate the historical context of the Renaissance theatre to 11–14-year-old pupils?	. . . photographic, video or written evidence of particular plays in performance?
. . . video material of physical theatre companies or performance artists?	. . . the work of theatre-in-education companies or education programmes of national or touring companies?
. . . theoretical work on performance analysis accessible to 16 + students?	. . . specific productions of plays or other performance events that might challenge Key Stage 4 pupils?
. . . a range of ways to facilitate drama workshops, using exploratory conventions such as teacher-in-role, hot-seating, role-on-the wall?	. . . how drama related to different artistic movements such as Expressionism, Realism or Symbolism?
. . . a range of poems and stories which might provide a starting point for drama?	. . . visual images, music or sound effects that might be used in pupils' drama?
. . . the structures of language in a range of forms of written work?	. . . the linguistic differences between spoken and written English, and recognizing different registers and forms of spoken English?
. . . the work of puppeteers, animators, storytellers which would appeal to 11–14-year-olds?	. . . plays suitable for pupils in the 11–14 age range to read and perform?

Information and communications technology

ICT is regarded as so important in education that it is now a compulsory component in all initial teacher training courses. Regional bodies responsible for teacher training throughout the UK have issued documents stressing this importance and outlining exactly what newly qualified teachers are expected to know and be able to do.[6] It is also important to remember that the political interest in ICT at initial teacher training level represents an aspiration towards an education service in which all pupils are able to use ICT in their work, and where all teachers are able to integrate it purposefully into their administration and lessons. Although progress is rapidly being made in this area, this is not yet a reality in every school.

In terms of subject-knowledge, there are three interrelated aspects in ICT which student-teachers need to acquire. They will need to know how to:

- use ICT in their own work, both in lesson preparation and in their personal and departmental administration;
- use skills specifically related to drama as an art form;
- to apply their skills to the drama classroom.

The application of ICT to the subject of drama is explored in more detail in the next section (see pages 50–2). What is in focus here is student-teachers' own ICT skills.

What counts as ICT?

Because new technologies are constantly being introduced, there has been an understandable reluctance by teacher training agencies to offer anything other than a broad definition of what might be included as ICT in education. For drama specialists it is encouraging to note that, in addition to computers, a wide range of other technologies are also mentioned. For example, the Internet, CD-ROM and other software, television and radio, video, cameras, stage lighting, tape recorders and other audio-visual equipment are all regarded as valuable in supporting teaching and learning. There is plenty in this list which has an immediate application to both creative practice and research work in drama. Finding out how to use different types of hardware and software need not be a terribly time-consuming task, and auditing existing knowledge is an important first step. Having identified areas for further development, student-teachers are well placed to go about upgrading their skills in a systematic way by drawing on the support systems available in their training programme and by seeking help from appropriate colleagues in placement schools. As one newly qualified teacher reported: 'If you don't ask, you're not going to get. That's a lesson I learnt quick! I think you have to be quite responsible for your own development really.'

Auditing ICT skills

Consider the 'ICT skills' chart and tick the column associated with the statement which best indicates your level of skill:

Column A: I have no idea, or I don't understand this;
Column B: I have some idea, but I may need help;
Column C: I can do this without help;
Column D: I can show other people how to do this.

ICT skills

Can you . . .	A	B	C	D
use a word processor to draft and redraft a text, e.g. an essay of lesson plan?				
format and save work on a floppy disk?				
connect to and use a printer?				
use word processing facilities such as tabs, tables, spell checker, etc.?				
use a computer to produce work which incorporates both text and graphics?				
use a computer to design graphs, charts and diagrams?				
use a computer in association with a digital camera?				
use a computer to manipulate numerical information (spreadsheets)?				
use a computer to sort and select information (databases)?				
access CD-ROM-based information?				
use the computerized library catalogue?				
access information on the Internet?				
use e-mail?				
use standard stage audio equipment (e.g. microphones)?				
use standard stage lighting equipment (e.g. manual and computerized boards)?				
use presentational software?				
use an electronic whiteboard?				
use standard video and audio recording equipment?				

Methodology and pedagogy

In the course of their training, student-teachers are likely to observe a variety of teaching methods in drama lessons which are grounded in, and informed by, different pedagogic principles and theories of drama education. Contemporary teaching methods in drama are indebted to years of research and practical experimentation in the subject, and have evolved in response to changing educational climates. Individual drama teachers often extend their practice by synthesizing a range of ideas and strategies into their work, developing their work through reading, attending courses and reflecting on experience. As a result, their understanding of drama education becomes 'embodied'; that is, they do not necessarily follow the work of a particular theory or practitioner slavishly, but generate, adapt and interpret a variety of teaching methodologies which cohere with their particular situations and personal rationales for drama education. This practical application of thinking and research may be referred to as *praxis*, a term which means the practical application of theory.

In order to start evolving their own praxis, student-teachers need to be able to draw from and reflect upon a broad canvas of theories and observations. Simply reading published teaching materials to get ideas for next week's lesson, or attempting to copy ideas which seemed to work without thinking about their educational purpose is unlikely to help new teachers develop a coherent methodology. Nor is it likely that drama teaching driven by such 'atheoretical eclecticism' will lead to progression in pupils' learning.[7] Rather, investigating how theoretical expositions of drama teaching have shaped and influenced contemporary classroom practice provides student-teachers with a basis upon which to form their own judgements.

Historical background

It is not the remit of this book to provide a detailed history of drama education; there are already illuminating published accounts that explore how drama education is indebted to the thinking and practice of a host of twentieth-century pioneers.[8] Nor is it the intention to give a detailed analysis of the ways in which contemporary writers and practitioners have adapted, re-interpreted and challenged the work of their predecessors. However, whilst acknowledging that in every historical account there is necessarily an element of interpretation, the aim here is to identify some of the key influences and movements in drama education. By placing drama education in an historical context, the intention is that this sketch will whet the appetite for further reading and study.

Placing yourself in history

This discussion task is best completed with a group of people of different ages. The aim is to share your own experiences of being taught drama, and to try to work out what you were learning. Share your responses to these questions:

- To what extent did you experience designated drama lessons in primary and secondary school?
- Describe a lesson or activity you particularly remember.
- Did you take examinations in drama? Did any of you take 'speech and drama' examinations? Or GCSE and A level? How did they differ?
- What are your best and worst memories of drama in school?
- Did you join in school plays, drama clubs or youth theatres? If so, what kinds of plays did you put on?
- Did you have to change your clothes to do drama? Why? (Be sensitive to people over 40 here — they may recall doing drama in their vest and pants!)

Sharing memories and experiences of drama education will probably reveal how much ways of working in drama vary and how much the subject has changed over time. Those who received a state education in the last twenty years or so may recall how drama lessons focused on the exploration of social issues through improvisation and devised work. For some, drama may have been primarily concerned with working dramatic texts, acting out scenes and experimenting with different theatrical interpretations. Those who end up specializing in drama may have enjoyed participating in school plays or other forms of performance. In any case, throughout the history of drama education, the work has been characterized by an emphasis on practice, and on educational principles which accept that children learn best by doing.[9]

Drama education has a strong history of emancipatory values and aspirations for the personal and social development of young people. Successive exponents of drama have turned such ideals into a practical pedagogy and, in many cases, radicalized teaching methods. For example, the pioneering work of Harriet Findlay-Johnson in the very early years of twentieth-century drama sought to democratize the relationship between teachers and pupils.[10] This approach to education, in which pupils were encouraged to learn from each other as well as their teachers, signalled an interest in increasingly egalitarian teaching methods to which drama and arts education became closely allied. Whatever later criticisms there may have been of progressive education, it is undeniable that the movement heralded a freedom of expression which was a welcome antidote to the kind of rigid teaching methods, authoritarianism and propagation of dogma rarely witnessed or imagined in schools today.

Given its basis in principles of social democracy, drama became increasingly significant in the period following the Second World War. The 1944 Education Act was intended, as Philip Gardner points out, to end inequality of provision in secondary education, where the children of the middle classes received secondary education whilst working-class children had access only to elementary schools.[11] The advent of free secondary education for all led, in England and Wales, to the establishment of grammar, technical and secondary modern schools for children aged 11–15, 'with the provision for its subsequent extension to 16 as soon as circumstances permit'.[12] This tripartite system was based on psychological theories that claimed that children's intellectual abilities were innate. Inter-war research into child psychology recognized the importance of childhood play in education, and this began to secure drama's place in the curriculum, especially in the primary years. [13]

The concept that play is integral to the learning process has been central to drama education, although the relationship between play and drama has been differently theorized, interpreted and reconfigured over time. Initially harnessed to various forms of Froebelian and Piagetian models of child development, by the 1970s drama educators were emphasizing the social purpose of play and role-play in particular.[14] This way of thinking about drama and play coincided with the rise of comprehensive schools, which were established in response to the conclusion that the tripartite system of secondary education was socially divisive. For the first time in the history of state schooling, it was proposed that pupils of all social backgrounds were to be educated together. It was in this social context that drama became increasingly well-established in the secondary school curriculum.[15]

The introduction of public examinations in drama at 15+ and 18+ during the 1970s, together with the expansion of university drama departments in the same period, led to increased recognition of the subject as a discipline in its own right. In secondary schools the teaching of drama came to require increasingly specialized subject-knowledge in order to satisfy examination syllabuses. The necessity for older pupils to be able to demonstrate a practical and intellectual understanding of different theatre practitioners and plays in performance did not immediately seem consistent with practices that had evolved from child-centred notions of learning through play. By the 1980s, questions began to be raised about how drama in secondary schools should be defined.[16] The debates that ensued were complex, often heated and can only be summarized crudely here. In brief, the discussion turned on whether pupils should be educated *in* dramatic art or *through* drama. In other words, those advocating an education *in* drama suggested that all pupils should develop an explicit knowledge of dramatic form, theatre history and drama practices in order to enhance and develop their own creative work. Others argued that drama *in* education should focus primarily on the pupils' exploration of the social world *through* drama. It was an ideological debate about whether, and how far, drama education should be subject-centred or whether it should primarily regarded as a child-centred method of teaching.

Any linear history of drama education that implies that there has always been agreement between drama educators and that changes to the ways in which it has been taught and defined were usually consensual would be inaccurate. Nonetheless, through a process of constant review and robust debate, drama has been revitalized and successful in reinforcing its position in the secondary school curriculum. By 1997, Michael Fleming suggested that a new consensus in drama education had been reached, in which it had become widely recognized that 'the dichotomies between "process" and "product"; "theatre" and "drama"; "drama for understanding" and "drama as art"; "experience" and "performance" may now be seen as false polarities'.[17] This confident statement reflected the ways in which drama teachers had, in their own classroom practices, assimilated, challenged and redefined the work of drama education theorists. It signalled an approach to drama education in secondary schools in which pupil-centred and subject-centred approaches to learning had become increasingly balanced and synthesized.

Establishing an overview

Read through the entries on the chart below. How aware are you of the effect that any of them have had on your own drama career? To what extent are any of the events and publications mentioned influential in the way drama is taught and thought of in your placement school?

Drama, theatre and education policy: a selective tradition

The 'Potted history of drama education' which follows is intended to offer an indication of some significant dates in drama education and match them against developments in theatre and education. Other references, particularly in the field of theatre praxis, are offered only to give a broad historical context for drama education and they should not, of course, be read as a new canon. On the contrary, the chart can only offer what Raymond Williams called 'a selective tradition' and readers will no doubt wish to observe many and significant omissions.[18]

A potted history of drama education

Date	Drama education	Theatre praxis	Official reports
1911	Harriet Findlay-Johnson's *Dramatic Methods of Teaching* published		
1913		First production of Shaw's *Pygmalion*	
1917	Henry Caldwell-Cook's *The Play Way* published		

Date	Drama education	Theatre praxis	Official reports
1918			The Newbolt Report: *Play Up and Play the Game* states that: 'The pupils who take part in performances of plays must learn to speak well and to move well, and to appreciate character and express emotion becomingly'
1931			The Hadow Report makes the case for drama education on the grounds of it being a fundamental facet of child development
1933		Stanislavsky's *An Actor Prepares* published in English	
1944			Education Act establishes free provision of secondary education for all up to the age of 15 (later increased to 16)
1945		Joan Littlewood's Theatre Workshop founded	
1947	Peter Slade appointed drama adviser for Staffordshire		
1954	Peter Slade's *Child Drama* published		
1955		First English production of *Waiting for Godot*	
1956		English Stage Company founded; first production of *Look Back in Anger*; Berliner Ensemble in London	
1961–71			The number of teacher training courses offering drama as a first subject grows from 6 to 100
1963			*Half Our Future* – The Newsom Report. Drama promoted as being a subject especially suited to less able pupils because through it they could 'work out their own personal problems'
1965	Theatre in education movement founded; Belgrade TIE company established		
1966	*Development through Drama* by Brian Way published		*The Provision of Theatre for Young People in Great Britain*: Arts Council report recommending subsidy and funding for young people's theatre and theatre work with children
1967			The Plowden Report: now regarded as the bastion of progressive education in primary schools. Curiously the report contains only one paragraph on drama

35

A potted history of drama education *continued*

Date	Drama education	Theatre praxis	Official reports
1968	*Play, Drama and Thought* by Richard Courtney published; *Experience of Spontaneity* by Peter Slade	Abolition of censorship in theatre; Red Ladder Stage Company founded; publication of Brook's *The Empty Space*	Education Survey no. 2 DES argues that school drama relies too heavily on improvisation at the expense of dramatic literature, which is seen as an art form in its own right
1969			*The Black Papers*: Cox and Dyson critical of many aspects of progressive education
1971	Winnicott's *Playing and Reality* published	Founded: John McGrath's 7.84; General Will	
1974		Association of Community Theatres; Joint Stock; Women's Theatre Group	
1976	Betty Jane Wagner has published an exposition of Dorothy Heathcote's work *Dorothy Heathcote: Drama as a learning medium*	Jatinder Verma founds Tara Arts	James Callaghan speaks at Ruskin College and starts debate over the necessity and nature of a national curriculum
1979	Gavin Bolton's first book, *Towards a Theory of Drama Education*		
1982		First production of Caryl Churchill's *Top Girls*	*The Arts in Schools*: report published which made connections between drama and allied arts in education
1984	Bolton's *Drama as Education* published	Forced Entertainment Theatre co-operative begins	
1985			*Better Schools* published, a forerunner to the National Curriculum. Recognizes need for pupils to study 'music, art and drama on a worthwhile scale'
1986	David Hornbrook's critique of drama in education published in *New Theatre Quarterly*	First production of Jim Cartwright's *Road*	
1988		Timberlake Wertenbaker's *Our Country's Good* first performed	Education Reform Act introduced National Curriculum. Drama is not included as subject in its own right
1989	David Hornbrook's *Education and Dramatic Art* published		*Drama from 5–16* HMI report in Curriculum Matters series outlines what pupils might be expected to know, understand and be able to do at different ages

36

A potted history of drama education *continued*

Date	Drama education	Theatre praxis	Official reports
1990	1990 sees publication of classroom-based handbooks: Rex Gibson on Shakespeare in schools; Jonothan Neelands's *Structuring Drama Work*; and Andy Kempe's *GCSE Drama Coursebook*	Welfare State International's *Glasgow All Lit Up* takes place	*The Arts 5–16: a Curriculum Framework*, led by Ken Robinson, made the case for connectivity between the arts in education
1992	John O'Toole's *The Process of Drama* published; Gavin Bolton's *New Perspectives on Classroom Drama* published	Simon McBurney's production of *Street of Crocodiles* with Théâtre de Complicité	*Drama in Schools* published by the Arts Council of Great Britain. It made the case for a curriculum framework based in making, responding and performing. It had huge demand in schools
1994	Michael Fleming's book *Starting Drama Teaching* published		*Handbook for the Inspection of Schools*: OFSTED gives a framework for inspecting drama in schools
1995	Edward Bond's collaboration with *Big Brum Theatre-in-Education* results in *At the Inland Sea*; Cecily O'Neill's *Drama Worlds* published	Jez Butterworth's *Mojo* at The Royal Court signals a renewed interest in Issues surrounding masculinity in theatre	Annual report of Chief Inspector of Schools criticizes lack of progression and sense of purpose in much KS3 drama work
1996	*Research in Drama Education*: UK journal established to support international research; *Theatre Studies* by Simon Cooper and Sally Mackey published to support A level drama and theatre studies students	First production of Mark Ravenhill's *Shopping and Fucking*	*Setting the Scene*: Department of National Heritage stresses the importance of the arts to the economy
1997		Royal National Theatre and BT commission new plays for performance by young people' 'Connections'	
1998	David Hornbrook's edited collection *On the Subject of Drama*; Joe Winston's *Drama, Narrative and Moral Education* offers a theorized account of drama as moral education		*The Arts Inspected* HMI handbook documents good practice within their specified framework; *Drama Sets You Free* published by Secondary Heads Association in support of drama education

37

A potted history of drama education *continued*

Date	Drama education	Theatre praxis	Official reports
1999		Khan-Din Ayub's second play, *Last Dance at Dum Dum* performed, whilst his *East is East* released on film. Both show new representations of British Asian communities	*All our Futures*: a report undertaken by the National Advisory Committee on Creative and Cultural Education. It was chaired by Ken Robinson, with an impressive line-up of celebrities and respected artists, who criticized the lack of publicity the report attracted
2000			Introduction of revised National Curriculum in England and Wales; national review of examination syllabuses

The contemporary picture: making, performing, responding

Contemporary drama educators are indebted to the legacy of their predecessors in many ways. Whilst it would be wrong to suggest that all drama teachers are similarly motivated, there is broad agreement that drama education in secondary schools encompasses three interrelated practices: making, performing and responding.[19]

Whilst it is sometimes convenient to categorize dramatic activities into one or other of these three modes, drama practitioners often work consecutively in different elements of making, performing and responding. In the most straightforward interpretation of these three modes, however, pupils will be clearly working in one or other area. Put simply, such drama activities may include:

- discussing how to construct a scene which illustrates a particular point (making);
- presenting a rehearsed scene to classmates (performing);
- discussing the way groups represented particular ideas or issues in their scenes (responding).

This would be a particularly simplistic model of a drama lesson. More commonly, the movement from one mode to another is much less obvious than this linear sequence suggests; at any given moment elements of all three modes may be apparent in the activity. The balance and movement between each mode will reflect the teachers' values and praxis as well as the pupils' progression.

Making drama is a particularly elastic concept in that it incorporates spontaneous improvisation, role-play, devising and script-writing as well as rehearsing plays for performance. Sometimes drama teachers encourage pupils to explore issues and ideas by employing a range of drama strategies, such as hot-seating or teacher-in-role. Teachers may structure a sequence of activities so that the pupils are able to make characters and fictions which invite speculation and offer new insights. At other times, teachers may provide opportunities for pupils to make drama using specific genres or forms, and use the context of making drama to develop an embodied understanding of practices such as physical theatre or mime. In making drama, the knowledge, skills and understanding pupils demonstrate include:

- how to work successfully in groups and develop collaborative working practices;
- the ability to research and select resources, information and other relevant material;
- the exploration and development of their own ideas, thoughts and feelings and those of others through and in drama;
- the ability to represent and shape ideas in dramatic form in devised, scripted or improvised drama.

The term 'performance' can suggest something quite formal and polished. However, at Key Stage 3 in particular, the crafts associated with performance tend to be integrated into drama lessons so that pupils show elements of their work as part of the process of sharing ideas with each other and moving the drama forward. As pupils progress, and particularly if they choose to take examination courses in drama, teachers are likely to focus more explicitly on developing performance skills. Performing drama may be seen as involving:

- sustaining a role or roles using particular performance styles;
- giving a coherent interpretation of a role;
- communicating with an audience, using voice, gesture, movement, timing and space;
- creating a dramatic atmosphere using appropriate lighting, sound and design;
- working co-operatively with others as part of an ensemble.

Responding to drama involves pupils in reflecting on their own emotional experiences of drama, as well as learning to decode theatrical images and interpret dramatic performances. Making sense of dramatic experiences in this way involves pupils in developing and using a critical vocabulary which they can use to share their perceptions. Knowing subject-specific terminology and understanding how dramatic works relate to their historical and social contexts enhances pupils' appreciation and understanding of their own drama and that of others. Responding to drama might include:

- interpreting visual, aural and physical signs inherent in performance;
- using a critical vocabulary to describe and conceptualize dramas made and seen;
- analysing and comparing possible interpretations of a dramatic script or performance text;
- noting and communicating personal emotional responses and resonance.

An agenda for observation

In a lesson you observe, consider the balance between activities that predominantly involve *making*, *performing* and *responding*. Were there moments when all three modes appeared to be working consecutively and complementing each other? Consider which elements of the lesson seemed primarily child-centred and which were more obviously subject-centred. How did the teacher integrate knowledge, skills and understanding about drama into the context of the lesson in an implicit way? To what extent did he or she make the pupils explicitly aware of what knowledge, skills and understanding were being addressed and developed? In discussion after the lesson, try to establish the way in which the structure and format of the lesson reflected the values and overall aims of the drama teacher.

Local contexts and national requirements

The place of drama in government requirements for secondary education varies between the four countries which make up the UK, and there are no statutory National Curriculum orders specifically for drama in any region. Nonetheless, drama continues to flourish in almost all schools, and in the vast majority drama is offered as an examination option.[20] Not only is drama regarded as a specialist subject in its own right, it is also integrated into government documents in a range of other curriculum areas including English, literacy development, the expressive arts and ICT. Furthermore, various National Curriculum documents make it clear that all pupils should have access to an education that has cultural, creative and aesthetic elements. In order to fulfil the different governments' requirements whilst also maintaining the integrity of the subject, drama teachers in secondary schools have developed ways of working which reflect and support the local and regional contexts in which they are working.

Given the absence of coherent statutory requirements for drama, there is a tremendous amount of local flexibility over how to teach drama at Key Stage 3 and which examination specifications to choose at Key Stage 4 and beyond. This means that there can be considerable variance in the knowledge and skills taught and assessed in drama lessons. In terms of departmental structures and organization, however, it would be wrong to assume that where drama appears as a separate subject on the timetable there is also an autonomous drama department. Although independent drama departments exist, many specialist drama curricula are taught from within larger faculty structures, particularly in expressive arts faculties or under the auspices of English.

Organizationally, there can be some advantages of locating drama in larger departments or faculties. Although working in an autonomous drama department can be an exciting prospect it can also lead to a sense of isolation. In some schools there is only one drama teacher, and a small department may have limited influence in the school structure. It may also lead to some frustration if there seem to be fewer kindred spirits with whom to share and evolve new ideas or reflect on experiences. As part of a large and powerful English department or arts faculty, there is often a greater say in the formulation and application of whole-school policies and opportunities to collaborate with a wider range of colleagues.

Despite the benefits of linking drama with English, not all English specialists are experienced in or enthused by the prospect of teaching practical drama and this can result in patchy or negative experiences for pupils. In this context there is also a risk that the verbal and written elements of the subject are over-emphasized. If drama is used solely as a means of delivering the National Curriculum in English, elements of the subject involving, for example, movement, design and technology may be overlooked. Including drama as a part of an arts faculty has the advantage, for drama specialists, of providing support in terms of staffing and finance (useful for upgrading specialist equipment and buying-in professional companies and artists to contribute to the curriculum). It can be tremendously exciting and productive to collaborate with colleagues who understand creative processes and are keen to share expertise and explore joint ventures. Reported disadvantages of working within an arts faculty are that drama can lose some of its individuality and drama teachers may have less opportunity to marshal progression in specific aspects of the subject if they have to concede to more general aims.[21]

Student-teachers in drama working alongside teachers of English, dance, music and the visual arts are in a good position to explore how the drama curriculum might cohere with and complement pupils' learning in related disciplines. In terms of subject-knowledge, this means that student-teachers learn when and how collaboration may enhance pupils' creativity and learning, and when it is less appropriate or productive. The next sections will explore some of these issues, focusing in turn on the subject-knowledge required by official documents to teach drama as a specialist subject, as an element of English, to contribute to literacy learning, as part of an expressive arts curriculum, in relation to ICT and within whole-school learning policies.

Discuss

What practices, processes and subject content do you think drama shares with other arts such as dance, visual art and music? Find out how teachers in those subjects describe the different modes of activity involved in their discipline. What particular contribution do you think drama teachers might make to an English curriculum? Are there skills that you think you might usefully learn from other arts or English teachers which would be relevant to you as a drama specialist?

Drama and public examinations

There are well-established examination courses in drama throughout the UK. In England, Wales, Northern Ireland and Scotland most pupils have an option of taking a GCSE or Standard Grade in drama at the end of Key Stage 4. Some continue to study the subject post-16 in courses learning to AS, A level or Highers, or vocational qualifications such as GNVQ or GSVQ. In most cases, drama teachers have a free choice of specifications and syllabuses. This choice is likely to reflect the values and methodologies of drama teachers in the school, but sometimes other local factors are influential in their decisions. For example, there may be a tradition of working with a particular examination board or with a strong network of other local schools which share a particular syllabus. All examination syllabuses must satisfy criteria set by the respective regional qualifications and curriculum authority. As a result, despite differences of approaches, emphases and assessment weightings within syllabuses, there are also a number of common factors. For example, the most recent review of GCSE syllabuses in England and Wales has led to the requirement that candidates study at least one scripted play of significant length. In Northern Ireland the Department of Education has issued non-statutory guidelines for the teaching of drama at Key Stage 4 to complement the optional GCSE course.[22]

In order to ensure a smooth and coherent progression in terms of what pupils know, understand and can do in drama, the Key Stage 3 curriculum is likely to acknowledge and work towards the requirements of the particular syllabus chosen for examination at 15+. (The issue of progression is discussed further in Chapter 5.) Student-teachers in drama obviously need to acquire a sound understanding of any examination syllabus they will teach in order to do justice to the candidates; knowing the requirements of the chosen syllabus will also help them understand the philosophy and principles on which drama is built in their placement schools. Reaching this understanding is, in turn, more easily achieved with some knowledge of the alternatives. Just as it is important to recognize the opportunities for learning and potential limitations of different methodologies in drama, so reading and discussing different examination syllabuses helps student-teachers gain insights into their own emergent praxis and that of their colleagues.

Opportunities for advanced and higher level courses have been revised recently. Young people wishing to stay in full-time education in England, Wales and Northern Ireland have been offered a wider range of courses leading to qualifications through the introduction of the AS (Advanced Supplementary) Level. The AS represents one half of a full A level. All A level specifications designed for a two-year period of study incorporate units of work leading to an AS qualification in the first year. In Scotland there has been a similar move in which Highers and GSVQ qualifications have been revised into broader qualifications known as the 'Higher Still'. Candidates in the 16 to 18 age-range are thus generally expected to undertake study of a wider range of skills and subjects than before. This move brings UK qualifications more in line with most countries in mainland Europe.

Find, compare and contrast

Access copies of the examination syllabuses used in your placement school and produce a brief synopsis of their content and how candidates are assessed.

Compare this with synopses of other drama syllabuses produced by your colleagues in other schools.

Discuss the differences between each specification. What opportunities or disadvantages would each have in the context of your school?

Full details of GCSE, A Level, GNVQ and Scottish Standard and Higher Still Grades can be accessed from the following addresses:

Edexcel: www.edexcel.org.uk (GCSE, A level Drama and Theatre Studies, GNVQ)
AQA: www.aqa.org.uk (GCSE, A Level Drama and Theatre Studies)
OCR: www.ocr.org.uk (GCSE)
WJEC: www.accac.org.uk (GCSE, GCE Drama and Theatre Studies including Welsh language options)
CCEA: www.ccea.org.uk (GCSE – Northern Ireland only)
SQA: www.sqa.org.uk (Scottish Standard and Higher Grades)

Drama and English

Although drama is perhaps most obviously identified as a separate curriculum subject, it is also closely allied to the teaching of English. In part, this is due to the inclusion of plays in the study of English literature. A good deal of drama clearly involves the use of verbal language, and since the introduction of National Curriculum Orders for English, drama has found a place in attainment targets relating to speaking, listening, reading and writing.[23]

Precise references to drama in National Curriculum Orders for English suggest that it is included in the curriculum for very particular educational purposes. For example, not only are pupils expected to read and write plays in their English lessons, it is also acknowledged that drama provides a valuable context for speaking and listening. The National Guidelines for the teaching of English in Scotland summarize the place of drama in the English curriculum:

> Drama is an important area of the curriculum in its own right. It is of importance for Language in promoting pupils' listening, talking, reading, writing and thinking. It also creates stimulating and exciting activities in which pupils can exercise their imaginations. Visits from companies, or excursions to the theatre, are obvious ways of involving pupils with drama.[24]

In such an integrated approach to the teaching of English, where reading, writing, speaking and listening activities are designed to support and complement each other, drama makes a valuable contribution.

Programmes of study which refer explicitly to drama are most detailed in England, suggesting that there is more flexibility in how the subject is taught elsewhere. Nonetheless, as these programmes of study are fairly typical of the kind of guidance given in all regions, the drama elements of the National Curriculum Orders for English in England are summarized below. The chart also indicates how pupils are expected to progress from Key Stage 2 to Key Stage 4; student-teachers will need to acknowledge how the content of their drama lessons and pupil progression coheres with the wider demands of the National Curriculum in their particular region.

National Curriculum Orders for English in England

Key Stage	Breadth of study	Learning outcomes
2	Children's knowledge and understanding of drama is developed through activities such as:	Through these activities children are taught how to:
	improvisation and working in role;	create, adapt and sustain different roles, individually and in groups;
	scripting and performing;	
	responding to performances.	use character, action and narrative to convey story, themes, emotions, ideas in plays they devise and script;
		use dramatic techniques to explore characters and issues (for example, hot seating, flashback);
		evaluate their own and others' contributions to the overall effectiveness of performances.
3 and 4	Pupils are expected to participate in a wide range of drama activities and be able to evaluate their own and others' contributions such as:	Through these activities pupils are taught how to:
	improvisation and working in role;	use a variety of dramatic conventions to explore ideas, issues and meanings;
	devising, scripting and performing in plays;	use different ways to convey action, character, atmosphere and tension when they are scripting and performing plays (for example, through dialogue, movement, pace);
	discussing and reviewing their own and others' performances.	
	Within AT 2 Reading pupils should have the opportunity to read:	appreciate how the structure and organization of scenes and plays contribute to dramatic effect;
	two plays by Shakespeare;	
	drama by major playwrights;	evaluate critically performances of dramas that they have watched or in which they have taken part.
	recent and contemporary drama written for young people and adults;	
	drama by major writers from different cultures and traditions.	
	As a part of their study for AT 3 Writing pupils should learn how to write in a range of forms including playscripts.	

The study of plays is included in both English programmes of study and in drama syllabuses. Understanding drama in performance has become an increasingly important element of the English curriculum and many English teachers use practical approaches to dramatic texts in their lessons. However, pupils' responses to plays are assessed differently in the two subjects. In English, their understanding of dramatic literature is usually assessed through written work or through speaking and listening tasks, whereas drama specifications often require pupils to be assessed as practitioners. This distinction between the two subjects becomes increasingly apparent as pupils progress; in post-14 courses pupils are expected to comment on plays as literary critics in English whereas in drama they will explore and interpret scripts as performers, directors or designers.

English and drama specialists possess complementary skills and subject-knowledge, particularly in the field of dramatic literature, and there has been much productive co-operation in schools. In England, where all Year 9 pupils must take Standard Attainment Tests (SATs) which include a Shakespeare play, many English and drama teachers work together to ensure that pupils participate in dramatic interpretations of the text. However, where drama teachers are expected to apply their skills to teaching English, they will need to possess adequate subject-knowledge in order to identify what individual pupils have achieved in reading, writing, speaking and listening. In this context, there is a danger of making references to the National Curriculum too vague and tokenistic. For example, simply stating that a drama lesson will 'Address the Programme of Study for Speaking and Listening' is neither convincing nor likely to help student-teachers assess pupils' learning accurately. It is far more productive to make one or two specific references to the National Curriculum in unit and lesson plans so that particular elements of pupils' progress and learning can be assessed.

Research

Find out how the drama elements of the English curriculum are covered in your placement school. Do drama teachers undertake particular responsibilities in the teaching and assessment of speaking and listening skills? To what extent do drama specialists contribute to the teaching of reading and writing playscripts? Conversely, how do English teachers incorporate improvisation, role play and performance in their lessons? To what extent do English and drama departments correlate their work to ensure that all of the statutory requirements of the curriculum are met and unnecessary repetition is avoided?

In England, Paper 2 of the KS3 SATs in English requires pupils to answer questions on a prescribed Shakespeare play. Read some past papers. To what extent do you feel a practical approach to the study of plays would help pupils answer the questions?

Further details about National Curriculum Programmes of Study and subject guidance can be viewed on the following regional websites:

England: www.hmso.gov.uk/guides.htm
Scotland: www.scotland.gov.uk
Wales: www.acac.org.uk
Northern Ireland: www.deni.gov.uk

Details of Standard Attainment Tests in England and Wales can be viewed on: www.qca.org.uk/

Drama and literacy

One way of seeing the importance of drama to the development of literacy would involve making a simple syllogism: literacy is concerned with reading and writing; drama involves reading and writing plays; thus drama must help with literacy. However, literacy is also concerned with speaking and listening, with the languages of physical communication as well as the written word. This means that drama presents particular opportunities for literacy development.

Drama specialists know that spoken communication involves more than just speaking and listening. In drama, attention is drawn to *how* people speak and *how* they communicate. The tone, pitch, volume and timbre of the voice along with the pace and rhythm of their speech all combine to give meaning to their utterances. Meanings are also attached to particular accents or dialects and all these factors mean that audiences may interpret the sound of words alone in a great variety of ways. In drama, the complexities of communicating verbally are further revealed through an exploration of the visual images that may accompany what is being said. In their practical drama work, pupils not only come to recognize that the meanings of words are changed by the way they are spoken and the actions that accompany them, they learn how to change the way they speak to suit different situations, purposes and audiences.

Through concentrating on *how* language works in communication, drama teachers have a particularly useful platform from which to help pupils learn *about* language. In drama, words may be used, for example, emotively, poetically, persuasively and polemically. The choice of words becomes crucial not only because of their literal meaning but because of the way their sound may complement or jar with each other when they are spoken. Assonance and dissonance, rhythm and rhyme, for example, affect how the meanings of words are interpreted.

Communication is an interactive process in that the person communicating uses a vast range of verbal, visual and aural signifiers to create particular effects. In turn, the receiver interprets and decodes those signals. Being 'literate' implies an ability to both put words, movement and gesture together effectively and being able to comprehend and interpret their visual, physical and verbal meanings. There is more involved in literacy than simply being able to spell or read a series of words; without the accompanying ability to make both connections between words and interpret the gaps and the silences between the words nothing can be communicated and nothing understood. In drama it is precisely because attention is paid to *how* words connect with each other and with the context in which they are used that drama teachers may contribute to the pupils' development of comprehension. However, trusting that pupils' conceptual development and literacy skills will, by some process of osmosis, be enhanced simply by doing drama is to misunderstand the importance of deliberately planning opportunities to develop literacy.

In order to ensure that a comprehensive programme for literacy learning is planned, a National Literacy Strategy was imposed, somewhat controversially, on primary schools in England in 1998. Two years later secondary schools in pilot authorities began to trial a framework for literacy at Key Stage 3. The purpose of introducing the National Literacy Strategy to secondary schools is to encourage teachers of all subjects to see themselves as having a role in improving literacy. This is emphasized in the National Curriculum Orders issued in all subjects, where the following passages appear:

> Pupils should be taught in all subjects to express themselves correctly and appropriately and to read accurately and with understanding . . .
> Pupils should be taught the technical and specialist vocabulary of subjects and how to use and spell these words. They should also be taught to use the patterns of language vital to understanding and expression in different subjects. These include the construction of sentences, paragraphs and texts which are often used in a subject, e.g. language to express causality, chronology, logic, exploration, hypothesis, comparison, and how to ask questions and develop arguments.[25]

In terms of subject-knowledge, drama teachers may consider both how pupils are taught the specialist vocabulary of drama and how different types of language may be integrated into drama practice and their purposes studied explicitly.

Read and discuss

Read the National Literacy Strategy for Key Stage 2 carefully. Identify all the references to drama.

How do the drama activities included in the Framework for Literacy at Key Stages 2 and 3 relate to the existing drama curriculum in your school?

Read the QCA publication *Language for Learning in Key Stage 3* and discuss with your mentor the contribution drama may make to a whole-school approach to the development of language and literacy. Are any units of work specifically aimed at developing aspects of literacy? How do the drama teachers ensure that pupils are taught the 'technical and specialist vocabulary' of drama?

Any whole-school literacy strategy should not be seen as additional to National Curriculum Orders for English but rather as complementary to them. Extracts taken from the draft framework for literacy at Key Stage 3 piloted in English schools illustrate how closely linked drama activities are to the project of improving literacy in the secondary school.

Extracts from the draft framework for literacy at Key Stage 3

Year	Through a range of drama techniques, pupils will . . .
7	explore in role a variety of situations and texts or respond to stimuli; reflect on the insight this provides into the motives and perspectives of others;
	extend their spoken repertoire by experimenting with language in different contexts and roles;
	work collaboratively to devise and perform scripted and unscripted pieces, which convey understanding of character, relationships and issues;
	develop a performance, which establishes and maintains the attention of the audience;
	reflect on and evaluate their own and others' performances;
	develop strategies for anticipating, visualizing and problem-solving in different contexts.
8	reflect on their participation in drama and analyse their development of dramatic techniques, e.g. *keep a reflective record of their contributions to dramatic improvisation and presentation*;
	develop the dramatic techniques that enable them to sustain a role;
	explore and develop ideas, issues and relationships through work in role;
	explore the language, structure and dramatic effect of scenes and plays;
	create complex or challenging dramatic performances which hold the attention of the audience.
9	recognize and evaluate the skills and techniques they have developed through drama;
	use a range of drama techniques to explore alternative ideas and meanings, e.g. *by playing out hypotheses, by changing perspectives*;
	examine the dramatic impact of a scene or play by Shakespeare, and identify the contributions of the writer, director and actors;
	recognize and respond to symbolism, subtext, mood and emotion as well as to actions and overt meanings;
	evaluate a performance which they have seen or in which they have participated;
	understand how thinking about issues and ideas can be developed through drama.

Research and discuss

How do the drama activities included in the draft Framework for Literacy at Key Stage 3 relate to the existing drama curriculum in your school?

Discuss with your mentor the extent to which the drama department considers itself a vital part of the whole school literacy strategy. How explicit is their contribution to the improvement of literacy in the school? Are any units of work specifically aimed at developing aspects of literacy? How do the drama teachers ensure that pupils are taught the 'technical and specialist vocabulary' of drama?

Drama and the expressive arts

In many schools throughout the UK drama is taught as part of an expressive arts or performing arts curriculum. This usually means that drama is taught separately by subject-specialists, but that common approaches to arts education are also recognized. There are both pragmatic reasons and theoretical principles which inform the decision to develop an expressive arts curriculum. First, a fragmented arts provision may sit uneasily in a context where all other subjects are grouped together into broader curriculum areas such as science, technology or humanities. Second, a well-planned expressive or performing arts curriculum can enable pupils to recognize common ways of working and transferable skills. Sometimes it is suggested that an arts curriculum leads to a dilution of subject specialism in drama, but this need not be the case. After all, no one suggests that when both French and German are included in a Modern Foreign Languages curriculum pupils learn an incomprehensible mixture of the two languages!

The relationship between the arts in education is summarized in the Scottish document, *National Guidelines: Expressive Arts 5–14*. In the introduction to the guidelines, it is recognized that the arts' role in education is to develop pupils' 'creativity, imagination and personal response', but that each arts subject 'represents a unique combination of ideas, skills and knowledge'.[26] In making this distinction between shared educational objectives and separate artistic skills, practices and knowledge, these guidelines suggest a theoretical basis for arts education which is typical of many expressive arts curricula and examination specifications. In the Scottish guidelines, the 'Outcomes' column is common to all arts subjects, but the 'Strands' are specific to drama.

Scottish National Guidelines for Expressive Arts 5–14

Outcomes	Strands
Using: Materials	Investigating and experimenting
Techniques Skills	Using movement and mime
Media	Using language
Expressing Feelings	Creating and designing

Ideas
   Thoughts
   solutions
	Communicating and presenting

Evaluating and appreciating	Observing, listening, reflecting, describing and

In practice, the success of an expressive curriculum often depends on a good culture of collaboration between different arts teachers. Where most of the curriculum is taught as separate arts subjects, sharing expertise can add a new dimension to the pupils' learning. The work of Year 10 music and drama groups may be enhanced through collaboration on a unit of work about Brechtian theatre and songs, for example, or dance and drama classes may benefit from uniting for work on physical theatre. Where there are robust artistic reasons for collaboration, pupils and teachers can find the process of working on expressive arts or performing arts examination courses at 15+ and 18+ very rewarding. Conversely, if drama is only tenuously linked by theme or idea to other arts subjects it is usually repetitive and lacking depth.

Research task

Observe lessons in music, dance and/or the visual arts. Discuss possibilities for collaboration in your placement school with other arts teachers.

Look up expressive or performing arts examination specifications on the Internet (see page 224 for websites). What potential advantages or disadvantages do you see in this way of working? How does it cohere with your own praxis and experience? What might you learn from working in an expressive arts curriculum?

ICT and the drama curriculum

Not only does ICT form an important part of industry and commerce, innovations in technology have played a significant part in entertainment and leisure. From the point of view of drama education, individual artists and theatre companies have been quick to integrate new technologies into their work. Inevitably, there has been considerable research into the impact of ICT on pupils' learning; the guidance issued by the Scottish Office makes this very clear. Referring to a report published in 1997, it claims that ICT has six main effects on learning:

- improved subject-learning;
- the development of network literacy;
- improved vocational training;
- improved motivation and attitudes to learning;
- the development of research skills;
- social development.[27]

While some schools may still be some way from realizing these aims, it is clear that the judicial use of ICT in the school curriculum is set to increase. The issue for student-teachers is how to develop the kind of subject-knowledge which enables them to select ways of working with ICT in the classroom which significantly enhance pupils' learning. They will also need to know how to discriminate between ICT resources which are genuinely educationally beneficial and those which are frills or distractions.

Some ICT skills have an obvious application to the drama classroom, whilst others may be more appropriately used in student-teachers' own organization and the preparation of teaching materials. For this, student-teachers may use some of the following skills:

- use of word processors to write lesson plans;
- design of worksheets, posters and displays;
- devising spreadsheets and tables to record pupils' progress.

In the drama classroom, student-teachers will need a working knowledge of specialist ICT equipment. This may be used both by teachers to enhance their own practical work with pupils and as an explicit element in the drama curriculum where pupils are taught to use it for themselves. Specialist equipment in drama includes:

- computer-aided lighting and set-design packages;
- computerized lighting desks;
- sound-wave software and other audio equipment;
- digital cameras;
- video editing equipment;
- powerpoint projectors.

In all areas of the curriculum, pupils are expected to use ICT to exchange and share information, to research aspects of the subject, and to use computers to draft and present their written work. Many of these are transferable skills, and familiarity with the ICT National Curriculum or guidelines should enable student-teachers of drama to draw on pupils' existing knowledge and extend their skills. Furthermore, as drama often relies on practice rather than written work for assessment, recording pupils' work using video or digital cameras is a particularly useful strategy.

Acquiring ICT skills and becoming proficient in applying them to classroom practice can be daunting. It is sometimes difficult to know what questions to ask, and the jargon of even the most benign ICT technicians can be intimidating. However, those starting training courses with little working knowledge of ICT need to elicit extra support as quickly as possible. As evidence of their learning, all student-teachers will find it useful to keep a weekly log of how different ICT opportunities are presented both in the classroom and in other educational contexts. The following table shows how one student-teacher responded to the challenge of learning more about ICT and how to apply it in her teaching.

Upgrading ICT skills

Week	University or other training course	Independent study	Classroom teaching	Administration
1	Have to complete first drama assignment on word	Get a password. Sort out how to access colour printers	Discuss ICT provision with drama mentor	Read booklet provided by university ICT resource centre
2	Micro-teaching using powerpoint	Edit text and video	Year 7 pupil showed me use of fonts to suggest intonation on drama script	Sorted out how I might use video next week in Year 9 lesson
3	Analysed camera angles and genre in Orson Welles's version of *Macbeth*	Edited different film versions of Lady Macbeth's sleep-walking scene on to one VT	Projected downloaded images of Lady Macbeth on OHP	Looked up pupil's self-assessment records kept on disk
4	Video recorded part of drama workshop on assessment of group work	Logged on to DV8 website	Used OHP in class to show image as stimulus for improvisation	Set myself up on the staff computer

52

Research and application

- Find out what ICT equipment is available in your placement school and how it is used by different teachers.
- Access the last OFSTED report for your placement school on the Internet. Print off the section related to English and drama.
- Review a number of CD-ROMs to discover how they may be used to support learning in drama.
- Download some information about a period of theatre history with which you are unfamiliar.

Drama and whole-school learning policies

There are some aspects of education which transcend subject boundaries and are integral to all areas of the curriculum. These 'key skills' have been identified as:

- communication;
- application of number;
- information technology;
- working with others;
- improving own learning and performance;
- problem solving.

In addition, schools are expected to help pupils develop a number of 'thinking skills' in order that they can focus on how to learn.[28] Such skills would include:

- information-processing skills;
- reasoning skills;
- enquiry skills;
- creative thinking skills;
- evaluation skills.

In primary schools, generalist class teachers are in a good position to ensure that these skills are integrated into the pupils' overall experience. By contrast, divisions between subjects in secondary schools sometimes mitigate against consistent and coherent approaches to the way such things are tackled. In order to address this, many schools have developed whole-school learning policies to which all subject-teachers are expected to contribute. In some schools, drama teachers take specific responsibilities for covering aspects of these areas, such as personal, social and health education, but even where this is not the case, student-teachers will need to know how these policies and practices impact on their own teaching and subject-knowledge.

Teaching pupils *citizenship* has gathered momentum in recent years. As a part of the taught curriculum, citizenship sets out to inform pupils about legal and human rights and responsibilities and different forms of government. It also aims to encourage young people to think about political, spiritual, moral, social and cultural issues, and it is in this aspect of citizenship education that drama has a specific contribution to make. Part of the programme of study for citizenship states that pupils should be taught to:

- use their imagination to consider other people's experiences and be able to think about, express and explain views that are not their own;
- negotiate, decide and take part-responsibility in both school and community-based activities;
- reflect on the process of participating.[29]

Micro-teaching task

In groups of four, two people take on the roles of parents/carers and one adopts the role of a drama teacher. The role of the fourth member of the group is to observe and listen carefully to the ensuing discussion and act as a timekeeper. It is a parents' evening. Using appropriate National Curriculum and other guidelines, the drama teacher has to explain to the parents how drama contributes to their children's spiritual, moral, social and cultural development. The parents may wish to ask for concrete evidence of this learning or query the values that appear to underpin the programme. How does the drama teacher respond in a way that will clarify things for the parents?

After an agreed time (most parent–teacher interviews will last for no more than ten minutes), the observer calls an end to the discussion and feeds back to the role players. What assumptions and expectations did the parents appear to have? How useful, clear and relevant were the teacher's response to their concerns and questions?

1 For an excellent example of how to encourage a range of cultural reference points in drama teaching, see B. Wooding (2000) 'Authoring our Identities' in H. Nicholson (ed.) *Teaching Drama 11–18* (London: Continuum), pp. 89–100.

2 See L. S. Shulman 'Those who Understand: Knowledge Growth in Teaching' in L. Tickle (2000) *Teacher Induction: The Way Ahead* (Buckingham: Open University Press), pp. 42–3.

3 For a fuller discussion of the moral values attributed to canonical art, see F. Mulhern, (1981) *The Moment of Scrutiny* (London: Verso). His analysis of Leavis and 'the Scrutineers' illuminates the birth of the canon in education.

4 The ways in which the academy legitimated judgements of taste was famously discussed by Pierre Bourdieu in P. Bourdieu (1984) *Distinction: A Social Critique of the Judgement of Taste* (London: Routledge), see especially pp. 257–94. Feminist, Marxist and post-colonial critics, in particular, have theorized the role of the interpreter.

5 See S. Grady (2000) 'Languages of the Stage: A Critical Framework for Analysing and Creating Performance' in H. Nicholson (ed.) *Teaching Drama 11-18* (London: Continuum), pp. 144–59.

6 DfEE (1998) *Initial Teacher Training National Curriculum for the Use of Information and Communications Technology in Subject Teaching* (London: HMSO); The Scottish Office (1999) *SOEID Guidance on the Use of Information and Communications Technology (ICT) within Courses of Initial Teacher Training* (Edinburgh: SOEID).

7 The concept of 'atheoretical eclecticism' is discussed in more detail on page 90.

8 For contrasting accounts of the history of drama education, see G. Bolton (1998) *Acting in Classroom Drama* (London: Trentham Books), pp. 32–48; D. Hornbook (1998) *Education and Dramatic Art* (2nd edn) (London: Routledge), pp. 3-58; A. Martin-Smith (1996) 'British Conceptions of Drama in Education' in *NADIE Journal*, vol. 20, no.1, pp. 57–76.

9 This is based on the philosophy of John Dewey, whose work had a profound influence on progressive education. See G. Bolton, *Acting in Classroom Drama*, pp. 31–2 and B. Cohen (1969) *Educational Thought: An Introduction* (London: Macmillan), pp.74–93.

10 See G. Bolton, *Acting in Classroom Drama*, pp. 3–26.

11 For a more detailed discussion of the history of this period see P. Gardner (2000) 'The Secondary School' in J. Beck and M. Earl (eds) *Key Issues in Secondary Education* (London: Continuum), pp. 3–12.

12 White Paper on Educational Reconstruction, 1943. See J. S.Maclure (1973) *Educational Documents* (London: Methuen), pp. 206–9. The aspiration to extend the school-leaving age to 16 was not realized until 1971.

13 This is a particular concern for Peter Slade, who commented that drama was suitable for all pupils, especially those at secondary modern schools, but also including those at grammar schools. He thought that dramatic play would aid their moral judgements later in life. See P. Slade (1958) *An Introduction to Child Drama* (London: University of London Press), pp. 90–1.

14 Dorothy Heathcote was the most famous pioneer of this approach. For a detailed description of her work at the end of the 1970s see B. J. Wagner (1979) *Dorothy Heathcote: Drama as a Learning Medium* (London: Hutchinson).

15 First Report of the Public Schools Commission (The Newsom Report) (1968). See J. S. McLure, *Educational Documents*, pp. 332–41.

16 See D. Hornbook (1985–6) 'Drama, Education and the Politics of Change', *New Theatre Quarterly*, no. 4 and no. 5. See subsequent symposia in *New Theatre Quarterly*, nos 7 and 8.

17 M. Fleming (1994) *Starting Drama Teaching* (London: David Fulton), p. 7.

18 R. Williams (1961) *The Long Revolution* (Harmondsworth: Penguin Books), pp. 52–3.

19 These modes of activity are expressed in slightly different ways in different regions and by different agencies, showing that they have proved to be useful in articulating what the drama curriculum might include and how pupils progress through it. OFSTED refers to '*making and presenting drama; appreciating and appraising it*'. In Northern Ireland the modes are condensed into just two terms, *making* and *appraising*. In the Scottish expressive arts curriculum the terms *using*, *expressing*, *evaluating* and *appreciating* may be seen as addressing similar areas of study and experience.

20 79 per cent of schools in the UK offer drama at 15+. See Secondary Heads Association (1998) *Drama Sets You Free* (Bristol: SHA Publications), p. 92.

21 For a discussion of collaboration between drama and dance teachers in an arts faculty, see H. Nicholson and R. Taylor (1998) 'The Choreography of Performance' in D. Hornbrook (ed.) *On the Subject of Drama* (London: Routledge), pp. 112–28. For comments about progression in an arts faculty, see National Drama (1998) *The National Drama Secondary Drama Teacher's Handbook* (London: National Drama) pp. 4–10.

22 Department of Education, Northern Ireland (1993) *Key Stage 4 Programmes of Study: Drama* (Belfast: DENI).

23 Interestingly, in an acknowledgement of the complexity of communication, the Scottish curriculum for English links together *listening* and *watching*: The Scottish Office Education Department (1991) *National Guidelines: English Language 5–14* (Edinburgh: SOED), pp 26–9.

24 Ibid., p. 68.

25 DfEE (1999) *The National Curriculum Handbook for Secondary Teachers in England, KS3 and 4* (London: HMSO), p. 40.

26 The Scottish Office (1992) *National Guidelines: Expressive Arts 5–14* (Edinburgh: SOED), p. ix.

27 The Scottish Office (1999) *SOEID Guidance on the Use of Information and Communications Technology (ICT) within Courses of Initial Teacher Training* (Edinburgh: SOEID), p. 5.

28 DfEE (1999) *The National Curriculum: Promoting Skills across the National Curriculum* (London: HMSO), pp.22–4.

29 DfEE (1999) *The National Curriculum: Citizenship* (London: HMSO), p. 16. The teaching of citizenship in schools in England will be a statutory requirement from 2002.

3 Planning

Planning

There is a huge difference between planning drama activities that will keep pupils occupied in their lessons and planning for learning. Some student-teachers may have experience of running drama clubs and workshops for young people. They may have found it relatively easy to lead games and activities that children find fun and exciting. However, planning sequences of lessons designed to help pupils progress intellectually, creatively and artistically represents a more complex challenge.

When student-teachers observe good drama lessons, the careful planning that lies behind the practice is often difficult to detect. Asking to see lesson plans may not help much as experienced teachers rarely plan individual lessons in the kind of detail expected of student-teachers. As we discussed in Chapter 2, their knowledge of drama education will, to a greater or lesser extent, have become 'embodied'. This can make their practice look deceptively effortless and intuitive. The point is that good practice is characterized by an emphasis on what pupils are *learning* rather than primarily focusing on what they are *doing*. The activities the pupils undertake will be designed and planned to support particular learning objectives rather than introduced as an end in themselves. This kind of planning requires relating theory to practice. It demands both a specialist subject-knowledge of drama and an understanding of the different ways in which individual pupils think, feel and learn.

Principles of planning

One of the challenges that faces drama teachers is how to plan clearly defined learning objectives and structured lessons *and* allow for the kind of flexibility which leads to creative and innovative drama. These two demands sometimes seem to be in tension, particularly to drama practitioners who know that the most exciting work often seems unplanned and develops from dramatic moments which are unexpected or unforeseen. Successful drama education requires teachers to base their plans on theories of learning which both recognize that pupils are best supported when the work is carefully structured and acknowledge the open, dialogic and 'unfixed' qualities of drama. Planning in this way relies on three interrelated theories of drama and of learning. First, it takes account of the aims, values and content of the drama curriculum. Second, it is based on an understanding of the relationship between structured learning and creative practice. Third, it draws on research into practical teaching methods and pupils' learning styles.

Policies and praxis

It was suggested in Chapter 2 that in many schools drama is described in terms of the interrelated elements of making, performing and responding. Although each of these elements will doubtless occur in all lessons and units of work, exactly how they are interpreted and emphasized will depend on the subject-knowledge and values of the teachers who devised the drama curriculum, the needs of the pupils they teach and the ethos of the school.

Decisions about the relationship between policy, praxis and curriculum content will be made as part of the process of long-term planning. It is now a legal requirement that schools will have written policy documents which outline and rationalize what is being taught. In relation to each curriculum subject, it might be expected that such a policy would:

- state the principal aims of the subject;
- explain how the subject-specific work relates to the broader curriculum, for example to National Curriculum Orders for English or by contributing to cultural, aesthetic, social and moral education;
- identify how work in the subject addresses issues such as equal opportunities and health and safety;
- briefly explain what sort of activities pupils will undertake and how their progress will be monitored and their achievements recorded.

The most useful subject policies are short, concise and easily understood. The policy for drama teaching in a school provides student-teachers with a clear point of entry into understanding how drama teachers select both *what* to teach and *how* to teach it. Learning to teach involves student-teachers asking questions and identifying why teachers operate in particular ways as well as trying out things for themselves.

A model for drama teaching?

Throughout this book the need for student-teachers to develop an informed rationale for their own drama teaching is emphasized. This is particularly relevant to the process of planning, where key decisions about the content of the curriculum are made. In order to consider different models for drama teaching, student-teachers may wish to apply the five models of English teaching identified in the Cox Report (1989)[1] to drama, and discuss which are most relevant or important in this context:

- *personal growth* – the focus is on the development of the individual child's imagination and emphasizes the relationship between language and learning;
- *cross-curricula* – English is seen as both a subject and a medium of instruction; without adequate language skills learning in other areas of the curriculum is impeded;
- *adult needs* – teachers prepare pupils for adult life by emphasizing the vocational and logistic aspects of spoken and written language;
- *cultural heritage* – schools are responsible for helping pupils appreciate the work that has shaped thought and belief;
- *cultural analysis* – pupils are helped to develop a critical understanding of the world in which they live and the ways in which language, in whatever media, carries values.[2]

Policy and practice

Which of these models would most closely match your view of the role of drama in education? Do you think they have been informed by particular critical theories? Read the policy for drama in your placement school in the light of these models and discuss them with your mentor. Are some of these models reflected in the practical classwork of the drama teachers you are observing more than others?

Aims and curriculum content

However described, most drama curricula will specify the knowledge and skills which pupils will be taught and which they are expected to understand and acquire. Learning in drama takes place most effectively when it is contextualized, and this often involves choosing particular themes, issues, stories or genres because they seem an appropriate vehicle for teaching pupils particular dramatic skills. Contextualizing learning in this way avoids the potential superficiality of a skills-led curriculum in drama.

It is the knowledge, skills and understanding of drama, however contextualized within a unit of work, which provide the aims for that part of the drama curriculum. The aims thus reflect the 'bigger picture' and will stay consistent for the duration of the unit of work. The *content* of the unit of work needs, of course, to suit these aims. For example, the aim of a unit of work on a contemporary play may be to help pupils to understand how dramatic tension is created, whereas the aim of a sequence of drama lessons which takes Expressionist paintings as a starting point may be to explore how a variety of dramatic interpretations can arise from a stimulus.

In order to understand the relationship between lesson planning and pupils' learning it is more helpful for student-teachers to be told the aims of lessons rather than the content. For example, if they are told that the work is aimed at enabling pupils to develop roles or construct monologues rather than simply that it is 'about' evacuees they will be more able to identify the purpose of the activities. Recognizing the way lessons have been planned may also require student-teachers to have some background information about the class. For example, not all pupils share similar cultural or historical reference points. They bring expectations and experiences to drama which reflect the values and attitudes of their home and street cultures and this may well have implications for both the content and form of lessons.

Identifying aims through observation

How clearly do teachers outline what the lesson will be about at the beginning? Are there particular words or dramatic practices which are emphasized during the lesson? Are there visual displays designed to extend and reinforce the learning? Do the teacher's questions follow a particular line of inquiry? Are pupils encouraged to summarize their learning during the lesson? What sorts of things are pupils asked to comment on when they give feedback on group work or performances? How does the teacher demonstrate or model particular dramatic practices? To what extent do the aims of the lesson reflect drama policies?

Contributing to a drama curriculum which is already established requires student-teachers to prepare their teaching thoroughly. Although it may appear that much of the planning is already complete and delineated in the drama scheme of work, simply following predetermined lesson plans often leads to sterile teaching where neither student-teachers nor their pupils have much ownership of the work. At the other extreme, student-teachers who are invited to teach whatever they like may find it difficult to know what to do or where to start, and may not understand how their teaching fits into a broader picture of progression. Mentors thus need to offer student-teachers clear guidance about appropriate aims and learning objectives for particular lessons or unit of works but invite them to make suggestions about the content of the lessons. In this way, student-teachers can experiment with planning lessons whilst adhering to prescribed learning outcomes.

Structured learning and creativity

It can seem contradictory to state that a subject such as drama, which aims to enable young people to express their own ideas, thoughts and feelings, also relies on highly structured approaches to learning. There is, however, significant evidence that pupils are actually able to be *more* creative when they are given limited choices and when they are encouraged to frame their work within particular constraints.[3]

The concept of creativity has not been uncontested in drama education. In Chapter 2 it was noted how progressive educationalists reacted to oppressively traditional forms of education by allying artistic creativity to childhood play.[4] What was thought to be needed at the time was an environment in which young people could express themselves freely. One of the most positive legacies of this way of thinking is the view that, in drama, pupils should be encouraged to work practically to represent and shape their own ideas, feelings and values. However when pupils are left entirely to themselves, they are only able to express their ideas in dramatic forms with which they are already familiar. Consequently, their work may be predictable, repetitive and unimaginative. In redressing this balance, there has been an increased interest in teaching pupils more explicitly about different dramatic forms, genres and styles and in facilitating the creative exploration of the ideas of others as well as their own.

If one of the overall aims of a drama curriculum is to encourage pupils to become informed, creative and thinking practitioners, the challenge for teachers is how to introduce new ways of working whilst also valuing the contributions and interpretations of the particular pupils in the group. In order to provide this kind of structure for the curriculum, planning is divided into manageable segments: short-, medium- and long-term plans.

Short-, medium- and long-term planning

Detailed short-, medium- and long-term planning ensures that there is a sense of continuity and progression in the drama curriculum from one lesson to another, within a unit of work and from one unit of work to another.

- *Long-term planning* involves devising a curriculum map for each key stage. In designing the map teachers need to take account of national requirements, whole-school policies and, where appropriate, the demands of examination syllabuses. Such a map will plot how pupils will be introduced to a range of different dramatic styles, forms, techniques and genres and how their knowledge and understanding is deepened and extended as they move up the school. This sort of long-term planning is normally the responsibility of the head of drama but all drama teachers in a school will need to understand its structure and the thinking behind it in order to ensure consistency and coherence in the drama curriculum.
- *Medium-term planning* breaks down the long-term plans into more detailed units of work. These units (which, in practice, often last about half a term) identify the particular learning objectives and assessment criteria appropriate to that stage of the pupils' progression in drama. The knowledge, skills and understanding that drama teachers expect pupils to develop at that stage (particularly in the 11–14 age-range) is often contextualized in an exploration of a particular stimulus, theme or issue of the work. Different teachers may thus approach different learning objectives in different ways. The main thing is to keep sight in the medium-term planning of what the pupils have already done and where the long-term map will take them next.

- *Short-term planning* involves working out how the learning objectives of any given unit will be addressed through a sequence of individual lessons. Short-term plans will help the teacher focus on *how* to actually structure and deliver the lesson. Short-term planning is necessary in order to account for variables that may not be predictable or controllable by the teacher. For example, one week's lesson plan may need to be adjusted to account for a class missing the previous week because of unexpected events such as a fire drill or field trip.

One of the most difficult things to learn about planning is how to be flexible within the planned structure of a lesson. Student-teachers, when they first start teaching, often stick rather too rigidly to the procedure they have planned and find it difficult to know how to accept and develop the pupils' ideas without losing the plot of the lesson. Again, focusing on what the pupils are learning rather than considering solely what they are doing is the key to identifying how the lesson plan might be adapted while it is in progress. Responding to the pupils' ideas in this way, whilst still adhering to clear learning objectives, is often called 'reflection-in-action'; it is this ability to reflect-in-action which for many is the mark of a good drama practitioner.[5] Sharing the learning objectives with the pupils and so creating a community of learners in drama makes this easier – if pupils know where the teacher is trying to take them they will be able to suggest alternative routes themselves. For many drama teachers, engendering a culture of collaboration is central to the success of drama.

Teaching and learning styles

Within any community of learners there will be a diversity of approaches to learning. In drama education, it has long been understood that pupils learn best by doing, but it is also acknowledged that they may find different points of entry into the curriculum and learn by participating in a variety of ways. This has often been explained in terms of the content of the drama and because the issues explored seem relevant to pupils' lives. This is obviously an important factor but it is also the case that drama appeals to a wider range of learning styles than most other subjects in the curriculum, and so suits the abilities of a greater diversity of children. Drama requires pupils to engage physically as well as intellectually and emotionally with the work. Planning a curriculum which accounts for pupils' different ways of learning requires careful consideration.

According to the social psychologist Michael Fielding, pupils have different preferred learning styles. Learners can broadly be identified in the following ways:

- *auditory learners* – who prefer to learn mainly through talk and discussion;
- *visual/verbal learners* – who are supported by reading and writing, and by the use of visual images and pictures;
- *kinaesthetic learners* – who are helped when they become physically involved with the work, through movement and touch.[6]

What is interesting about this categorization of learning styles is that the kinaesthetic, visual, aural and verbal are all elements of practical drama; a range of learning styles is thus woven into the art form itself. Recognizing pupils' different learning styles provides a practical way of diagnosing individual needs and supporting pupils in tackling aspects of the work they find difficult. Experienced learners tend to be able to draw on a wide repertoire of learning styles. Including a range of activities in drama lessons that are differentiated to take account of different learning styles can encourage pupils to develop just such a repertoire.

Task: find your preferred learning style

In groups, compare how you remember telephone numbers – by the shape traced by your fingers, by seeing the numbers in your mind, by making up a tune or rhythm? When acting in scripted plays, how have you set about remembering your lines? Do you hear the characters' voices in your head? Visualize where you will be on the set? Walk around the room?

Differentiation

Considering learning styles in drama lessons is one approach to planning for differentiation in drama. A fully differentiated drama curriculum takes account of the different ways in which individual children learn and includes a diversity of drama practices. In practice, there are three main ways in which drama teachers plan for differentiation:

- differentiation by outcome;
- differentiation by task;
- differentiation by organization.

Although experienced drama teachers will tend to use a mixture of approaches to suit the context in which they are working, student-teachers may initially need to focus on each approach more explicitly in order to understand how the different models work.

Differentiation by outcome means that a whole class follows a shared structure or works on the same stimulus. Their different responses are supposed to illustrate their different levels of ability and achievement. This approach is undoubtedly important and plays a key role in assessment, but it has limitations in terms of teaching. If the work is only differentiated through outcome, there is a risk that pupils' individual needs remain undiagnosed and thus unsupported. Some may be insufficiently challenged while others sense they are failing because the task is beyond their comprehension or current capacity. The model calls into question the role teachers play in pupils' learning; to what extent and by what criteria will they intervene in order to help pupils learn?

Differentiation by task means that individuals or groups of pupils undertake different activities in the lesson. For example, it may be that some pupils have particular skills in choreography, and they are invited to take responsibility for the movement in a piece of devised work. Some members of the class have literacy difficulties and so require special support in text-based work. Perhaps one group is always prone to trivialize improvisation work and are thus given specially prescribed criteria to work towards. The advantage of differentiating by task is that, at best, it provides the opportunity for pupils to both extend their strengths and address new or more challenging aspects of the subject. The disadvantage is that in a traditional curriculum, differentiation by task has often been dependent on the pupils' abilities in verbal literacy. At worst it can be used as an excuse for bad practice. For example, sometimes tasks may be set in drama which both are inappropriate to the needs and potential of individual pupils and fail to recognize the skills associated with different elements of the art form. Giving the able readers the best parts in a play while shoving the 'slow-learners' off to sort out the costumes or 'do the lights' might well be one way of differentiating by task, but is it justifiable and productive? Does it, for example, take account of pupils' different learning styles? To what extent will it help pupils progress in areas in which they are not already quite competent?

Differentiation by organization requires teachers to structure group work so that pupils of similar or different abilities and skills can learn from and support each other. In most secondary schools, drama is taught in mixed ability groups. Successful groupings within these classes depends on the teachers' knowledge of the pupils' abilities and needs. Differentiation by organization is one way of valuing the diversity of skills and experiences pupils bring to the drama classroom. This is a very complex aspect of differentiation in which local factors may be extremely important. For example, social expectations associated with gender may be a significant factor in pupils' willingness to engage in some drama activities. In an attempt to achieve equality, different schools promote various approaches to this issue, and a balance is often struck between single-sex and mixed groupings. Furthermore, drama teachers will need to be particularly aware of how different religious beliefs may impact on elements of the drama curriculum and, in particular contexts, teachers may need to provide alternative activities for pupils who are forbidden by their religion to watch videos, be videoed or to engage in activities which involve physical interaction with members of the opposite sex. In multicultural classrooms, drama teachers may also wish to focus in their planning on how to value a diversity of ethnicities and cultural experiences in the organization of pupils' groupings and classes. In all cases student-teachers are well advised to seek advice from other teachers; in particularly interesting and complex situations it is likely that there have been discussions with parents and other members of the community in order to reach consensus about curriculum content and organization.

- Planning is very carefully structured for short-, medium- and long-term learning.
- Drama activities undertaken in lessons support teaching and learning objectives.
- There is potential for pupils' creativity within a clearly defined curriculum framework, especially when the pupils are a party to the intended learning outcomes and feel they have a voice in the shape and direction of the work.
- Planning should take account of different learning styles.

64

Ingredients of planning

Learning how to plan drama involves understanding how the different ingredients which make up a lesson, a unit of work and an entire drama curriculum work together to enable effective learning. Effective learning is only really achieved when the relationship between the principles of planning and the practice of the classroom is fully recognized. Long-term planning and devising units of work takes a lot of time and thought. Having done this, however, experienced teachers develop ways of planning individual lessons quite quickly and are able to adapt their plans while a lesson is in progress (which is often what makes them seem so effortless to the observer). There are no magical short-cuts for student-teachers in this process but many find that working to a set framework for lesson planning is helpful.

So what are the ingredients of planning? The terminology can sometimes seem confusing, and although some terms appear rather similar, they each have a distinctive function and purpose. Including the following ingredients of lesson planning in all short-, medium- and long-term plans helps student-teachers to keep their work focused and purposeful. This kind of detailed record keeping also helps them discuss their own progress as student-teachers.

- *Aims* indicate the long-term focus of the learning, and make the theory informing the practice explicit.
- *Teaching objectives* break down the aims into statements which set out what will actually be taught in the drama classroom.
- *Learning objectives* identify what the pupils will learn as a result of the teaching.
- *Continuity and progression* focuses attention on how the teaching takes account of the pupils' past and future learning.
- *Assessment criteria* indicate the aspects of drama on which the pupils will be assessed.
- *The syllabus or curriculum framework* which the pupils are following, as part of a public examination, national or local curriculum, will need to be consulted to ensure that planning coheres with specifications and requirements.
- *Organization and procedure* shows the way activities, resources, timings and structure set out to meet the teaching and learning objectives.
- *Differentiation* is the term used to show how the abilities and needs of individual pupils or groups of pupils might be met.

- *Homework* may need to be set to develop pupils as independent learners and to support classroom practice.
- *Evaluation* of the lesson is necessary in order to reflect on how the planning enabled learning to take place. A careful evaluation provides invaluable information for future planning.

Micro-teaching: planning parts of lessons

Unlike a recipe for a culinary dish, there are no set rules about which ingredient should be added first in the process of planning. Some teachers prefer to begin by considering the aims of the curriculum or unit of work, then selecting materials and strategies to address them. Others begin with a theme or stimulus for a drama and then work out how their ideas can be used to present opportunities for learning in drama. The important thing is that all the ingredients are eventually added, and that they conform to the values of the drama curriculum as a whole. In order to ensure continuity in the curriculum, most teachers will plan for long-term learning first, and then break the work into medium-term units and then into individual lessons. Student-teachers learn to plan by working the other way round. That is to say they will most likely start by planning parts of lessons, progress to individual lessons and only move to planning units of work and for the long term at a later stage in their training or induction period. The following sections of this chapter mirror this line of student-teachers' progression.

Student-teachers are likely to begin by planning work for small groups or by taking a small part in a lesson. It is most helpful to student-teachers when this sort of micro-teaching is carefully structured and supported by their drama mentors who can give them the opportunity to practise a range of teaching skills and strategies before they are faced with an entire lesson. The role of the mentor in student-teachers' progression from observation to whole-class teaching is discussed in Chapter 7; the purpose of this section is to identify the practicalities of planning activities at this level.

Planning just ten minutes of a lesson can take student-teachers a long time when they first start. The fact that it is so time consuming can be a good thing if it means that student-teachers are recognizing the complexity of teaching by making crucial links between teaching and learning rather than simply dreaming up wacky activities to fill lesson time. The process does speed up with experience.

There are a variety of drama activities, both small groups and whole-class teaching, to which student-teachers might contribute. In many cases, student-teachers are only in school two or perhaps three days a week in the early stages of their training. It is important that they can prepare their contributions to lessons and find ways to ensure continuity from one week to another. There are some tasks that can prove invaluable here. For example, student-teachers who have used digital cameras to capture dramatic moments in one lesson might learn how to give feedback to a group if they bring the prints mounted on a display with captions from the pupils' dialogue to the following week's lesson.

Micro-teaching: some drama activities

Small-group work

- Working with specified groups in the devising process.
- Introducing new resources appropriate to the theme or issue to support learning.
- Filming or taping groups work in progress.
- Scribing improvised dialogue.
- Demonstrating craft skills such as mask-making or puppetry.
- Providing writing frames which help pupils script their own work.
- Assisting with ICT tasks such as video editing or storyboarding.

Whole-class work

- Using digital cameras to capture or frame dramatic moments.
- Reading a story or poem to the class.
- Handling the feedback from performances of work in progress.
- Giving instructions in some part of the lesson.
- Taking on a particular role in a drama.
- Explaining a particular concept or skill.
- Finding and introducing a short video clip to illustrate an aspect of drama.
- Demonstrating a particular skill such as how lighting creates a dramatic atmosphere.

Student-teachers will learn most from micro-teaching when the task is very focused. They need to feel sure that they have interpreted the drama teacher's plan properly, so some discussion about the activities they intend to include both before and after the lesson is ideal. Issues surrounding collaborative teaching are identified in more detail in Chapter 7, but it is important to emphasize here that this way of working not only supports student-teachers in their planning but it can also provide productive and lively experiences for pupils.

Short-term planning: individual lessons

When they first begin to prepare individual lessons, student-teachers will probably be asked to tailor their plans to fit unit of works in which the aims, teaching objectives and dramatic forms are already identified. This offers student-teachers the chance to experiment with different methods and materials but involves careful consideration of all aspects of planning. Using a lesson-planning pro-forma has proved to be a particularly helpful way of ensuring that they do this. In practice, individual lesson plans should not be lengthy documents. It is better to write plans reasonably succinctly so that they can be read easily while the lesson is in progress.

Lesson-planning pro-forma

Date	Date of lesson	*Period* Time and place of lesson
Class	Name of class	*Ability range* Indicate NC levels or general ability range in the class, e.g. mixed ability, set (1/6)

Lesson length Duration of the lesson

Aims
Write in the aims of the unit of work of which this lesson forms a part. These aims will stay consistent throughout the unit of work and will form the basis of the assessment criteria.

Teaching objectives
In this section of the lesson plan, you will need to write down the two or three points you intend to *teach* in this lesson in order to address the overall aims of the unit.

Learning objectives
This indicates what two or three points the pupils will *learn* as a result of the lesson. They will echo the teaching objectives, but it is important that you indicate what they are learning in your planning so that the relationship between teaching and learning is made explicit.

Continuity
Note how the work in this lesson relates to previous work the group has done. This section ensures that you make connections between work they are currently undertaking and work undertaken before.

Progression
Note what opportunities the lesson will provide for pupils in this group to progress in their knowledge and understanding and drama skills.

Programme of study/examination syllabus
If the drama undertaken in this lesson is linked to aspects of the National Curriculum, literacy framework or to an examination syllabus, you should record how the work complies with it. Be specific.

Assessment
Record the assessment criteria for the unit of work here which will relate to this particular lesson. Briefly note what evidence of learning you will expect to see.

Organization, resources and ICT
Make brief notes here to help you to organize the classroom or drama studio to facilitate learning. Does the furniture need to be set out in a particular way? How will the pupils be grouped? Are there pupils in this class who may need particular support for aspects of the drama undertaken in the lesson? How will any in-class support be allocated during the lesson?

You should also consider how ICT or other resources will be prepared and organized. Are you using lighting or sound effects? Recording equipment? Do you need to lay out props or craft materials for the pupils?

Procedure

This section can seem to be the most important part of the planning, as it provides the structure of the lesson. You will need to record the stages you and the pupils work through during the lesson, the resources you will need and the timing of the lesson. It needs to be set out very clearly as you may wish to refer to it during the lesson.

Differentiation

Note here how the work will be differentiated in order to address the needs of individual pupils and/or groups.

Homework

Note here what homework you are setting, if any, and how this relates to the next lesson. Consider also how you will set the task, e.g. writing it on the board, explaining orally, issuing a printed slip.

Evaluation

Following the lesson you will need to consider how it worked out in relation to your planning. In addition to noting what the pupils appeared to learn from it and how you knew, you will need to note what *you* have learnt from it and how this will inform your future teaching.

How to write a lesson plan

Constructing a lesson plan in drama requires a good knowledge of the teaching methods which are part of the drama teacher's craft. Whatever the learning objectives the drama is designed to develop, the most common questions raised by student-teachers concern how the procedure of the lesson might be structured into a coherent learning experience. Issues which relate specifically to drama here include:

- Should there be a warm-up? What is the value of games or warm-up activities? How can they be linked to the aims of the lesson?
- How might the lesson be structured? How will the timing work?
- Should the work progress in ways which encourage all pupils to participate in the drama? How can more reluctant participants be brought into the work? How can pupils be organized to work in a range of groups?
- How many different activities should be included in an individual lesson?
- How might new dramatic genres, forms and vocabulary be introduced?
- How might the drama build on the pupils' own experiences as well as present new challenges?

All these questions provide excellent starting points for planning. Good drama lessons usually contain a variety of activities; if there is too much repetition, it is likely that the pupils do not quite have a varied enough diet. In the sample lesson plan shown, there are different activities planned which meet the teaching and learning objectives.

Sample lesson plan

Date: 06.01.00	Period: 4 (1.25– 2.25p.m.)
Class: 7	Ability range: mixed
Lesson length: 1 hour	

Aims	To encourage students to explore the physicality of poetic language; to experiment with dramatic atmosphere through making and performing sounds and movement; to investigate the voices of the protagonist and other characters; to develop a dramatic and critical vocabulary.
Teaching objectives	To develop creative skills using words as a stimulus for creating soundscapes with physical reactions. The words of the poem are then introduced as a whole piece and the students will critically analyse the poem.
Learning objectives	To experiment with words and phrases using different sounds/voices and to choose the most dramatic in order to physicalize the sound. To revise critical vocabulary with regards to analysing poetic structure.
Continuity	This unit uses making and performing skills that the class has used in previous units, but introduces the use of words and specifically poetry as a stimulus to creativity.
Progression	This unit will build upon this work on the poem; students will use it to create their own poems to work on.
Programme of study/ exam syllabus	In exploring this poem for dramatic potential the students will be practising the skills outlined in English in the National Curriculum for Reading: Extract meaning beyond the literal, explaining how choice of language and style affects implied and explicit meanings. Analyse and discuss alternative interpretations, unfamiliar vocabulary, ambiguity and hidden meanings. Plus the poem will be used to 'extend pupils' ideas and their moral and emotional understanding'. In dramatic terms the poem will be used to introduce dramatic tools such as freeze frame, sound collage and spoken thoughts as monologue.
Assessment	Formative. In this unit the students will be assessed on their ability to: use words and poetry as a stimulus to using sound and movement dramatically; work together effectively in small-group and class context.
Organization	Whole-class introduction to the scheme of work and whole-class Chinese whispers. Split the class in two for word-level work: 'bathing' other in sound. Same halves to work on phrases, then pair up to work on phrase and movement.
Procedure Timing and Resources	1.25 Register and settle. 1.30 Warm up from where they are sitting: close eyes and be aware of breathing. Now stand, find a space and focus on breathing again. Add a physical action, using just the arms, that reflects the movement of the breath in the body. Open eyes and keep action going. Add a sound that goes with the movement of the arm. 1.40 Stand in a circle: focus on breathing as a basis of sound/voice, plus looking at movement and sound and words. Word game/voice work – the whisper – Chinese whispers: send it around both directions until the sentence meets somewhere in the middle. How different are

Sentences:

'The sacks in the toolshed smell like the seaside.'

'Be careful your feet aren't sticking out.'

1.50 Divide the group A/B around the circle. The poem we are doing is called 'Hide and Seek'. So think about how the words make you feel: what feelings do you associate with/go with the idea of hiding and seeking? A = 'hide'; B = 'seek'. In a minute we listen to the words with eyes shut to concentrate on the sounds and think about how the sound affects us.

One person in the middle of the circle to listen very carefully. (Could perhaps try a sound/thought tunnel or have the As saying it to the Bs?)

The group not speaking should shut eyes and listen to the sounds of the words; the group speaking should concentrate on me: I will indicate with my hands when they should get louder and softer.

Ask As to step forward.

2.00 Give out phrases from the poem – they should think about many ways to say the phrase using different levels of pitch and voices, then say them out loud.

2.05 As to teach Bs the phrase: repeat exercise.

2.10 People with the same phrases pair up: find out which is the best way of saying the phrase, i.e. a way that reminds you of the feelings associated with hide and seek. Once decided, think of a simple action and freeze to go with the phrase (demonstrate). Give them time to practise: show some work that will invite comment from the group.

2.20 Evaluate and clear up.

2.25 End of lesson.

Differentiation	By outcome: learning aurally using the spoken word as a stimulus; kinaesthetically using movement to express meaning associated with the words; visually using the printed poem as a stimulus and also reading the pictures created by the performances.
Homework	Diary entry about the game of hide and seek.
Evaluation of students' learning and your teaching	This is an excitable group who coped reasonably well with some of the focus and concentration part of the lesson, but they do find it difficult to settle. I made a hasty decision to cut some of the warm-up due to the late start and went into the word-level work. While Chinese whispers went very well (i.e. they managed to learn a phrase and whisper it to each other), they had more difficulty with the word association (NB: introduce the hide/seek element with word association next time: due a full word association game) and the volume control. This had a lot to do with not being able to concentrate (only a few of the students) in the circle. The girl in the middle did well to analyse what she heard. I then returned to the breath, movement and sound part of the warm-up to end the lesson and calm them down again. This was where the best work was achieved. And this involved a deal of learning for myself: The group members work better in their own spaces rather than in a circle; the concentration is better. They need very clear instructions and more demonstration throughout the session in order to be better able to proceed with the work.

Sample lesson plan *continued*

> They need more time: cramming too much into the plan for the post-lunch lesson; settling at the start of the lesson takes a lot longer than five minutes as they need time to calm down and also think about the work that it is coming up: set expectations early.
>
> They set themselves targets for next week:
> listen to one another and be sensible.
>
> Mentors to check individual targets with me before lesson.

Balancing a range of drama activities with time for reflection and explanation is a difficult skill to acquire. Student-teachers often initially plan far too much material for one lesson and leave pupils little time to assimilate their learning and to relate the drama to their previous and future work. In order to avoid falling into this trap, it is helpful to consider the lesson from the pupils' point of view, and imagine how long they might need to complete any given activity well. One way of doing this is to log the time it is anticipated each part of the lesson will take. Viewed in this way, the procedure for part of the lesson above shows that the pupils are engaged in different but related activities.

Logging a lesson

Procedure	Teacher	Pupils
3.25 Register and settle	Give instructions, read list of names	Sit, listen, answer register
3.30 Warm up from where they are sitting: close eyes and be aware of breathing. Now stand, find a space and focus on breathing again. Add a physical action, using just the arms, that reflects the movement of the breath in the body. Open eyes and keep action going. Add a sound that goes with the movement of the arms.	Explain, narrate, instruct	Physical warm-up: breathing exercise, movement, non-verbal sound
3.40 Stand in a circle: focus on breathing as a basis of sound/ voice, plus we will be looking at movement and sound and words. Word game/voice work – the whisper – Chinese whispers: send it around both directions until the sentence meets somewhere in the middle: how different are they? Sentences: 'The sacks in the toolshed smell like the seaside.' 'Be careful your feet aren't sticking out.'	Explain, describe. Question, listen	Listen Vocal exercise Discussion
3.50 Divide the group A/B around the circle. The poem we are doing is called 'Hide and Seek'. So think about how the words make you feel: what feelings do you associate with/ go with the idea of hiding and seeking? A = 'hide'; B = 'seek'. In a minute we listen to the words with eyes shut to concentrate on the sounds and think about how the sound affects us.	Explain, question	Listen, speculate and discuss Create soundscape/ listen to

Scripting lesson plans : a case study

Student-teachers often have innovative ideas for drama but they may sometimes find that, when they are actually in the classroom, they become tongue-tied or, conversely, ramble on for far too long. Very detailed planning of individual lessons becomes less necessary with experience, but in the early stages many student-teachers' plans can look rather like scripts. This shows that they have thought through exactly what they will need to say to the class.

Case study lesson plan 1 was one of the first written by a student-teacher. She had been asked by her mentor to take 10–15 minutes of a Year 7 drama lesson. In writing this plan she considered what the pupils would be doing in the lesson, and made detailed notes about her own role and interventions. This helped her to keep firmly focused on the teaching and learning objectives and ensured that what she said enabled the pupils to make connections between their practical drama and their conceptual understanding of character. Although she did not stick rigidly to her 'script' in the lesson, the fact that she had thought about each moment in this detail gave her confidence in the classroom. She could refer quickly to her plan in the lesson – the use of different fonts, capitals, italics and colours highlighted different elements of the lesson.

Case study lesson 1

Date: 15th October   *Location*: Studio

Class: 7 Th. (mixed ability)   *Duration*: 50 mins

Unit title: 'GIANT'

TEACHING OBJECTIVES
To introduce the concept of 'character' and how external factors may affect character's mood (cause and effect).

LEARNING OBJECTIVES
To understand the concept of 'character' as something that is not static but as something that is affected by external factors (cause and effect).

PROCEDURE
- All sitting in a circle on the floor.
- Recap last week's lesson:

    Let's just cast our minds back to last week's lesson.
    If you remember, we began the lesson by talking about a mountain.
    And when we looked closely at the mountain, we saw it was shaped like a giant person.
    And then we talked about all sorts of activities that might go on on that mountain like farming, or picnicking or hang-gliding.
    And then we acted out some scenes about the sort of people that we might find on that mountain, and what sort of characters they might have.

- Introduce what we're going to do today:
  I want you to think about the giant person that is in the mountain. Just imagine that the giant has a character.
- Ask for a volunteer.
  Pupil and I are now going to bring the giant into the room, and as we place the giant before you, I want you to tell me what patterns and shapes you see in it.
- Unleash fabric in centre of circle and ripple it with volunteer.
- Ask what they see in fabric.
  Looking at the shapes the ripples are making, what kind of mood do you think the giant is in?
  What do you think may have made the giant in that mood?
  (e.g. maybe it's quite agitated and nervous because the strong winds indicate that a big black storm is approaching.
  e.g. maybe it's in a happy, lively mood because it's springtime.)
- Ask class to get into groups of five.
- Give each group a pen and two bits of coloured paper the same colour.
- TWO MINS FOR THIS: each group must first think of a mood that the giant's character might be in and write it down on one piece of the coloured paper in big clear writing.
- Each group must then think of a reason for the giant to be in that mood, and write it on their other piece of paper.
- Quieten class
- In turn, one member of each group must put:
  a) their mood on the giant, then
  b) their reason for the giant to be in that mood.

HOMEWORK
Write up the 'I have seen' poem spoken by giant. Minimum ten lines. First half positive, second half negative. Illustrate it.

This plan shows how closely short-term planning is connected to classroom management. This student-teacher has anticipated issues of classroom management, and whilst keeping a firm grasp of the focus of the lesson, has found ways to encourage pupils to respond flexibly and imaginatively to the work. As she progressed through the training period her plans showed less need for this kind of detailed scripting. Whilst she found that she didn't need to write down all her own words or actions, she continued to script those aspects of the lesson which required complex definitions and descriptions of specific dramatic terms and concepts. For example, an A level class were working on Timberlake Wertenbaker's *Our Country's Good*, and using the text to explore Stanislavsky's theories of rehearsal. Case study lesson plan 2 illustrates that the student-teacher had developed her layout and own form of shorthand which she could recognize and interpret quickly in the lesson.

Case study lesson plan 2

Procedure

1. Register and recap internalization of 'sense' and 'emotion' memory.

2. Explain today's class, moving away from introspection to another of Stan's system theories: *tempo-rhythm in movement* as linked to *subtext*.

3. 'Wherever there is life there is action; wherever action, movement; where movement, tempo; and where there is tempo there is rhythm.' (Stan).

> *Theory*: that each actor has two rhythms: outer and inner.
>
> Inner = internal state of actor.
>
> Outer = state that actor chooses to show others (e.g. *subtext*).
>
> These two rhythms are surrounded by the inner and outer rhythms of other actors,
>
> e.g. like a number of metronomes ticking at the same time but at a different pace with different beats.
>
> Different rhythms of one actor (e.g. inner and outer) *and* how these contrast with other actors' rhythms creates *tensions*.
>
> *Importance of keeping rhythms distinct and separate.*
>
> *How does tempo-rhythm affect movement?*
>
> *N.B. the strength of stillness – silence is also a tempo-rhythm (them to note down).*

4. Warm-up exercises:

> Work in pairs
>
> Devise a short scene that uses inner and outer rhythms.
>
> How do these affect overall atmosphere of piece?
>
> Decide which actor moves the most and which is the least mobile – use informed judgement.
>
> Rehearse.
>
> Perform.
>
> Evaluate. (Examples for this: a) interviewee has squits, whilst interviewer actually planning to leave company quite soon; b) fiancés – just become engaged, but they have different agendas; c) death bed – little boy unaware of imminent death. *N.B. not all tempo-rhythms have to have a 'but' to them – but these highlight the point more clearly.*)

5. Read through *Our Country's Good*, Act 1, Scene 7: 'Duckling and Harry rowing in a boat.' Discuss their background – who they are, etc.:

> e.g. *Duckling*:
>
> Brutality of her past and her present environment make her fear consequence of committing to Harry; mutual suspicion – convict and gaoler.
>
> Craves freedom and space which Harry won't give her.
>
> How social forces (class and status) have psychological effect on sexual relationships.
>
> e.g. *Harry*:
>
> Destroyed through experience of transportation.
>
> Sexual paranoia – infatuated by Duckling.

Certain that Duckling's been unfaithful – jealousy – guilt referred, having hanged rival Handy Baker – Harry dies later on.

Discussion on inner/outer rhythms in that scene and what we know about characters already.

6. Rehearse, in pairs, a section each.

Perform.

Evaluate.

Comparing these plans shows the student-teacher's clarity of thought, her subject-knowledge and her awareness of different learning styles in her teaching. Because from the outset she considered the learning opportunities presented by the drama, she was able to plan for pupils' progression. Both plans show that she has considered the pupils' previous knowledge, skills and understanding of drama in her planning; together, they demonstrate her progression as a teacher. The work on Stanislavsky and *Our Country's Good* shows a real understanding of medium-term planning, and how this particular lesson contributed to the unit of work.

Short-term planning

- Consider all the ingredients of planning to ensure that learning objects are clear and that pupils are given the opportunity to progress.
- Consider the lesson from the pupils' point of view as well as the teacher's.
- Try scripting parts of the lesson at first as a way of preparing what needs to be said.
- Find ways of varying the activities and strategies to reinforce the pupils' learning.
- Allow time for pupils to make the drama their own and to consolidate their learning.

Medium-term planning: units of work

While short-term planning is primarily concerned with how a drama lesson is actually taught; medium- and long-term planning show how the aims and content of the curriculum are related. Learning in drama is not a linear process. There will be many forms and skills which pupils revisit, re-examine and employ in new contexts over a period of time. What must be avoided is unnecessary and stultifying repetition. Constructing units of work which gradually introduce new approaches to drama and explore new topics ensures that there is continuity and progression in the curriculum.

In drama, units of work are usually designed to cover a half a term's lessons. The unit of work establishes how the content of the drama curriculum will further the pupils' knowledge, skills and understanding. The content of the unit may focus on the exploration through drama of particular themes or issues, or it may include a particular play, dramatic genre or style. Of course, it is entirely possible that it will tie together a number of these elements. For example, extracts from *Oh, What a Lovely War!* could be used to inform and stimulate an exploration of the tragedy of the First World War in tandem with developing skills in devising and a working knowledge of Brechtian techniques. What should be explicit from the unit of work is the learning outcomes the work is intending to achieve and how the pupils' achievement will be recognized. Where drama is taught as a separate subject, learning outcomes should be described in specifically *dramatic* terms.

How to write a unit of work

At some stage during initial teacher training, most student-teachers will be expected to write and teach their own units of work. Most schools have developed their own way of documenting units of work which should contain all of the ingredients of planning described earlier. Where this is the case, it is sensible for student-teachers to adopt the same format if they feel they understand it and are comfortable with it. Sometimes, groups of schools in a particular area will follow the same format for writing units and this can be useful for exchanging ideas. Recently published source books for drama teachers will provide models for unit plans which student-teachers might usefully read, discuss and adapt to their own purposes.[7]

Quite often, student-teachers are so full of ideas it is difficult for them to know which to choose to work on with pupils. It is easy to become over-ambitious in the planning stages with the result that the student-teachers are worn out but the pupils have understood and produced very little. Answering questions such as these is a prerequisite to effective medium-term planning:

- What should the pupils have learnt by the end of the unit of work?
- What drama skills will they have practised and developed?
- How will the unit of work enhance their knowledge and understanding of drama?
- What practical activities will they have undertaken by the end of the unit?
- How does this unit build on their previous work and invite them to revisit their drama skills?
- What opportunities for reading, writing or design elements does the unit contain?
- How does the work provide evidence for assessment?

The unit plan should provide a clear reference point for the work in much the same way as individual lesson plans do, although it may look more condensed (see following Sample unit plan). In this example, it indicates how the unit ensures curriculum continuity and pupil progression. What is more sketchy here is the way in which individual lessons within the unit will be structured, organized and resourced.

Student-teachers can find it helpful to decide how the activities they wish to include will be divided between the available lessons. This means that they start by planning 'backwards' – in other words they will *begin* their medium-term planning by considering what they expect pupils to have achieved by the *end* of the unit work. This gives a clear focus for the work, and can help to divide the plans and activities into manageable segments. A clear structure for a series of lessons enables student-teachers to see how they might:

- manage the overall time-scale;
- build time for reflection and consolidation into each lesson;
- ensure that knowledge, skills and understanding are developed at an even pace (i.e. pupils are not bombarded with too much information at once or expected to use skills before they have completely understood them);
- end each lesson in a way that will leave the pupils looking forward to the next one;
- ensure that homework produced after one lesson informs the next;
- move towards an appropriate way of finishing the unit, for example, by allowing time for group presentations and/or some kind of summative assessment task.

The ability to 'plan backwards' by starting with learning outcomes becomes particularly relevant when pupils are following examination courses or if they are working towards end of Key Stage tests. The discipline of summarizing work in this way often shows that whilst long lists of aims and assessment criteria may look impressive, it is impossible to do them justice in the time available.

Sample unit of work

Topic of the work: *Sparkleshark* by Philip Ridley

| *Class*: Year 9 | *No. in Class*: 30 | *Ability range*: Mixed |
| *No of lessons*: 5 | *Lesson length*: 60 minutes | *Room*: Drama studio |

Aims
- To enable pupils to explore and interpret a dramatic script in practical work.
- To enable pupils to understand the relationship between the languages of the stage and the representation of social issues.

Continuity and progression
This work builds on the two previous units of work on script-writing and improvised agit-prop theatre.

Assessment criteria
Pupils will be assessed on their ability to:
- explore ideas represented in the play through improvisation and rehearsal techniques;
- sustain a role and contribute to the realization of an extract of the play;
- reflect on the dramatic atmosphere and effectiveness of the play.

Learning outcomes
By the end of this unit all pupils will have:
- explored the dramatic representation of isolation and community, fantasy and reality through movement, spontaneous improvisation and rehearsal;
- understood how the device of the fairy story is used metaphorically in the play;
- used rehearsal techniques such as hot-seating and thought-tracking to explore the emotional memories of the characters;
- read the play and realized an extract in performance;
- engaged in critical discussion and reflective writing.

Suggested activities

- Pre-session task to gather images, newspaper articles, music related to contemporary urban life.
- Class share and discuss material in small groups. Create dramatic image based on information. Respond to images and record words to describe them.
- Using dramatic images, create whole-class movement piece.
- Teacher narrates urban scene using key ideas – isolation and community.
- Whole-class discussion of dramatic atmosphere created in movement.
- Give out first two pages of play, just stage directions, no dialogue. In threes, read stage directions and decide who they are for. Colour code: director/actor/designers?
- Improvise dialogue. Give out slips of paper with dialogue on it. Pupils decide where it fits.
- Spotlight two or three versions. Class discuss and record information given in opening, expectations raised and questions they or the audience may have.
- In small groups, the class given different extracts of the play. They must decide what they think has just happened. Find a way of telling their part of the story to other groups in improvisation. See improvised version of whole play.
- Return to discussion of information, expectations and questions raised in first scene. What has seeing an improvised version of the whole play added?
- Preparation for design task: contrast use of props, set, costume, sound effects with the metaphor of the fairytale. Discuss juxtaposition of urban reality and fairytale fantasy. How might this be represented in design terms?
- Journey of the characters: all those playing a particular role meet. Hot-seat character at beginning and end of play. Choose line which best sums up feelings. Draw a chart to show where and how the character changes. Write explanations for this change as metaphor in a fairy story, shared in the following lesson.
- Journey of the play: each group decides on the most significant moment in their scene in the play. Create stage picture for this moment and thought-track characters. Digital cameras record this moment. What does this tell the audience? What do the opening and closing images of the play tell the audience?
- Using their stage picture as a key moment, small groups rehearse a short performance of one part of their scene. Use three key digital images as notation for SM book. Each group must use design features such as: gobo or gel as part of lighting design, key props, sound effects tape.
- Rehearsed readings performed. Groups asked to respond by focusing on key elements such as dramatic atmosphere, juxtaposition of fantasy and reality, dramatic representation of moments of transformation or change.

Resources and ICT

- Copies of the play.
- Digital cameras.
- Large sheets of sugar paper and felt pens.
- Tape recorders, and four lanterns on a stand.

Differentiation

- By organization: pupils in mixed gender and ability groups of threes, fours and fives.
- By task: each group must designate responsibility to pupils for technical effects, props and stage management.
- By outcome: all pupils will explore ideas in practical drama and realize an extract of the play.

Homework

Three lots of homework will include:

- Research exercise: find a newspaper article, image or piece of music which reflects contemporary urban life for young people.
- Writing activity: write the moment of transformation or change for one character using the metaphor or a fairy story.
- Design exercise: plan and execute one element of design (lighting, sound effects, costume, set).

Medium-term planning

- Provides a clear framework for continuity within a series of lessons.
- Enables pupils to focus on a particular aspect of drama practice.
- Identifies learning outcomes.
- Offers evidence for assessment and assessment criteria.

Long-term planning: mapping the drama curriculum

Long-term planning entails detailed consideration of how the principles and values of the drama curriculum are translated into a practical structure. As process requires some experience of how different theories and approaches to drama education relate to classroom practice, it is most usually undertaken towards the end of the training year. However, understanding the process of long-term planning is an essential part of professional development.

In planning for the long term, drama teachers will try to find ways of integrating myriad different factors into the curriculum programme. These will include, for example:

- knowledge and understanding of the nature and purpose of drama from different times and places; experiencing different genres and dramatic form, e.g. melodrama, kathakali, soap opera, Noh theatre, naturalism, physical theatre, Greek tragedy;
- dramatic skills, e.g. spontaneous improvisation, script writing, direction, set, lighting and costume design, rehearsing scripts;
- elements of drama, e.g. use of voice, movement, pace, rhythm, timing, gesture, symbol, climax;
- exploratory strategies and rehearsal techniques, e.g. hot-seating, slow motion, role-on-the-wall, flashback, still images;
- topics with potential for exploration through drama, e.g. stereotypes, the evacuees, the environment.

Deciding how to integrate these different elements into a map of the drama curriculum is not easy. There is no obvious sequence in which to introduce pupils to, for example, different genres or periods of theatre history any more than there is an unassailable logic to dealing with bullying in Year 7 but homelessness in Year 9 rather than the other way round. Learning in drama takes place most successfully in the context of practical exploration, where it is recognized that pupils need both to revisit elements of drama practice and to be introduced to new areas of learning. As it is not a linear process, long-term planning in drama requires the planner to make decisions about exactly how they want the pupils to progress in drama, and how the curriculum can facilitate this learning by bringing them new challenges.

Task: fantasy curriculum map

The aim of this exercise is to plan your fantasy drama curriculum for Key Stage 3. It works best if you work as a group of six. Sub-divide into pairs; one pair should focus on Year 7, another on Year 8 and another on Year 9. Each pair should divide a large piece of paper into six boxes. Each box represents a unit of work. In each box write the title of the unit of work (the content), the dramatic knowledge, skills and understanding practised or developed in the unit, the National Curriculum attainment targets addressed if relevant. When all six boxes are completed, compare with the two other groups and decide what adjustments need to be made for this to be a complete Key Stage 3 drama curriculum.

Continuity, progression and the whole curriculum

Drama has a significant role to play in pupils' personal, moral and cultural education, and the drama curriculum is closely allied to an education in and for citizenship. This relationship will very possibly be spelt out in the school's policy for the teaching of drama. In the process of long-term planning, opportunities for the exploration of values and the development of the moral imagination need to be charted on to the drama curriculum map in order to try to ensure that, over their whole school career, pupils have the chance to explore a welter of ideas in a variety of dramatic forms and engage in a breadth of drama experiences. Long-term plans might, for example, include a programme of visits to the school by professional artists, trips out to the theatre and in-house productions. Such planning requires drama teachers to address questions about provision and entitlement. For example, should all pupils be expected, at one time or another, to contribute to performance? Should all pupils work in spontaneous improvisation? How many and what type of plays should pupils be expected to study as part of their drama and English studies in secondary school?

To ensure that there is progression within the drama curriculum, and that pupils are not simply applying different ideas or issues to dramatic structures and ways of working, the curriculum map should show how they are introduced to different dramatic forms and styles. However morally interesting an issue is, it is not very challenging for pupils to undertake a role-play on sexism followed by a similar role-play on drugs. Furthermore, the increased influence of critical and performance theory on drama education has meant that progression cannot be regarded as moving from spontaneous improvisation to the performance of canonical plays. Student-teachers may well have practised and studied a variety of dramatic forms such as devised drama, carnival or street theatre as part of their drama degrees. Similarly, the drama curriculum in school should not assume that there is a hierarchy of dramatic forms or techniques.

One way of thinking about progression is to consider how pupils move from implicit understanding of the dramatic forms and styles they employ to more explicit knowledge about drama. This is a point made by Michael Fleming, who also notes that learning in drama does not 'progress in a neat linear sequence'.[8] As such, the pupils' progression in drama is often described in terms which recognize that successful drama requires pupils to be emotionally or aesthetically engaged in the work. At Key Stage 3, teachers may encourage pupils to become engaged in the work by structuring the drama for them but, as they progress, they should become increasingly independent as artists.

Long-term planning

- Gives a clear framework for progression.
- Reflects the values, policies and principles of the drama teachers.
- Recognizes that learning in drama is not a linear process.
- Ensures that pupils are given new creative and intellectual challenges.

Evaluation and planning

At the end of each lesson, student-teachers are usually expected to reflect on their learning and evaluate their teaching. More is said about the process and purpose of evaluating lessons in Chapter 5. Suffice to say here that, in the early stages, evaluations are most likely to focus on classroom management issues, as this can seem the most pressing or obvious area to address. However, student-teachers also need to use their evaluations of lessons to inform their planning, and this involves learning how to focus on the pupils' learning in the lesson rather than their own performance.

Many training institutions support this approach to reflection and evaluation by setting written assignments which specifically require student-teachers to consider the pupils' learning in response to their teaching. On a practical day-to-day level, mentors who see student-teachers in schools are in a unique position to help them use lesson evaluatations to inform their planning. In the following three sample lesson evaluations, the student-teacher learns to give herself subheadings so that she comments on the pupils' learning as well as her own teaching.

Sample lesson evaluations

February: Year 12
I should have linked all the components of the lesson together to drive the learning objective home. I linked the text work to the warm-up, but not the warm-ups to the introduction. My introduction was delivered in too much of a lecturer-type way. I thought I had been really explicit, but I should have tested that they really understood. I enjoyed the lesson – really nice group.

1 March: Year 10
Student learning and my teaching: I think my use of questioning worked well as a way of developing them as independent learners. I realized today that intonation is very valuable for pupil learning – it guides them almost subliminally.

Future lessons: maybe if I set one group's ICT homework a lesson earlier then the groups could have used the suggested websites for research during the lesson.

21 March
Student learning: I'm trying to concentrate on what they actually *grasp* as opposed to just making them do lots of tasks without really learning. I think most of them did grasp the point of the lesson.

My teaching: As a consequence, I need to watch the pace of the lesson.

Future lessons: Striking a balance between pace and ensuring learning objective is learned.

These evaluations not only offer information about the work undertaken by the pupils, they also provide evidence of student-teachers' progression. As a newly qualified teacher, this student-teacher later reflected that the evaluation of 21 March showed 'me on the cusp of delivering cohesive lessons in terms of pupil learning'.

NOTES

1   DES (1989) *English for Ages 5–16* (The Cox Report), paras 2.20–2.25.

2   Later research revealed that English teachers rejected the cross-curricular model, arguing that all teachers had a responsibility to help pupils with the language demands of different subjects. Beyond that, teachers recognized that their work took account of all of the other models, though with different emphases, some of which arose from external influences. For example, while many English teachers reported a sympathy with the *personal growth* model, there was a grudging recognition that elements of the National Curriculum appeared to overvalue notions of a *cultural heritage*. Such a position may feel familiar to some drama teachers (see Chapter 2, 'The trouble with canons', pp. 24). For a fuller discussion of this area see A. Goodwyn (1992) 'English Teachers and the Cox Models', *English and Education*, vol. 28, no. 3, pp. 4–10.

2   For a theorized account of creativity in relation to drama education, see S. Bailin (1998) 'Creativity in Context' in D. Hornbrook (ed.) *On the Subject of Drama* (London: Routledge), pp. 36–50.

4   See, in particular, P. Slade (1954) *Child Drama* (London: London University Press) and B. Way (1967) *Development Through Drama* (London: Longman).

5   In his influential account of teacher development, Schon describes 'reflection-in-action' as:

    a reflection (which) gives rise to on-the-spot experiment. We think up and try out new actions intended to explore the newly observed phenomena, test our tentative understanding of them, or affirm the moves we have invented to change things for the better . . . What distinguishes reflection-in-action from other kinds of reflection is its immediate significance for action.

    D. Schon (1987) *Educating the Reflective Practitioner: Towards a New Design for Teaching and Learning in the Professions* (New York: Basic Books), p. 29.

6   M. Fielding (1996) 'How and Why Learning Styles Matter: Valuing Difference in Teachers and Learners' in S. Hart (ed.) *Differentiation and Equal Opportunities* (London: Routledge), pp. 81–103.

7   See, for example, A. Kempe and M. Ashwell (2000) *Progression in Secondary Drama* (London: Heinemann).

8   M. Fleming (1994) *Starting Drama Teaching* (London: David Fulton Publishers), pp. 139–40.

Managing the Drama Classroom

My first aim is to leave the course a confident, knowledgeable, approachable and above all a good and enthusiastic teacher able to handle any situation and know how to get the best out of it.

I hope to be able to communicate with ease and be concise when giving instructions and inspire confidence in the pupils.

Key points for becoming a good drama teacher: understanding and listening, encouragement, enthusiasm, trusting, involvement, firm discipline.

These statements, written by student-teachers at the beginning of their training year, show that they have very clear ideas about what kind of teachers they wish to become. However, at this stage a great many student-teachers also admit to being concerned about their ability to manage a classroom. Recognizing the complexity of classroom interactions is an important part of the learning process for student-teachers, and drama classrooms have distinctive qualities and particularly dynamic relationships.

In a four-year study, 12–16-year-old pupils were asked to comment on the qualities teachers possess which are most likely to increase their commitment to learning. Many of their observations relate directly to classroom management. They suggested that effective teachers:

- enjoy teaching the subject;
- enjoy teaching students;
- make the lessons interesting and link them to life outside schools;
- will have a laugh but know how to keep order;
- are fair;
- are easy for students to talk to;
- don't shout;
- don't go on about things (e.g. how much better other classes are, or how much better an older brother or sister was);
- explain things and go through things students don't understand without making them feel small;
- don't give up on students.[1]

These insights closely mirror the qualities described by the student-teachers quoted at the beginning of this chapter. In drama, a subject which relies on social interaction and collaborative practices, student-teachers need to become skilled enablers who can encourage pupils to work together and share ideas productively. Furthermore, drama has an aesthetic dimension in which pupils can become personally and emotionally involved which requires student-teachers to consider how to create the kind of working atmosphere which encourages artistic engagement in the work. Whilst this is one of the facets that engages and attracts many young people to the subject, it contributes to the complexity of teacher–pupil relationships in the drama classroom. In practical terms this means that, in addition to the kind of classroom management skills which are generic to all successful teaching, student-teachers in drama need to learn how to manage the aesthetic qualities inherent to drama in which bodies, timing, space, movement, pace and rhythm are integral to the process of learning. It is thus very misleading to suggest that classroom management in drama is solely concerned with maintaining discipline.

Within the training process, student-teachers are likely to receive considerable support from experienced teachers who are able to share their classroom management skills. In most training programmes it is very unlikely that student-teachers will be left on their own with a class until they are quite confident. The presence of an experienced drama teacher in the room ensures a disciplined environment in which student-teachers can learn how to organize their drama lessons. This chapter is intended to provide practical advice about how drama specialists might acquire a range of crafts as classroom managers, and how theories of classroom management can assist student-teachers in sustaining a productive environment in which pupils may work creatively and imaginatively.

Managing learning

Learning to manage a classroom is intimately connected with managing learning. One of the challenges which faces student-teachers of drama is finding a balance between maintaining a well-ordered classroom and endorsing the kind of flexible approaches to learning required for creative work. Drama is a collaborative art form that often relies on ensemble work; pupils need to participate in the lesson actively and interactively and this places particular demands on student-teachers. Pupils cannot be forced to join in, and they certainly won't become emotionally or aesthetically engaged in the work unless they feel drawn to it. However, it is counter-productive for student-teachers to feel that they must always create magical moments for pupils in drama lessons. A successful drama curriculum is characterized by good working relationships where the learning is clearly structured and pupils understand the purpose of the work. Managing learning in drama, which both is structured and recognizes what John O'Toole has called 'the unpredicted meanings' of drama, requires an understanding of how classroom interactions between pupils and teachers facilitate learning and the motivation to learn.[2]

Student-teachers of drama will find the theories of social psychologists Vygotsky and Bruner are particularly helpful in developing effective day-to-day management of the drama classroom. Both of these influential education theorists have emphasized the importance of social interaction in learning, arguing that talk plays a central role in children's intellectual development. Vygotsky identified two forms of speech, 'communicative' speech which involves dialogue with others and 'inner' speech which exists inside the child's head. Both forms play an important part in cognitive development. He described inner speech as 'a dynamic, shifting, unstable thing, fluttering between word and thought' whereas, in communicative speech, thoughts need to be explained if effective communication and dialogue between people is to take place. In suggesting that inner speech holds the kernel of thought which communicative speech formulates and explains, Vygotsky wrote that, 'a thought may be compared to a cloud shedding a shower of words'.[3] It is this process of explanation and social interaction which brings inner thoughts to cognition, not always as fully developed ideas, but also as speculations and hypotheses which are further formulated, clarified, questioned or challenged in dialogue with others. Interestingly, Vygotsky invokes Stanislavsky's rehearsal methods in support of this premise, and argues that thought is 'engendered by motivation i.e. by our desires and needs, our interests and emotions'.[4] This emphasis on the relationship between thought and language is particularly important for drama education, which recognizes that communication is not confined to verbal language, but includes the physical languages of movement, space and sound.

The implications of Vygotsky's theories of inner and communicative speech to the management of the drama classroom are two-fold. First, it suggests that learning is best achieved when the classroom is organized so that different forms of social interaction are facilitated. This means that teachers will need to provide opportunities for pupils to work together in pairs and small groups as well as in whole-class work. Furthermore, student-teachers need to make time for the learning to take place. Pupils will learn from moments of reflection as 'inner speech' within the drama, in which they might formulate thoughts. However lively and exciting it may seem, leading pupils through a succession of unconnected spontaneous improvisation exercises is unlikely to give time for the kind of depth of thought required for interesting drama. An approach to learning which accommodates both inner speech and communicative speech as suggested by Vygotsky is more likely to motivate pupils to learn; classroom management is always much easier when pupils are motivated.

The second implication of Vygotsky's theories for classroom management in the drama classroom concerns the role of the teacher. If children learn best through social interaction with their peers and their teachers, then drama teachers have a responsibility to provide a framework for learning which will help pupils question, speculate, challenge, surmise and summarize in order to clarify and interpret their own feelings and ideas. In suggesting that drama teachers are, at different times, managers, animateurs, facilitators and actor/dramaturges, Jonothan Neelands invokes the work of Vygotsky and Bruner.[5] Each of these roles, he suggests, indicates the importance of social interaction between teachers and pupils in the drama classroom, and recognizes the dialogic and aesthetic qualities of drama as an art form and medium for learning.

In an assignment completed very early in the training year, one student-teacher in drama reflected on the implications of reading Vygotsky for her teaching.

> I could now articulate that social interaction develops thinking, which led to new fragile ideas about the implications for my own classroom. From the Vygotsky-inspired structure of our university seminar and from observations at school I began to crystallise these ideas too: the importance of social interaction to learning affects the teaching and learning styles we provide our students. The teacher's role becomes one of facilitating rather than delivering knowledge. They have a responsibility to take into account the ways in which children learn new ideas. They must provide continuity, carefully connecting new subjects with 'previous achievements' in order for students to cleave new ideas onto existing rocks of knowledge. Different children will have different rocks of knowledge which necessitates careful differentiation. They must also provide supportive social structures in order for them to clarify and solidify new crystals of knowledge.

As we have already pointed out, pupils themselves recognize that effective teaching requires a combination of good subject-knowledge, detailed planning and constructive classroom management. In addressing this latter point, student-teachers need to be able to recognize when and how pupils are learning, and when they are ready to accept new challenges. For this, they need to foster skills in listening and observation as well as explanation, instruction and demonstration. Bruner calls this process 'scaffolding', a metaphor he uses to explain the ways in which pupils are provided with new challenges, information, knowledge and skills at appropriate moments in their development and learning.[6] The ability to offer 'scaffolding' for pupils' learning is particularly relevant in a drama curriculum which aims to encourage pupils to experiment with different practices and new ideas in the process of learning. For student-teachers of drama, learning how to question, recognizing when to intervene and finding different ways of encouraging pupils to experiment and move forward is central to the craft of classroom management.

Approaches to classroom management

Schools are, on the whole, orderly places in which pupils enjoy good relationships with most of the staff. This is because the non-teaching and teaching staff, along with the pupils themselves, tend to want much the same thing. This kind of co–operation depends on a shared ethos in the school, where specific values are upheld within the institution. This requires members of the school community to reach a consensus about expectations and behaviour which, in a pluralistic society, is not always easily achieved. Student-teachers are often quick to observe how the ethos or 'feel' of the school impacts on individual classrooms; the values of schools differ greatly and can be repressive as well as liberating.[7]

If education is to have positive effects it must meet the needs of all involved. A composite list of these needs drawn from research into different classroom management practices comprises the following:[8]

- *Survival* – people must feel safe in the environment. Any threat to their sense of physical, mental and emotional security will be a distraction from the focus of the learning.
- *Autonomy* – people perform better if they see a purpose to the task and feel they have some control over its nature and outcomes.
- *Competence* – people perform better when they *experience* success. In the case of teaching, trying to help pupils *feel* they are achieving is not as effective as helping them identify exactly what it is they are achieving. As N.E.Curry and C.E.Johnson point out, 'children need coaches, not cheerleaders'.[9]
- *Self-esteem* – as most children grow older and experience more of the world their concept of their own social, emotional, academic and physical abilities develops, as does a concept of what they would like to achieve. Low self-esteem may arise when pupils do not achieve competence in the skills they value or if they have achieved competence but have not recognized it. Low self-esteem also occurs when the pupils set too high an ideal for themselves or unrealistic ideals are set for them. Whatever the cause, low self-esteem adversely affects learning and behaviour.
- *Relatedness* – in addition to understanding the nature and purpose of any given individual task, people need to be able to structure their experiences in a way that enables them to make connections. Although a great deal of what is learnt in the context of the education system may not appear directly relevant to the everyday lives of the pupils, their performance and behaviour is improved if they can see 'the big picture' and how individual learning experiences relate to each other.
- *Fun* – sometimes accused of being austere in his didacticism, Brecht famously said that the main purpose of theatre was in fact to entertain: if it did not entertain then it could not educate. It may well be an overly romantic and unrealistic notion to suggest that all learning is fun, but it is both possible and desirable to create a lively learning environment that can help pupils engage with their work.

An agenda for observation

Use this list of factors when observing a series of drama classes. The apparent success or otherwise of the lesson may be a result of the way the teacher is attending to the combination of them.

How do these factors relate, in practice, to pupils' perceptions of what makes an effective teacher as listed on page 84?

Managing the drama classroom is not dependent on the projection of charisma. Rather, it involves knowing what policies are at work in the school and what support systems are available to both staff and pupils. Asking for support in situations that seem difficult or confusing is not an admission of failure; it is an entirely sensible strategy which shows sensitivity towards the complex codes that inform and create the sense of community in the school.

Managerial functions of the drama teacher

Some potential drama teachers believe that young people inherently like drama, that drama teachers are universally loved and make the kind of deeply productive relationships with their students that other teachers can only dream about. If you want to be a drama teacher, don't believe a word of myths such as these! Drama teachers, like any other teachers, have to work for any respect and warmth afforded to them. Student-teachers who suppose that their being new, probably young and involved in a 'cool' subject like drama may make the pupils warm to them quickly. Sometimes the student-teachers may respond by relaxing too much in their company. Once the novelty wears off however, it is an uphill struggle to reassert discipline in the classroom and establish a professional standing amongst colleagues.

It has been proposed that all teachers, regardless of subject specialism, have two key functions.[10] The first function is to ensure that all individual pupils acquire the content of the curriculum as a whole while promoting positive attitudes to learning in general and their subject specialism in particular. The second function is a managerial one which promotes order through instituting procedures and limits. According to Doyle, the parameters of the teacher's managerial role are set by six goals.

- *Order* – the first goal of school discipline is to establish and maintain order so that an environment is created in which learning is not only possible but probable. In an ideal situation the instructional and managerial functions are intertwined so that the good management of the school environment contributes to an engagement with the learning. In turn, the content of what is learnt reinforces the need for an ordered approach to personal and social development.

- *Compliance* – authoritarian theories of education often mention self-discipline when what they actually mean is that pupils will simply comply with externally set behaviour controls. However, insofar as they help children to learn that they operate within a social and cultural context and that certain types of behaviour may assist or disadvantage them, the notion of compliance may be seen as a justifiable educational goal.
- *Self-discipline* – while authoritarian theories regard self-discipline as the result of internalizing externally set controls, humanists emphasize the value of pupils constructing and adhering to their own codes of conduct.[11]
- *Emotional regulation* – one of the goals of creating an ordered environment is to allow pupils to express their feelings appropriately and in ways that distress neither themselves nor others unduly. By these means pupils learn how to cope with their own and other people's feelings.
- *Co-operation* – a third goal of discipline is to enable pupils to propose solutions to social issues through co-operating with each other. In addition, some humanists identify the need to balance individual, personal needs with those of the communities in which they live and work.
- *Integrity* – this goal concerns teaching young people how to make ethical choices based on an understanding of the relationship between social responsibilities and personal rights. Integrity is contingent upon moral principles; promoting integrity requires teachers to recognize their own moral principles.

Idealistic views about working with young people without sanctions or rules in an atmosphere of shared and equal enthusiasm for learning tend, in practice, to be jettisoned depressingly quickly. This loss of idealism sometimes leads student-teachers to adopt unnecessarily draconian and reactionary methods of behaviour management and classroom organization. This is a pity; most teenagers can, at times, exhibit generosity and lively enthusiasm as well as challenging behaviour. Developing into an effective teacher involves student-teachers inspecting their own attitudes, assumptions and expectations and understanding why the pupils may not always seem to share the same values and aspirations or respond to the drama as they would wish. Becoming an effective classroom manager, particularly in drama which relies on co-operative behaviour, is not about teachers imposing authority or asserting their superiority; on the contrary, student-teachers are helped if they learn to recognize their own fallibility.

Theories of classroom and behaviour management will support student-teachers in creating an appropriate learning environment for drama. Louise Porter suggests that *atheoretical eclecticism* is unlikely to promote good classroom and behaviour management.[12] Being eclectic means selecting the practices most appropriate to a given context and situation from a variety of theories. She suggests that whereas *atheoretical eclecticism* is characterized by the haphazard gathering and application of ideas without any underlying guiding principles, *synthetic eclecticism* seeks to integrate compatible approaches, and this is more likely to result in comprehensive theories that are finely tuned to a particular context. Without a clear rationale, student-teachers are unlikely to be able to explain why methods sometimes fail and what else could have been done. Furthermore, a grounded theory of classroom organization and behaviour management is likely to lead to the kind of consistency required for effective learning.

Expectations

Before visiting the drama teachers in your placement school, list in order of importance five principles that you think should underpin the managerial function of the drama teacher. Should teachers, for example, place compliance to external controls above all else? Or the promotion of pupil autonomy? Where would you place physical well-being? Co-operation? Emotional regulation?

Where does your list appear to place you amongst different theories of behaviour and classroom management? What theoretical position does the drama teacher in your placement school appear to hold? To what extent is this consistent with the ethos of the school as a whole?

Observing the management of drama

Some drama teachers make the whole thing look deceptively easy. Through observations and questioning, student-teachers need to try to fathom out what is really going on in terms of the teachers' decision-making processes and how their actions reflect the theoretical model or models in which they are grounding their practice. Is it that they have tremendous charisma but are actually pretty lazy and 'fly by the seat of their pants'? Or is it that they have thought through what they want the pupils to learn from their teaching and considered different ways of achieving these objectives so that they can accommodate new circumstances without being fazed?

Indicators of consistency

Read the policy and schemes of work for drama in your placement school. Pick out any words that seem to indicate particular values in terms of expectations of how pupils should behave and operate. Is there, for example, an emphasis on drama *empowering* pupils to make their own decisions? Perhaps there is an emphasis on *group co-operation*.

Review some of your observations of drama lessons and conduct further ones in order to gauge the extent to which the actual content and conduct of the lessons reflect the stated philosophy of the drama curriculum.

Preparation and organization

The negative stereotype of the drama lesson is that it is noisy and uncontrolled. In more generous moments, casual observers (such as headteachers popping in to show prospective parents around) sometimes smile reassuringly before backing away from what they apologetically describe as 'organized chaos'. Chapter 3 offered detailed guidance about how to make sure that any activity taking place in drama lessons is purposeful and anything but chaotic. In terms of classroom and behaviour management, good personal organization will certainly help student-teachers project positive signals to drama classes. Having good plans, knowing what resources are needed, where they are and how to use them promote a sense of confidence; this kind of detailed organization means that student-teachers are better prepared to tackle the more unpredictable challenges presented when the pupils arrive at the lesson. This confidence will be projected to and reflected back from the pupils.

Many drama rooms offer exciting possibilities for creating a stimulating environment for learning. Pupils who are taught in a well-equipped drama studio may justifiably expect that the specialist equipment will be used. Student-teachers can help themselves considerably by thinking about what sort of ambience and atmosphere they want to create in the drama space. Using a rig of coloured stage lights as an alternative to fluorescent strip lighting can make a huge difference to the mood of a group. A particular lighting state may be used at the start of a lesson to generate certain expectations or a sense of intrigue. Alternatively, the lesson may start with normal lighting then revert to stage lighting in order to change the dynamic at a key moment or to enhance the aesthetic value of the pupils' own work. Similarly, it may be effective to have the class enter while a piece of music is playing, or introduce some appropriate music to underscore particular sequences later on. Consider, for example, the stimulating impact of having a class enter the drama room in silence in order to soak in a particular image that has been installed using props, costumes, lights and sound. If the resources are there to catch the pupils' imagination and interest then why not use them? Drama invites pupils to work in a range of learning styles and, as an art form in its own right, drama enables young people to communicate through all the senses; drama in schools has a part to play in educating the senses by appealing to them. Having said that, using the drama resources to the full should not just be an exercise in 'icing the cake' but a means of addressing sound educational objectives. Overusing resources can detract from the pupils' learning. It can be self-defeating if the novelty value which can be used so effectively to create a stimulating and engaging classroom atmosphere quickly wears off.

Auditing the resources

Some schools appear to have astonishing facilities for teaching drama as a specialist subject while others have very little. However, appearances can be deceptive. Although a purpose-built studio may have a well-equipped lighting rig and highly sophisticated sound system, how accessible and easy to use is it during standard drama lessons?

Spend some time acquainting yourself with the technical resources in your placement school by finding out where they are and how they are operated. Find out also about costumes, make-up, props and rostra. You will need to discuss the rules concerning the use of any equipment with your drama mentor before you use anything.

Starting the lesson

If at all possible, teachers should greet the class at the door. If it is appropriate, they might chat informally to the pupils as they arrive or line up. For example, finding out where the pupils have just come from and what they remember of their previous drama lesson serves a number of purposes, not least of which is building relationships with individual pupils and setting a friendly atmosphere. The pupils' entrance into the drama room must also be carefully monitored to ensure that it is orderly and safe.

It may be that there is a system for lesson beginnings already in place in the school. For example, pupils may have been taught that they are to sit quietly in a circle on the floor or stand silently facing the teacher. There may be rules regarding footwear, watches and jewellery. If there is a particular system already in place student-teachers are well advised to investigate the principles upon which it is based and use it for the sake of consistency.

Many schools will insist that a register is taken every lesson. It may be usual for this to happen at the start of the lesson, with the rationale that taking a register is an effective way of calming the pupils down and establishing an appropriate working atmosphere. Alternatively, it may be more productive to get on with the lesson and check attendance while the class are engaged in group work. (Consider this: a school has a policy taking the register formally each lesson. It operates a 5 period day and 2 tutor periods. Estimating that taking the register takes on average 3 minutes, this means that 21 minutes each day are spent on registration. That's 105 minutes each week. Over a 36 week year that's 3,780 minutes. Over five years that's 18,900 minutes or 315 hours. Given an average 6-hour teaching day, that's equivalent to around 10 weeks' worth of teacher contact time spent either saying 'Yes, miss/sir' or hearing others say it. Imagine how much could be learnt in that time!)

The pre-lesson check

- Make sure that you are in the classroom before the class arrive.
- Is the room laid out as you want it?
- Do you have all the resources you need to hand?
- If you want to draw the pupils' attention to a display or information on the board will they be able to see it?
- Have you considered using stage lighting or the sound system to create an intriguing/appropriate atmosphere?
- Have you practised writing on the board/OHP?

- If you intend to use any words that you are unsure how to spell yourself, have you prepared a cue card to help you?
- Are you making the most effective use of the lighting and sound resources available?
- What is going to stimulate the students and help establish and maintain a productive working environment?

Health and safety in the drama studio

Every school should have a clear overall policy on health and safety and student-teachers should become familiar with it. Drama studios, like science laboratories and technical workshops, are potentially very hazardous environments. For this reason, drama teachers are advised to have clear guidelines which reflect the particular demands of drama spaces and working practices. Finding out about safety procedures – how to respond to a fire alarm, for example – should be one of the first things covered in the induction into a new school. More is said about the legal and professional responsibilities regarding health and safety in Chapter 6, but it is also worth linking the relevance of health and safety issues to classroom management.

Working in the classroom

The question of who does the talking and who creates the action is central to drama teaching. One of the principal aims of drama education is to encourage pupils to explore ideas for themselves. Good drama teachers know how to listen to pupils. They are able to develop the pupils' own ideas by observing their work carefully and judging when to intervene. Mentors can draw attention to this by recording individual pupils' contributions to the drama in student-teachers' lessons, a process which ensures that learning to listen to pupils and observing their work constructively becomes a priority.

Explaining, demonstrating and setting tasks

Explanations should be kept short and to the point, demonstration should be used to support and stimulate rather than showcase the teacher's skills, and tasks should be purposeful and manageable. However, it is worth considering the implications of such bold statements in a little more depth.

If a lesson has been planned well, it will be clear what tasks are to be set and how long pupils will work on each activity. In the chapter on planning, it was suggested that well-prepared lessons offer the pupils the chance to use their own creativity while progressing in their knowledge, understanding and skills. Varying the way in which lessons are structured will help to engage pupils' interest and there are likely to be fewer management and behaviour issues in drama when teachers use a variety of teaching strategies and different stimuli. While some of these things can be dealt with at the planning stage, really effective teaching is always dependent on how such strategies are actually employed in the classroom. An awareness of pace and rhythm, for example, is as important for the drama teacher as it is for the playwright. An exciting and exhausting opening has to be followed up carefully. If the change of mood or pace is too abrupt the pupils may have difficulty in adjusting and keeping a focus on the learning objectives.

Regardless of the shape and structure of the lesson, student-teachers will need to acquire skills in presenting material and explaining tasks, and know when to demonstrate things. Acknowledging that there are different learning styles suggests that using a range of stimuli and providing explanations in different ways is likely to enable pupils to understand the work. However, it is not always productive to bombard pupils with different resources, no matter how exquisitely presented, and offering explanations in too many different ways may be unnecessarily time consuming.

Pupils like to work with well-presented stimuli. It sets an example for their own work and signals that the teacher is affording them time and respect. Student-teachers who hand out badly presented materials are likely to find them returned in a much worse state, if at all. It can be very useful therefore to have printed and visual resources neatly mounted and laminated. Expending time preparing materials in this way is especially worthwhile if it is intended that materials will be used several times. It may be easier and just as appropriate to use an OHP to show the group a picture or poem but again attention needs to be paid to the quality of the resource and its presentation. It is also important to find ways to distribute or collect materials; it is always the best-presented resources and most attractive new books that pupils are tempted to keep.

Observation task

Observe carefully how effective teachers hand out and gather in materials. Do they hand things out themselves or ask the pupils to pass things around? Are books and sheets numbered? Counted in and out? How time consuming is the whole process?

Unless there is a good reason for withholding the information, it is usually a good idea to explain to the pupils what the focus of the lesson is early on. There is no need to ramble on about this. Something as brief as 'This lesson we are going to continue looking at Victorian melodrama by focusing on the types of characters you might find in many of the plays at that time' will be perfectly adequate. Later in the lesson there will be opportunities to expand on this and highlight the learning objectives more specifically.

Many drama lessons start with a recap of the previous lesson's work. The problem with asking an open question such as 'Who can tell me what we did last week?' is that only a few pupils may be bothered to think about it or answer and any forthcoming information is likely to be a bit of a hotchpotch. Recapping previous work may well be an educationally valid activity in drama if it is focused and structured, but this is not always the case and student-teachers need to consider the real purpose of spending time on it. If recapping is necessary the following strategies may have advantages:

- The pupils are given two minutes to talk to the person they are sitting next to about previous work. The expectation, made clear to the class, is that each pair should be able to contribute one detail of what was explored or learnt.
- When the class enter a number of sheets of sugar paper are already laid out on the floor. Pupils gather around them in small groups and quickly jot down words representing what they recall.
- Having used a digital camera in the previous lesson to record key moments, the teacher hands out the prints to different groups and asks them to comment on what was going on at the time the picture was taken.

Ideally, student-teachers will seek to engage the class in an activity as quickly as possible. To facilitate this, it can be very useful to support a task described orally with a written resource. For example, if the task is structured and there are a number of points or steps that the pupils need to remember and work through, then a printed slip carrying instructions or a pre-prepared sheet on a flip chart will be a helpful guide. Attention should certainly be paid to the volume, tone, pitch and pace of the voice (see the section on 'teacher talk' later in this chapter). Trying to get pupils to construct a deeply sensitive scene by bellowing out instructions will be as effective as trying to jack up the pupils' energy levels by droning on like Eeyore.

Micro-teaching tasks: giving instructions

- Work with a colleague. One person should draw a simple picture on a sheet of paper. It may be an object such as a stereotypical house; it may convey an emotion, for example a person crying; or it may be an abstract design – a square with an irregular triangle attached to one side. The exercise involves sitting back to back and explaining as carefully and clearly as possible exactly what is shown on the picture so that your partner can draw a version for themselves. Dimensions, shapes and the spatial relationship between features need to be precisely highlighted. Having finished the task, discuss how clear the instructions were and how difficult is was to give them economically.
- In a group, take it in turns to try to explain how to play a drama game. You may find some form of demonstration is helpful. In reflecting on the task, focus in particular on the structure of the explanation. Was there a logical linear sequence to it? Or did it jump confusingly about?

- Consider and try out different ways of dividing a whole class in smaller groups. Exactly how will you number them and have them move so that you get groups of the required size? Discuss the part moving and gesturing played in making the instructions clear.

Some student-teachers in drama may find themselves being told not to demonstrate skills on the ground that this is egotistical and may intimidate pupils who will think themselves unable to achieve the same quality. Here is what one PGCE student reported being told by a professional tutor in school:

> I was told that children don't respond well to a teacher demonstrating in drama because it's that 'hey, look at me and what I can do' thing; they see it as an opportunity to show off. But I found that quite patronizing. Isn't that a part of teaching – to help pupils learn by demonstrating? I mean, in other subjects there are different ways but drama is a practical subject. P.E. teachers have to demonstrate practices and rules so why shouldn't teachers in drama?

Clearly, drama lessons are not provided as showcases for student-teachers' acting talents no matter how impressive they may be. However, it may be that demonstrating how a movement, gesture, tone of voice or use of pause can create a dramatic effect may be far easier, clearer and economical on time than attempting to explain in words alone. Sometimes it is appropriate for drama teachers to model particular ways of working by joining in the pupils' drama, by working in role or by careful repetition of new vocabularies and concepts. Modelling dramatic practices or language can be integrated into the lesson and may be less self-conscious than demonstrating particular skills to the whole class. In different contexts both demonstrating and modelling can be useful teaching strategies and provide effective ways of encouraging pupils to use the knowledge and skills of drama for themselves.

Recall and reflect

Think about things you can do in drama because someone demonstrated them to you. How did they avoid intimidating or embarrassing you? Can you imagine any other ways of explaining to someone how to do these things?
Observe drama teachers at work and discuss their use of demonstration with them.

Like stage managers, drama teachers need to manage time and work with a system of signals that others know and understand. Student-teachers should be wary of becoming slaves to the famous 'elastic minute' whereby far too much time is allowed for relatively simple tasks. It is important, however, for student-teachers to learn how to maintain the structure of the lesson but also be flexible over timings where this is appropriate. Sticking rigidly to the time allocated on the lesson plan when the pupils have made it clear that they really need more time to complete a task well can impede their learning and cause a lot of frustration. In any case, it is always extremely useful for the drama teacher to at least try to leave a few minutes for reflection at the end of the lesson and make sure that the bell does not catch them unawares and ruin a dramatic or sensitive moment.

Different teachers will have their own means of recapturing the attention of the class. The most effective way of achieving pupils' attention is to consistently use the same type of signal so that it becomes a convention that is plainly understood and to which pupils readily adhere. Student-teachers need to find out what their mentors' systems are for this. They may, of course, after negotiation with the mentor, choose to instigate a system of their own but they will need to explain the device to the pupils and be prepared to reinforce the rule several times before it is assimilated.

Checklist

- Keep explanations short and to the point.
- After explaining and perhaps demonstrating what the pupils must do, briefly recap.
- Reinforce the task with a written resource where it will help to do so.
- Think carefully about what size groups you want the pupils to be in and how you will get them into these groups. (You may also need to think about how certain pupils are integrated into groups.)
- Before setting groups off on their own, make sure they know where the task is taking them, e.g. 'remember that you are going to share these scenes, so think about which direction you will want us to see them from'.
- Finish your instructions or comments strongly rather than fading out or leaving points half made.
- When monitoring the work of groups, listen to what the students are saying before interrupting and offering advice.
- Encourage students to reflect on their own progress, e.g. 'how are you getting on with this? What's your best idea so far do you think?', but do not keep interrupting the work with questions or new information.
- Do not digress or let pupils take you off on tangents and do not be afraid to stop a pupil who you suspect is doing this, e.g. 'I'm sure that what you want to say is interesting but I'm not sure that it's going to help us with this work, so I'm asking you to stop there'.
- Give a strong clear visual and/or aural signal when you need to call the class back together. For example, go round to each group and warn them that you intend to draw small group work to a close. Then stand in a central position in the drama room, clap your hands loudly, then raise one arm in the air and wait.

Responding to students

Once in the classroom, drama teachers must find the right balance between setting the tasks and exercises that will help the pupils achieve the desired learning outcomes, and gauging the pupils' moods and attitudes in order to judge whether they need more encouragement or firmer control. There are a number of special factors at work in the drama space that can both help and hinder this aspect of classroom management. Having a background in the study of drama ought to prepare student-teachers well for a number of aspects of classroom management. For example, an understanding of proxemics and how status is signalled through the physical distance between characters is invaluable in ensuring that pupils are not unnecessarily intimidated yet nevertheless feel the presence of the teacher. As a general rule, drama teachers need to find a position so that they can see everything and be seen by everyone no matter what sort of activity is under way. Even when talking to groups or individuals, they will want to frequently scan the room visually, making eye contact with pupils and using facial expressions to reinforce relationships. A smile offered to a pupil who catches the eye can be tremendously encouraging for them (forget the rubbish spoken about 'don't smile until Christmas'!), while a raised eyebrow can effectively remind a pupil that their behaviour is verging on the unacceptable. This sort of direct eye-to-eye contact is often all that is needed to keep pupils on task and the atmosphere pleasant. Being physically close to pupils, using an encouraging tone and sitting alongside them on the floor will help establish pupils' confidence in the teacher's ability to deal with them sensitively as individuals. Conversely, issuing a brief instruction or 'warning shot' across a space can, when reinforced with a strong clear tone, give the teacher tremendous status without projecting malice or threat.

Their specialist knowledge of how space, sound and light can communicate meaning enables drama teachers to use an array of techniques in their classroom management but this in itself means watching out for a number of pitfalls. For example, subdued lighting can be used very effectively to create a dramatic mood but student-teachers must understand that in such a state pupils will not necessarily be able to see them clearly and vice versa. This is an especially important consideration when working with pupils who are hearing impaired and need to see clearly the faces of those speaking. Standing against a window or with their back to a strong stage light can also be disconcerting for pupils who only see the teacher's silhouette. Similarly, careful use of music can help generate an appropriate atmosphere. On the other hand, it may simply add to the overall level of noise leading inexperienced teachers to shout instructions over it. The absence of desks and chairs and the flexibility of the specialist drama space can, when managed well, enhance a sense of autonomous learning and lead to greater inter-pupil co-operation; as many a poorly prepared cover teacher will testify, it can also inspire a good deal of unnecessary running around! The project for student-teachers is to observe closely how experienced drama teachers manage such a space and work towards being able to monitor the whole room and make contact with each student for themselves. Effective management of individuals and the whole group in a space as flexible, and potentially dangerous, as the drama room requires teachers to divide their attention. For example, while making eye contact with one pupil over the space, the teacher may be listening to and helping another.

When they arrive in the drama studio, pupils are most likely to assume that they will be actively participating in drama. Talking, writing, looking and listening may well also be a part of the teacher's plan. Firmly establishing early on that these also constitute valid activities in the study of drama will help avoid confrontations which can arise when the teachers' and pupils' expectations do not match. Blaming pupils for exhibiting a negative attitude towards something they were not prepared for is obviously unlikely to do much to cement good relations because it simply isn't fair (a concept that young people are acutely concerned with when it affects them directly!). It is sound educational practice to let the pupils know what is expected of them and give them adequate time to prepare for this. By the same token, it is worth remembering that most people tend to respond more positively towards those who afford them respect and actually use the social graces they demand for themselves; in other words, if teachers want pupils to say 'please' and 'thank you' to them they should model this themselves.

One of the principles which underpins all classroom management is the need to treat pupils fairly and with equal respect. However, one of the most important lessons student-teachers can learn is that treating pupils equally does not mean treating them in exactly the same way. Some pupils have particular behavioural difficulties that affect their learning, and others may be going through a difficult time which means they have trouble concentrating. In both cases, the support of school systems and other members of staff is very important. Pupils who suffer from behavioural difficulties may well receive support from teachers with expertise in special needs who will be able to give student-teachers advice on how to work most effectively with individual pupils. If pupils are experiencing troubled times which are affecting their moods or behaviour, pastoral tutors will be able to suggest the most appropriate way to encourage them to work. In both cases, it is crucial for student-teachers to know what to expect from pupils and how to set reasonable expectations for their behaviour. Other pupils in the class quickly learn to adapt to pupils who present behavioural difficulties, provided that it does not dominate the lesson or threaten them personally and they can see that the teachers' attitude to these pupils is fair and consistent rather than indulgent or unnecessarily harsh.

Relationships in the drama class

Ask yourself the following questions:

- Do you know all the students' names? (Only knowing and using the names of the 'naughty' ones will reinforce their poor self-image and do nothing to help you build relationships with the other members of the class.)

- Are you treating individual pupils in the class fairly? Do you know which pupils have particular behavioural difficulties and respond appropriately to them? Do you tend to rely on certain students to answer questions? Do you tend to give the same students responsibilities in the class each lesson, e.g. packing equipment away, working the lighting/sound equipment?
- How 'present' are you? Can the students always find you when they look up? (If you dress in a way too similar to them they may not.)
- Are you being consistent so that the students know what you expect of them and what they can expect of you?

Dealing with difficult issues

One of the reasons why drama is often so popular with young people and, indeed, why drama teachers are often liked and trusted, is that the content of the drama curriculum can offer opportunities to tackle contentious and sensitive issues. There are, however, particular challenges presented by this aspect of drama teaching. It may seem, on the surface, politically and morally correct to suggest that, in drama, pupils have the right to express their own feelings and beliefs. However, student-teachers need to consider what they propose to do when those beliefs turn out to be sexist, racist or in any other way offensive and at odds with their own moral codes and that of the micro-cosmic society of the school. What must be separated out here is the dramatic *representation* of beliefs, attitudes and behaviour, and the unmitigated expression of the pupils' own beliefs. For example, the drama teacher may help a class explore issues such as bullying by working on extracts of *Lord of the Flies,* face up to racism via David Leland's *Made in Britain* or discover how to identify and tackle sexism through use of Boal's forum theatre techniques. In all these cases, pupils may be invited to portray values and attitudes in roles that demonstrate, for example, bullying, sexism or racism. However, it is important that these are discussed *as* drama. Drama can be affective and lead to personal and social change but it is more likely to do so when the power of metaphor and symbol are recognized and employed. Simply lifting the lid off contentious issues and allowing pupils to say what they think may have an appeal to Jerry Springer fans but raises a number of questions for student-teachers:

- what will the pupils learn about drama?;
- what will such a free exchange of potentially offensive views do to the dynamic of the class?;
- in what way will such an exchange positively contribute to the pupils' personal, social and moral education and preparation for citizenship?

In a similar vein, student-teachers need to consider how different factors in the content of the lesson may, if not handled in a firm and consistent fashion, lead to a breakdown in classroom discipline. One thing student-teachers will almost certainly face is the use of swearing. Another is fighting. In both cases, it is always wise to establish what the policy of the department or faculty is before making unilateral decisions. Many drama teachers will hold that allowing pupils to swear is contingent upon the age of the pupils, the content with which they are working and the level of potential offence caused by their choice of language. Asking the pupils why they think it is appropriate and necessary may be an educationally valid exercise in itself. In the case of fighting, the drama curriculum may well include a unit in which the pupils are taught to stage fight safely and effectively. Until then it is safer in every respect to encourage, as alternatives to pupils thumping and kicking each other, the use of tableaux, slow motion or the Greek messenger device. 'It's all right, Miss, it's part of the play!' is often an excuse used to avoid thinking carefully about what is represented in the drama, and it may lead to pupils getting hurt.

Sometimes drama teachers face a different kind of problem arising from the content of the drama. It may be that the issue is of a particularly sensitive nature such as death, child abuse, divorce, abortion or addiction. Once again, the aim must be to create a safety margin through objectifying the issue, inspecting the situation as it relates to the fictitious dramatic characters and considering how the drama might be interpreted by and affect an audience. Even so, student-teachers may observe or experience occasions when the emotion is too hot for a member of the group. Having a pupil suddenly run from the room in tears because the drama has touched a nerve is an awful experience for a teacher and especially disturbing for student-teachers. One solution would be never to tackle anything contentious. However, this would result in excluding most of the really good plays, stories, poems and works of art from the drama teachers' repertoire of resource material. Equally, no drama teacher should assume that the trauma of homelessness or sexual abuse, for example, are 'social issues' from which members of their own classes are exempt. If student-teachers are planning to include such difficult material in their lessons, they must check with their mentor to ensure that, as far as possible, it will not upset particular members of the class. Drama mentors may well be able to advise on the relevant history of individual pupils, or if members of the class may have particular religious or cultural objections to the content of the lesson. Nonetheless, however carefully advised, sometimes pupils do get upset as a result of the work undertaken, and drama teachers need to find ways of coping with this. Continuing with the work when a particular pupil has clearly signalled they find the content difficult may be considered unforgivable, though it may not be prudent to draw attention to an individual pupil by instantly stopping the lesson. When a reaction has not been predicted it is important to take a number of simple steps to recover the situation.

- Settle the rest of the class. It may be appropriate to ask them if they know what the problem is. If they do, the details are not up for discussion. The point is to appeal to their best nature and ask them not to make a big fuss about what is obviously a difficult issue for one of their classmates.
- Check outside the room to see if the pupil is still around. You may be able to invite him or her to return to the lesson, sit quietly or go and see an appropriate colleague.
- Use the school's support system. As soon as possible alert the member of staff responsible for the pupil's pastoral well-being such as their tutor, head of house or year head.
- Try to talk to the pupil on their own at a later time in the presence of a colleague. It may be appropriate to apologize. It will certainly be necessary to explain the purpose of dealing with the issue in the context of drama. One of the intentions of such a talk is to reassure the pupil that no hurt was meant and so re-establish trust in the relationship.
- Discuss the situation with the drama mentor and drama teacher for the group. No student-teacher should be left alone with a class for long, and the mentor may well have witnessed most of the incident.

Teacher talk

Whether setting a task or commenting on behaviour, it is always worth trying to be clear and concise in drama lessons. Pupils need to be sure about what is being asked of them and have the time to get on with it. This requires an awareness of both what is being said and how it sounds to pupils. Student-teachers in drama should have particular expertise in the use of voice, which may be seen as one of the most important tools teachers possess. In some countries trainee teachers are obliged to undergo extensive voice training and thereafter have frequent checks on their voices. The voice depends on the use of muscles; like any muscles they need warming up if they are to perform efficiently. Drama student-teachers tend to have a good supply of songs and other vocal warm-ups for use in practical work; it is advisable to use them as a part of their preparation for teaching.

It is helpful to consider how and when to use three basic 'types' of voice in the drama classroom:

- *The teacher voice*: this is the voice most often used. It will probably be slightly louder than the normal talking voice and geared towards talking to the whole class in order to explain and give instructions. Sometimes it might get a little louder and dominant in order to gain attention, or become slightly quieter and softer in order to elicit answers to questions and encourage responses.

- *The big voice*: student drama teachers will often work in big spaces or situations in which the pupils are generating a lot of noise. Sometimes it is necessary to project the voice forcefully in order to gain the attention of the whole class or focus on inappropriate behaviour. The effective 'big voice' is not a shout or holler. It certainly should not be shrill, strangulated or sound unnecessarily threatening and confrontational. The 'big voice' can become an invaluable tool. However, it should be used sparingly both in order to retain its value and avoid damaging the vocal chords. Finding the 'big voice' may take some practice. It involves opening the vocal chords and really drawing on the power of the diaphragm. Student-teachers may need to spend some time in the space alone listening to the resonance of their voice there. It can be very helpful to enlist the help of mentors or colleagues to give feedback on what the voice sounds like in the space at different volumes.
- *The narrator's voice*: this is the voice which might be employed when telling young children a story or trying to scare the living daylights out of friends on a dark and stormy night! It is a mistake to think that by using it secondary school drama students will be patronized. On the contrary, lowering the volume, softening the tone and carefully controlling pitch and pace can be a terrifically effective way of generating a productive atmosphere and motivating pupils of all ages to engage with the drama. Actually discussing the technique with older secondary age range pupils can help them relate it to their own voice work.

Some student-teachers can find it difficult to gauge the language level of different age and ability pupils. The aim is not to talk too much or use words the pupils will not understand. This is not to say that student-teachers should not introduce new words to pupils; on the contrary, this is part of scaffolding their learning. What is required is a sensitivity to how the pupils, as an audience, are responding to what is being said. The faintest glazing of the eyes may indicate the need to stop the flow and check that the pupils have understood. When new terms are introduced it is essential that they are carefully but succinctly explained and it is useful to write the word on a board so that the pupils can see how it is spelt.

The eyes have it!

Eye contact is an extraordinarily powerful means of communicating. As well as receiving sensory information the eyes also seem to transmit it. A lively and effective communicator not only uses the right words and speaks them in an engaging way, they also use their eyes. In fact, we seem to be acutely aware of moments when there are discrepancies between what people are saying out loud and what their eyes seem to be saying. Student-teachers who try to motivate classes by telling them that their work is really good and very interesting when their eyes are palpably deadened by boredom may wonder why the pupils remain unimpressed.

Sometimes it is as if the eyes can send out laser beams – when they lock on to the target it can have a dramatic effect not only on that person but on others in the vicinity. Perhaps we have all at one time or another come across teachers who are experts in using their eyes in this way; pausing mid-sentence, momentarily holding their pose, fixing on to a pupil and radiating the message, '*Just don't . . .*'.

As with the use of the voice, student-teachers of drama should have a good understanding of the impact this element of body language can have and may quickly find that they can build the technique into their classroom practice. As hinted at above, effective eye contact is not just a question of showing in the eyes alone what is being thought or felt. Positioning is vital – the pupils must be able to see the teacher and, like an actor engaging an audience with a piece of direct address, the teacher must be able to scan the audience, giving each and every member the feeling that they are being spoken to personally. When a pupil is not engaged, holding the rest of the body still and stopping speaking for a moment draws attention to the eyes. In the classroom situation, once the attention of an inattentive pupil has been gained, the slightest movement of the head may be all that is needed to make the pupil desist in their behaviour, sit down, move to another position, explain themselves or whatever. Some teachers are very good at this even in a crowded school hall – so good in fact that student-teachers observing them have reported how a shiver ran down their own spine! It is a minimalist approach reminiscent of Pinter's plays, about which a critic once said, 'the lack of bloodshed never persuades us to believe that blood cannot or will not be spilt'.[13]

Training your pupils

There are a number of exercises which you can try to help you remember the importance of eye contact and tutor your use of it.

- As a group, walk around a studio space, weaving in and out of each other. Try to make eye contact with someone. Once contact has been made try to hold it for as long as possible even though you are still moving around. When contact is broken because too many other people have come between you, simply make contact with another player. Develop the exercise by, variously, agreeing as a group to try to communicate interest, loathing or lust! Discuss how pre-deciding what was to be communicated affected not only the ways the eyes worked but what happened to the way people moved.
- As a group, sit in a circle. One person volunteers to stand and tell some kind of story (maybe just what they have done so far that day). Their task is to try to include all of their audience through eye contact. Meanwhile, the listening audience silently count to 20. If the speaker has not made eye contact with them by the time they reach it they must hum. The speaker must then find out who this is and make eye contact with them to stop the hum without interrupting their narrative flow. This is a very helpful exercise for learning how to 'scan' a class and communicate a particular message to one pupil while speaking to others.

Rebukes and punishments

There will inevitably be times when student-teachers have to take positive action in order to maintain a productive working environment. Having to reprimand pupils sometimes does not necessarily signal a failure to teach or make effective relationships. On the contrary, it may be an important part of a pupil's socialization. This being the case, it is important that pupils are treated individually. It is unfair and unproductive to accuse any group of young people as being 'the worst in the school/I have ever taught/in the entire world, etc.' on the grounds that a few members of the class are difficult. It is certainly unjust to punish a whole class because of the actions of a minority.

Using a firm tone of voice when speaking to students who have overstepped the mark does not necessarily indicate an overly authoritarian approach, especially if the voice does not sound threatening or confrontational. Instructions and rebukes should be unambiguous. A clear, firm 'Sally, turn around and stop talking' is more effective and sets a better example than a bellowed 'Oy you! Pack it in'. Similarly, it is preferable to comment on the behaviour in question, not the personality of the pupil: 'That was a very silly thing to do!' rather than 'Sally, you are the most stupid person I've ever met'. Better still, though not always practical in a busy lesson, is to ask the pupil to consider why their behaviour is unacceptable.

It is important for teachers to show pupils that although their bad behaviour may be frustrating and disappointing, they have not been permanently cast as troublesome or difficult. The teacher–pupil relationship has to move forward, so it is best for the teacher to make it clear that once they have said their piece or set a punishment the event is over and done with. Pupils need the opportunity to re-establish themselves but it also can be a mistake to reward them too quickly. For example, a pupil who has been rebuked may well offer to run an errand involving going out of the classroom, but do they yet deserve such trust? On the other hand, a pupil who has been rebuked may be the first to put his or her hand up in response to a question. Inviting them to answer, if it seems that they are volunteering in good faith (look at their eyes!), can signal that the relationship is back on an even keel.

Punishments should follow the offence as soon as possible and be unequivocal. Pupils must know what they have done wrong and exactly what the punishment will be. It is not very wise to punish pupils by letting them out of something they do not want to do anyway: 'Right then, Brian, you can sit out while the rest of us sing this lovely song from *The King and I*.' Conversely, it is far from educationally sound to punish pupils with things that are, in other contexts, educationally desirable: 'Right! You can just sit down here and write an essay about this play!'

Punishments and rebukes are best administered on a one-to-one basis rather than before an audience who may support the miscreant. Ideally, student-teachers should try to offer alternative punishments which sound reasonable and put the onus on pupils to take responsibility for their own decisions. They might say, for example, 'Now, you can either do this at home tonight and hand it in tomorrow morning, or come in this lunchtime and do it while I'm here'. Clearly, such a cool approach is not always possible in the mêlée of a drama lesson where the teacher may spot a pupil doing something dangerous or offensive and needs to respond instantly. If pupils have been rebuked during the lesson it is a good idea to see them briefly at the end. This may be to issue a punishment, extract an apology or explanation from them or help them understand why they were rebuked. Either way, if at all possible, the dispute needs to be settled before they leave the classroom. However, teachers should avoid being long-winded about this – if pupils are late for their next lesson they may get into more trouble which does little to establish good relationships with them.

Positive reinforcement

As with rebukes, encouraging specific behaviour or outcomes is more effective than throwing around generalized compliments which can sound insincere and carry little value. The very concept of *praise* has been questioned by some educationalists who see it as simply reinforcing the imbalance of power between teachers and pupils which may in itself be destructive.[14] However, most teachers recognize that positive recognition of particularly interesting ideas, good behaviour and lively contributions to the drama is very encouraging for pupils. Comments such as 'you've all done very well' might be true, but it is more useful in terms of progressing learning to pick out particular examples of work and say exactly why they were so interesting. Such comments bolster the pupils' sense of achievement, offer clear examples of what is valued in drama lessons and help to establish a positive group feeling in which pupils respect and praise each other.

Just as it is important for teachers to avoid bland comments on work such as 'good', it is helpful both to class discipline and subject learning to invite the pupils to make positive comments about specific aspects of their own and each others' work. Pupils will find it easier to do this if they are given an agenda to work with rather than being asked simply to say what they liked or did not like about something, for example, 'I want you to pick out three things that were said in that scene which helped us believe in those characters' or 'Tell us what you felt was the most dramatic image in that piece'. When groups of pupils have all been working on the same sort of scene, student-teachers may wish to consider the educational value of (and time involved in) reviewing each one. Whatever the situation, it is useful to involve the audience by differentiating the agenda. For example, one section of the audience may be asked to focus on the performers' use of voice, another on use of space and the third on the dramatic interpretation of the content. In this way, the pupils' own reflective and evaluative comments are more likely to be pertinent and supportive; they may also provide teachers with evidence to assess the pupils' abilities in speaking and listening and responding to drama they have seen.

To be of any value, rewards and privileges must be justified. In this context, it is particularly useful for experienced teachers and student-teachers to work collaboratively. Experienced teachers, who know the usual standard of work achieved by members of a class, will be able to recognize when individual pupils have made good progress and warrant praise. Drama is most often taught in mixed ability groups, and there will be significant differences in levels of achievement. However, praising rubbish and defending the indefensible will devalue standards and rapidly lead to a loss of respect among the pupils. Giving out dozens of merits, credits, house points or whatever may make student-teachers popular on a very short-term basis but it can soon lead pupils to see them as a 'soft touch'. (It is often the case that beyond Year 8 pupils see the whole business of merits as being pretty 'uncool' and issuing them may cause more embarrassment than delight.)

Using the system

Drama teachers are part of the larger enterprise of the school as a whole. Student-teachers must also of course recognize their responsibility towards supporting the general aims and standards of the school. Inevitably some students, like their teacher colleagues, will find aspects of the system frustrating and they may find themselves philosophically or morally at odds with it. The training year is really not the best time to set about 'kicking the system' though. On the contrary, student-teachers need to understand and use every aspect of the support network in place in the school rather than alienating themselves from it.

It is most likely that the school's support system for pupils and teachers will be explained as a part of a professional studies programme. Student-teachers of drama must then ensure that they are clear about how these systems work in drama lessons. It is important to remember that the purpose of any support system is to try to help the educational process rather than offer punitive measures to those pupils who are less than fully engaged with it. In many schools, there are learning support assistants who work alongside individual pupils who have particular learning difficulties and student-teachers will need to understand their role and function in drama lessons. For example, having another adult presence can present tremendous opportunities to use strategies such as teacher-in-role. Support assistants who are willing to take active roles in whole-class work will also need to pay special attention to their assignment. This means that student-teachers will need to be absolutely clear about their aims and expectations for the work.[15]

Making links

Talk to your drama mentor to find out about the following:

- How are pupils' Individual Education Programmes used and monitored in the context of drama?
- What classes/pupils are accompanied by a learning support assistant? To what extent are they likely to be willing to be actively included in the work of the class as a whole?
- Does the drama curriculum offer particular children any specially differentiated programmes of work? How is this organized and monitored? What special resources are available?
- Who should be contacted first when a pupil or drama class is becoming unacceptably disruptive? How should this contact be made?
- Do drama teachers set detentions or other punishments on their own or as part of a bigger faculty or teaching team? What are the guidelines and limitations of such punishments?

Ending the lesson

Having the end of the lesson creep up unawares can be very frustrating for all involved and is sometimes quite destructive. Pupils may justifiably be annoyed if the drama teacher has said that they will see or do something at the end of the lesson but has left insufficient time to fulfil the promise. Poor time management such as this can cause a problem at the start of the next lesson when pupils insist that they still have work to finish off or show.

Check:

- that time is left for some reflection on the work;
- that specific examples of good work are highlighted;
- that chairs and other equipment are tidied away and organized ready for the next class;
- that resources such as books and worksheets are collected;
- that homework is set and written into diaries where appropriate;
- that the class is dismissed calmly and efficiently rather than pupils being allowed to race from the room on the first ring of the bell. (It is a good idea to stand by the door as pupils leave the room just as you should have done when they entered. This allows you to ensure they leave safely while providing another opportunity for you to praise individual pupils.)

Coping with disaster

It happens. Although it may sound clichéd when even the most experienced and seemingly unflappable of drama teachers tells a student-teacher that it has happened to them, they will doubtless be speaking the truth. One of the reasons that these teachers are so good is that they have had such experiences, reflected on them and used them to develop their practice. It is more likely that any teacher claiming never to have had a disastrous lesson or a run-in with a pupil is either lying, deluding themselves or joking.

There is a big difference between *learning* good classroom management and simply *coping* with boisterous pupils who regard the inexperience of student-teachers as an excuse to misbehave. However, it is also very irresponsible for training programmes to allow student-teachers to be left alone with a class until well into their training year. Even so, some student-teachers will find too many lessons difficult and perhaps unbearable. Teaching is a very tough job and certainly not the right career for everyone.

For the vast majority of student-teachers, having the odd duffer is no cause for total despair and abandonment of aspirations to become a teacher. It may sound a little flippant, but it is generally worth remembering that:

- no-one except your mentor or the class teacher saw it (and they probably really felt for you!);
- the pupils will probably forget it much quicker than you;
- it will make you stronger in the long run if you are prepared to reflect honestly on the experience;
- it's over – tomorrow is another day.

More seriously, student-teachers can usefully assess the functionality of their own beliefs in order to gain a perspective on their relationships in the classroom situation and move towards a clearer sense of their own professionalism. Doing so is the first step in altering an unacceptable situation.

Teachers' functional and dysfunctional beliefs

Look at the table of 'Functional and dysfunctional beliefs'. Consider which statements you feel to be true for you. Have you always felt like that? If not, why do you feel it now? Do you want to feel like this? If not, what can you do and who can you go to in order to try to change the situation?

Functional and dysfunctional beliefs

Dysfunctional beliefs	Functional beliefs
I must always be a perfect teacher.	I would *like* to do a good job and can take steps towards achieving that aim.
All of the pupils must always be interested and involved.	Pupils are responsible for their own feelings. I can guide them but not force them.
I should have the solution to every problem.	I don't have to know everything but be open to learning what I need to know.
I should look after others and not waste time thinking of myself.	Other may sometimes be disappointed in me because I don't do what they want.
I must not allow myself to get tired, sick or inefficient.	I want to do things well but accept that I am not perfect.
I cannot allow myself to relax until the job is completed.	I can rest when I want or think I need to.
My colleagues should like and respect me.	I'd like to be respected and can feel lonely and isolated when I am not but can take steps to improve relationships.
I need to worry about the bad things that have happened or could go wrong.	Worrying about things that might go wrong is unlikely to stop them from happening. It's better to focus on the good things that are going on now.
I have to have someone to rely on as I cannot survive on my own.	I like to have other people in my life but do not feel entirely dependent on them.
The problems I have now are because of what has happened in the past. I cannot change how I operate as a person.	Ways of tackling stress and improving the way I work can be learned.

111

NOTES

1   J. Ruddock, J. Day, and G. Wallace (1999) 'Students' Perspectives on School Improvement' in C. Day (ed.) (1999) *Developing Teachers: The Challenges of Lifelong Learning* (London: Falmer Press), pp. 18–19.

2.   J. O'Toole (1992) *The Process of Drama* (London: Routledge), pp. 226–7.

3   L. Vygotsky (1962) *Thought and Language* (Massachusetts: MIT Press), p. 150.

4   Ibid.

5   J. Neelands (1998) *Beginning Drama 11–14* (London: David Fulton Publishers), pp. 40–52.

6   This process is not only confined to teachers; other experienced learners can also scaffold pupils' learning. See J. Bruner (1986) *Actual Minds, Possible Worlds* (Cambridge, MA: Harvard University Press), p. 73.

7   See L. Tickle (2000) *Teacher Induction: The Way Ahead* (Buckingham: Open University Press), pp. 42–5, for a fuller discussion of this point.

8   L. Porter (2000) *Behaviour in Schools* (Buckingham: Open University Press), p. 216.

9   N. E. Curry, and C. N. Johnson (1990) *Beyond Self-esteem: Developing a Genuine Sense of Human Value* (Washington, DC: National Association for the Education of Young Children), p. 53.

10 W. Doyle (1986) 'Classroom Organisation and Management' in *Handbook of Research on Teaching* (3rd edn), ed. M. C. Wittrock (New York: Macmillan), p. 395.

11 A. Kohn (1996) *Beyond Discipline: From Compliance to Community* (Alexandria, VA: Association for Supervision and Curriculum Development), pp. 5–6.

12 Porter, L. (2000) *Behaviour in Schools*, p. 13.

13 J. Elsom (1976) *Post-war British Theatre* (London: Routledge and Kegan Paul), p. 108.

14 H. G. Ginott, quoted in Porter, *Behaviour in Schools*, p. 96.

15 A particularly helpful chapter dealing with the potential of working in this way is 'Working in Partnership' by Jan Beats and Penny Barrett in A. Kempe (ed.) (1996) *Drama Education and Special Needs* (Cheltenham: Stanley Thornes), pp. 130–56.

112

Monitoring, Assessment, Recording, Reporting and Accountability

Now, what I want is, Facts. Teach these boys and girls nothing but Facts. Facts alone are wanted in life. Plant nothing else, and root out everything else.

In Dickens' novel *Hard Times*, Thomas Gradgrind has an unerring faith that an education based on factual knowledge rather than 'fancy' will create docile, obedient citizens. For Gradgrind – the personification of utilitarianism – imagination and creativity threatened moral order; educating young people to think for themselves was socially dangerous.

When the National Curriculum was first introduced, there was considerable concern amongst drama teachers that the increased emphasis on monitoring and assessment would lead to the kind of curriculum forced on Gradgrind's children. After years of progressive education, in which drama and the arts held an important place, it was feared that subjects that invited creativity and encouraged questioning would become increasingly marginalized. Furthermore, and perhaps equally worrying, there were concerns that drama education would have to change so radically to comply with a new educational climate that its special qualities would be lost. The fear was that teachers would be expected to test only pupils' knowledge and understanding of facts and to establish rigid, easily measurable learning outcomes.

Some might argue that this picture of education has become a reality. In our experiences, things have not been so bleak for drama education. Rather than accepting a model of assessment of which Gradgrind would approve, drama teachers have worked hard to find ways to monitor and assess pupils' learning which both value the pupil-centred qualities of drama teaching and propose subject-specific assessment criteria. This balance is often reflected in drama department assessment policies, in approaches to monitoring pupils' learning and in examination assessment criteria.

Nonetheless, the renewed focus on monitoring, assessment, recording, reporting and accountability has brought about debates about what is taught and what pupils are actually learning in their drama lessons. Once considered an authoritarian practice which would interfere with young people's creativity, it is now widely accepted that assessment is an integral part of teachers' planning and, when used judiciously and sensitively, has a positive impact on pupils' learning. The purpose of this chapter is to raise some questions about monitoring, assessment, recording, reporting and accountability in drama and to offer practical advice about how to undertake assessment in the drama classroom.

Assessment autobiography

Make a list of the different ways in which you have been assessed in drama at different times. What were you assessed on? How and where was it undertaken? Did you know the assessment criteria? Equally importantly, were there times when you had drama lessons, but were not assessed? Did you have a say in your own assessment? What do your experiences show about the values of the different drama curricula or teachers?

Principles of assessment

In the context of education, the word 'assessment' may all too easily conjure up images of examination desks in rows and unseen tests. This form of assessment certainly exists, and its importance is frequently over-emphasized by traditional educationalists. In drama, however, it is only a very small part of the process of monitoring pupils' attainment. There are many different ways of assessing pupils. What is particularly important is to reflect on why assessment is necessary and how it is best carried out in order to benefit the pupils. Student-teachers should note that, in the criteria applied to their own professional training, assessment is grouped with monitoring, reporting, recording and accountability. This indicates that these aspects of teaching relate to each other in promoting pupils' learning.

Good assessment policies and practices in drama are able to fulfil the following purposes:

- they provide clear information about pupils' achievements;
- they assist in the diagnosis of any problems and difficulties that pupils may face;
- they offer insights into the relationship between teaching and learning.

Effective assessment can thus:

- help the teacher evaluate their own teaching;
- provide a way of recognizing and subsequently supporting individual pupils' needs;
- inform future planning lessons and schemes of work.

Assessment and learning

Learning in drama is not confined to the linear development of skills, nor would it comply with Gradgrind's educational values as it is not primarily concerned with the acquisition of facts. When pupils engage in drama, they revisit areas of learning and dramatic practices in order to consolidate their knowledge, skills and understanding as well as developing new ways of working. This is what Jerome Bruner has called a 'spiral curriculum'.[1] A spiral curriculum is built on principles which recognize that pupils learn best when they have ownership of the work, and when they are given the opportunity to revisit specific aspects of a subject in order to explore new ideas with increasing independence and complexity. Bruner's concept of a spiral curriculum does not assume, however, that pupils develop at their own pace irrespective of teacher intervention. On the contrary, as we identified in Chapter 3, he suggests that good teachers offer pupils support or 'scaffolding' for their learning. The concept of scaffolding links planning, progression and assessment. Enabling pupils to become increasingly informed and thinking practitioners of drama, in this context, requires teachers to make decisions about how and when to scaffold their learning. To do this effectively, teachers must use their knowledge of pupils' learning gained from different forms of assessment.

The relationship between practice and learning in drama means that assessment of pupils' work often forms part of the drama lesson itself. Unlike many other curriculum subjects, where evidence for learning is most usually found in written work, drama involves the related modes of making, performing and responding. Clearly, it is often the case that the teacher is able to assess pupils' knowledge and understanding from the way in which they articulate responses to their own and other people's work. However, as we pointed out in Chapter 2, the three modes of activity in drama are more frequently intertwined. This means that pupils' knowledge, skills and understanding of the art form are 'embodied', and can be demonstrated and assessed effectively in practice, within the form itself. It is precisely because this is recognized that *continuous* or *teacher assessment* forms a part of so many of the specifications for public examinations in drama. This also recognizes that pupils are aided when they have a chance to revisit areas of learning (the spiral curriculum) as well as being offered new challenges. Assessment policies and practices which reflect this approach to learning are likely to make the assessment criteria explicit to pupils, and they will be encouraged to be actively involved in the assessment of their own work.

Assessment criteria and the drama curriculum

New entrants to teacher training courses in drama sometimes seem wary of the whole business of assessing pupils in drama. Perhaps deeply impressed by child-centred philosophies of education and the part drama may play in this, they sometimes hold that drama cannot justifiably be assessed because it is almost entirely subjective. Assessment is seen to mitigate against encouraging pupils and so inevitably leads them to become de-motivated. On the other hand, student-teachers seem to have no problem explaining why they think one play, playwright or actor is better than another and tend to agree that they prefer feedback on their own work that makes it clear where they stand and what they must do to get better. In order to ensure that pupils are neither de-motivated by harsh assessment strategies, nor left uncertain about their progress, their work should be assessed according to appropriate criteria. And what counts as 'appropriate', in this context, is a matter of principles.

The model of assessment most usually employed by drama teachers is *criterion referenced*. This means that assessment criteria are identified in the drama syllabus or unit of work, and pupils' work is assessed according to these predetermined criteria and levels of attainment. An analogy is the UK driving test in which candidates must perform a series of set manoeuvres and correctly answer a number of questions. If they manage this they pass the test. There are no limits on how many people might pass the test in any one day, month or year – the project is to get as many people driving safely as possible. Criterion-referenced assessment procedures can be designed to encourage all pupils to succeed. By making the criteria explicit, it is argued, teachers and pupils know precisely what it is they are supposed to focus on in their teaching and learning.

Norm-referenced assessment, on the other hand, arguably fosters competitive approaches to teaching and learning because it aims to discriminate between high and low achievers. In this form of assessment the supposition is that in any given task a normal curve of distribution may be applied to the success rate of candidates. That is to say, that for every one achieving a top mark there must correspondingly be one achieving the lowest, with the greatest number of candidates achieving marks in the middle of the range. If too many candidates are seen to be gaining top marks, the assessment criteria are adjusted in order to re-establish a normal curve of distribution. Faith in the merits of this system periodically lead to accusations that examinations are too easy on the grounds that so many pupils are passing them.

It is not difficult to see why criterion-referenced, rather than norm-referenced, forms of assessment have found favour with drama teachers. Drama necessarily involves collaborative working practices, and to pit one pupil against another would severely inhibit creative work. However, criterion-referenced assessment in drama also has its critics. Michael Fleming, for example, has pointed out that some of the most exciting and productive learning in drama cannot be easily assessed, and to adhere rigidly to predetermined assessment criteria does not allow pupils and teachers to value moments of insight and imagination which are unexpected or unforeseen. If this is the case, it is a legitimate concern.[2] Drama is a dynamic, interactive and creative subject; any attempt to confine the practice of drama to over-prescriptive assessment criteria, or to define learning in drama as linear rather than spiral, misses the point of the subject and ignores its artistic and aesthetic qualities.

Subject-specific assessment criteria

The challenge, as Fleming has identified, is to define clear assessment criteria while planning lessons that have sufficient flexibility to allow for the unexpected and to recognize that valuable learning may occur beyond which the teacher initially planned.[3] Although many drama educators would subscribe to the view that a fundamental purpose of drama is to enable pupils to explore emotions and express ideas and values which are personally and deeply felt, it may be argued that assessing these beliefs and feelings is unjust and morally contentious. (How would you feel about your mentor grading you on your religious or political beliefs or on the depth of your love for someone?) In order to avoid making judgements about individual pupils which are intrusive or inappropriate, assessment criteria need to be subject specific. What particular aspects of *drama* are the pupils learning in a scheme of work? How are they representing or expressing ideas and values in dramatic form?

In short, if the objectives of a piece of work are clear, teachers will be able to identify what sort of evidence will illustrate that learning has taking place. For example, if one of the objectives is to teach the pupils that the meaning of words is modified by tone, pitch, volume and pace, the teacher will be listening out for the extent to which the pupils discuss and manipulate these elements of sound. Such observations of what the pupils are saying and doing enable teachers to ascribe a grade or level to the work of individual pupils. In this instance, for example, in order to assess the pupils the teacher might consider the extent to which they are able to:

- plan their work taking account of different sound qualities;
- vary their use of tone, pitch, volume and pace in order to communicate meaning appropriately;
- identify and articulate the way sound qualities alter the meanings of their own work and that of others.

In these contexts, the assessment criteria take account of making, performing and responding in drama. As we have already explained, pupils who have ability in one particular mode may need support in developing their ability in another. Designing assessment criteria which take account of all three modes of drama in this way is both fairer on the pupils and more likely to enable teachers to maximize progression amongst the whole group.

The following examples ('Assessing objectives') show how well-defined aims and objectives for a unit of work can be used to form manageable assessment criteria.[4]

Assessing objectives

Unit title: The Rime of the Ancient Mariner *Year*: 7

Aims:

- to identify, explore and realize the dramatic potential of a visual stimulus (Dore's engravings of scenes from the poem) and a poem;
- to consider how ideas can be represented symbolically and interpreted through different art forms.

Learning objectives:

By the end of the unit the pupils should know and understand:

- what gives a visual stimulus dramatic potential;
- how visual images can be used as symbols in drama.

They should be able to:

- read visual images for narrative;
- use gesture and physical expression imaginatively;
- use sound and visual images to present feelings;
- communicate mood and atmosphere appropriately.

Assessment criteria:

Evidence of learning will be sought in terms of the extent to which pupils are:

- using sound and visual images to present their interpretation of the stimulus;
- using gestures and facial expressions to communicate specific meanings;
- reflecting the mood and atmosphere of the stimulus material in their own performances;
- identifying and commenting on the way drama, poetry and visual art create and convey symbols.

Unit title: The Evacuees *Year*: 8

Aim:

- to explore a historical situation through role-play and improvisation.

Assessment criteria:

Pupils will be assessed on their ability to:

- build on their own and each other's ideas in role;
- use and interpret historical resources in spontaneous improvisation.

Unit title: Physical Theatre *Year*: 10

Aim:

- to encourage the expression of abstract ideas in visual imagery and movement.

Assessment criteria:

Pupils will be assessed on their ability to:

- demonstrate an understanding of visual images in movement;
- explore abstract ideas using a simple movement vocabulary.

In drama, it is important to set out to assess what is visible and tangible. Perhaps paradoxically, the more focused and limited the assessment criteria are, the greater scope there is for flexibility in the teaching and learning styles. Not everything that is learnt or taught in drama will be assessed, nor should it be. By selecting a limited number of assessment criteria for each unit, the pupils' work will retain purpose and focus without negating the possibility of creative responses and diverse interpretations. The criteria need to be introduced as they begin the work, reiterated as it develops and referred to in any reflection. It is not always possible to capture the magic of drama in the language of assessment criteria but pupils' progression is enhanced if they are involved in the process of assessment.

Principles of assessment in drama

- Assessment criteria are described in subject-specific terms.
- Subject-centred and pupil-centred approaches to teaching and learning are balanced and not seen as mutually exclusive.
- Learning in drama is recognized to be spiral rather than linear.
- Criteria for each unit of work are limited and focused.
- Discussion between teachers and pupils about progress and learning is paramount and highly valued.

The context of assessment

How drama is assessed, and what aspects of drama pupils are assessed on, depends on three related influences. As we outlined in Chapter 2, drama teachers will need to take account of different forms of government guidance such as National Curriculum Orders. The choice of examination specifications and the way in which drama is organized within an individual school's curriculum will also influence what is assessed, how and when. Finally, and most influential of all, are the drama teachers themselves who will interpret outside influences in ways which support their own praxis.

On their professional placements, student-teachers will need to understand the rationale for assessment in drama, fit into the model adopted in the school curriculum framework and learn how to apply it to their own practice. Many will work in departments where drama is taught as a separate subject and the assessment policies focus on elements of learning which are subject specific. However, as we pointed out in Chapter 2, drama may be taught in other curriculum contexts. It may, for example, be part of the English curriculum or part of citizenship education. In these contexts, the assessment will not be focused solely on the drama, but on the subject it illuminates. Student-teachers of drama will benefit from working on assessment with colleagues in cognate disciplines. For example, they might assist English teachers in the assessment of speaking and listening or written work on plays.

In the best cases, student-teachers will observe how teachers have worked together to formulate policies and practices for assessment. A coherent approach across the curriculum enables pupils to understand the practices of assessment and gain confidence as learners as they recognize that some skills are transferable. It helps, for example, if all teachers use the same symbols when marking written work. Complying with whole-school assessment policies does not necessarily mean that all subjects use similar assessment methods. It may well be deemed appropriate, for example, for Maths or Modern Foreign Languages to frequently give pupils short paper and pen tests to gauge their development of subject-knowledge. In drama where subject-knowledge is embodied within the processes of making and performing, such tests will be of limited value. Contributing to, and complying with, whole-school assessment policies has led drama teachers not only to share common approaches, but to effectively describe and communicate the special qualities of learning in drama to others.

Learning through comparing

Read the documentation which underpins the assessment of drama at Key Stage 3 in your placement school. Compare this to the policy and guidelines for assessment of at least one other subject. What similarities and differences do you notice about, for example:

- the nature and stated purpose of assessment;
- frequency of formal and informal assessments;
- the way achievement is recorded and reported (by numerical or letter grades, grade descriptor, etc.)?

Do the teachers in the different subjects:

- use a common language for assessment;
- employ similar forms of monitoring;
- share approaches to written marking and oral assessment?

Continuity and progression
Interview a group of pupils in the first year of their secondary school about their experiences of assessment. What changes have they noticed about the way in which they are assessed? Do they think they are being assessed in the same things?

At Key Stage 4, assessment in drama is most likely to be closely, if not wholly, allied to the requirements of the chosen examination syllabus. All current public examinations in drama (GCSE, Standard Grade, AS, A2 and Higher Still) require teachers to assess their pupils. On the whole, drama teachers appreciate the contribution this internal assessment makes to the overall grading, particularly when the process involves the opportunity of moderating work with colleagues. Cross-moderation at any level helps teachers sharpen their assessment practices. Most teachers find moderation more comforting than threatening when they see, more often than not, that their values and judgements are similar to their colleagues'. Student-teachers can learn a great deal from observing and indeed contributing to moderation sessions. To gain the most from such opportunities means scrutinizing the assessment criteria in advance and discussing with mentors how the activities incorporated in the moderation will afford the pupils the chance to meet them.

Research

Find out how the assessment of pupils in drama in your placement school corresponds to national criteria. What contribution do drama teachers make to the assessment of other subjects such as English?

Discuss with your mentor how the assessment criteria for drama used at Key Stage 3 relates to the examination syllabus used in Key Stage 4. How is progression from one key stage to the next monitored? What is the balance between internal and external assessment in the examinations syllabuses used by the school? What are the moderation arrangements?

Talk to pupils about the jump from Key Stage 3 to 4 and from 4 to 5. How difficult did they find the transition? What do they perceive they are being assessed on at each key stage? Do they think that the form of assessment used is appropriate to drama and helpful in their development of subject-specific knowledge, skills and understanding?

Most drama teachers would argue that whatever the context in which assessment takes place, and however it is undertaken, it is vitally important that the drama curriculum is not driven by it or that teaching methods are determined by it. What is rather required is a kind of symbiotic relationship between planning, teaching and assessment by which:

- planning is built on sound principles of progression involving the identification of learning objectives appropriate to each stage of a pupil's drama career;
- teaching is geared towards helping pupils understand what objectives they are trying to achieve and offering them a variety of ways of doing this;
- assessment registers the extent to which objectives have been met and the resultant information is used to inform and improve future planning.

In the next section, we shall look at how to achieve this relationship by employing different forms of monitoring and assessment without losing the kind of creativity and flexibility which is so important to teaching and learning in drama.

Monitoring and assessment

Drama teachers are continually engaged in the process of monitoring and assessing pupils' learning as part of their normal classroom practice. Even if the assessments are not always recorded, experienced drama teachers often know their pupils very well and can tell people how they are progressing in the subject. In order to build up a clear picture of their pupils' progress in drama, they will monitor their learning and assess their work in a variety of different ways.

In their chapter about assessment, John Raffan and Kenneth Ruthven make the distinction between *monitoring*, which they define as the activity undertaken by teachers to identify what and how pupils have learnt, and *assessment*, which is the process by which information about progress is elicited. They point out that monitoring pupils' work sometimes has a bureaucratic purpose, in that it may be used to provide evidence to external agencies of standards achieved; this will be discussed in more detail later in the chapter. But they also suggest that one description of the term 'monitoring' is more directly concerned with the process of pupils' learning: 'Monitoring means keeping up with your pupils' learning, the difficulties they are experiencing and the progress that they are making. The term also summarises the various procedures used by any organisation responsible for education, from schools to local and national government, to check on standards and progress.' Assessment, often used colloquially to suggest the testing or measuring of pupils' progress, is given a rather more eclectic definition by Raffan and Ruthven: 'Assessment refers to any process which gives information about pupils' learning. Informal classroom processes include the observation of pupils tackling a task, questioning them about their work, looking at their written work, recording, or listening in on their discussions. More formal processes include testing and setting assignments for marking, and the national system of tests and examinations.'[5]

This way of thinking about assessment values informal processes undertaken in the context of the classroom as well as more formal forms of assessment. Taken in this way, neither monitoring nor assessment are exclusively concerned with passing judgements about pupils' work, but can be regarded as integral to the pupils' learning process and the means by which teachers evaluate their own effectiveness.

Interview task

Ask a small group of pupils in Key Stage 3 to describe how their work has been assessed in drama. Ask them about the written reports they have received and how oral feedback is given to them. How do they, explicitly or implicitly, describe the criteria by which they think they are being assessed? To what extent do they see assessments as necessary in improving the quality of their work in drama?

Raffan and Ruthven's definitions of monitoring and assessment, whilst helpful, do not, however, entirely suit drama. Because drama is a collaborative, creative and enactive art form, teachers are very likely to participate actively in the work alongside their pupils. In drama, monitoring individual pupils' work will often be integrated into the lesson itself with drama teachers using a range of practical and creative strategies to gauge pupils' knowledge, skills and understanding. In addition to observing the pupils while they are on task, listening to them and questioning them, drama teachers might, for example, also note how pupils respond to strategies such as teacher-in-role. In drama, an overall picture of pupils' learning and progress may be developed:

- in the context of the lessons themselves by teachers watching, listening and interacting with pupils;
- as the result of reviewing practical work, reading written work and looking at other material kept in working notebooks such as designs or storyboards;
- as part of the process of the teachers' own reflections on their own practice as teachers in lesson evaluations.

Student-teachers' appreciation of the relationship between monitoring and assessment and how both are necessary to maximize pupils' learning is enhanced by an understanding of the different and complementary purposes of baseline, formative and summative assessment. The meanings of these terms may seem to be self-evident:

- *baseline assessment* gives teachers an indication of the pupils' experiences and abilities at the beginning of a course;
- *formative assessment* is that which is used to fashion the next stages in a pupil's learning;
- *summative assessment* measures the point reached by the pupils at the end of a study sustained over a period of time.

Baseline assessment

By the time pupils enter secondary education, they are likely to have had at least six years of drama education in one form or another. Some secondary schools will be furnished with data relevant to the pupils' attainment in drama in the form of individual profiles. Where liaison is particularly good, secondary school drama teachers may have had the opportunity to visit partnership primary schools, observe the sort of drama undertaken and gain a sense of the pupils' level of achievement. In most cases, however, student-teachers may find that secondary teachers have little or no information about the drama experience of new pupils. In order to start to plot their progress, drama teachers needs to establish a basic appreciation of what they know, understand and can do. This is called the baseline.

In drama, baseline assessment may involve engaging the pupils in a variety of tasks. Simply asking small groups to produce a dramatic response to a stimulus (which may be a poem, short story, picture or object) within a short time-span will reveal a good deal about the way pupils are able to, for example:

- identify the dramatic potential of a stimulus;
- help each other develop ideas;
- experiment with language, sound, gesture and space;
- create dialogue and other forms of dramatic speech;
- communicate through use of voice, gesture and movement;
- convey a dramatic narrative in a structured way.

By inviting the pupils to reflect on their own and each other's work the teacher will also gain an insight into their understanding of dramatic vocabulary and critical terms. Other aspects of the pupils' knowledge and understanding may be accrued from asking pupils to complete a simple questionnaire about their experience (e.g. plays seen or performed in, drama clubs and classes attended out of school, most memorable drama lesson) or providing them with a photograph or diagram of performance event, play-script or stage and asking them to annotate it appropriately.[6]

Baseline assessment is also used for pupils already in secondary education. Ideally, full and accessible records of pupils' achievements in drama will be kept in schools. However, teachers new to a school or taking on a new GCSE or A level class, for example, may wish to establish for themselves the pupils' depth and breadth of experience. In the case of baselining, pupils need to be clear that they are not being tested in order to give them a label, but so that the teacher can plan effectively how to start them on the next stage of their drama career.

Selecting stimulus material

Consider these three short pieces of text. Each was used by student-teachers to establish a baseline at different stages in a secondary school drama curriculum. In each case the class was told to use the text as the basis for a piece of drama of their own. This could involve finding an interesting way of presenting the text or taking an idea from it and developing something entirely new. Discuss how appropriate you feel each piece to be for the age group. What potential for development through drama do you think each piece has?

> Be not afeared: the isle is full of noises,
> Sounds and sweet airs, that give delight, and hurt not.
> Sometimes a thousand twanging instruments
> Will hum about mine ears; and sometimes voices,
> That, if I then had wak'd after long sleep,
> Will make me sleep again: and then, in dreaming,
> The clouds methought would open and show riches
> Ready to drop upon me; that, when I wak'd
> I cried to dream again.

> William Shakespeare, *The Tempest*

I won't be my father's Jack,
I won't be my mother's Jill,
I will be the fiddler's friend
And have music when I will.
Another tune, another tune
Come and play me a different tune.

Adapted from an old rhyme in the *Oxford Dictionary of Nursery Rhymes*, ed.
Iona and Peter Opie, Oxford, Oxford University Press, 1951

I could not dig: I dared not rob:
Therefore I lied to please the mob.
Now all my lies are proved untrue
And I must face the men I slew.
What tale shall serve me here among
Mine angry and defrauded young?

Rudyard Kipling

Research
Find three short pieces of text, music or pictures that you think could be used to
stimulate drama work at Years 7, 10 and 12 that would help establish what the pupils
knew, understood and could already do at each level. What criteria inform such a
selection?

Baseline assessment

- Establishes what knowledge, understanding and skills pupils are bringing to a new
  situation and environment.
- Provides opportunities for pupils and teachers to discuss what constitutes progress
  and learning in drama.
- Introduces the importance of using a dramatic vocabulary.
- Sets clear signals about the importance of collaborative working practices in drama.
- Helps pupils understand that what they already know and can do will inform future
  work.

Formative assessment

Formative assessment is integral to the process of teaching and learning. It may
be seen as the next logical step from establishing a baseline in that it addresses
two fundamental questions:

- have the activities undertaken by the pupils provided the opportunities for learning which
  were intended?
- what evidence is there that pupils are developing knowledge, skills and understanding?

Formative assessment enables teachers to help move pupils on from the
intuitive practice of drama to a more conscious understanding of dramatic ideas,

forms and structures. It is the means by which teachers keep pupils informed of assessment criteria and their individual progress. As such, formative assessment occurs in both the short and the long term. It is also consistent with Bruner's description of a spiral curriculum, as formative assessments encourage pupils to relate their previous learning to new contexts and thus become increasingly independent learners.

Valuing this relationship between practice and thought has led drama teachers to develop approaches to formative assessment in which the pupils themselves are included. The three central teaching strategies which enable teachers to make formative assessments are questioning, observation, reflection. Each of these activities forms an essential part of pupils' learning in and about drama. By creating opportunities for pupils to use these strategies to improve their own work, the drama teacher is, in effect, enlisting them to contribute to their own formative assessment. By working in this way teachers are able to deepen learning by reiterating the aims of a unit of work or learning objectives for the lesson and asking the pupils to relate the assessment criteria to their practice. The process of constantly assessing and reflecting becomes a part of the learning without breaking the flow of the lesson. Furthermore, working in this way does not preclude drama teachers becoming directly involved as active participants.

An agenda and task for observation: integrating formative assessment into drama lessons

Record a drama lesson on video. Observe and critically analyse how drama teachers use the three strategies of questioning, observation and reflection in their lessons in order to make formative assessments about pupils' learning. What opportunities do they provide for the pupils themselves to use these same strategies to reflect on their own work and contribute to the development of each other's? Looking for the use of the following strategies may help:

- *Questioning*: in and out of role, marking the moment, hot-seating, role-on-the-wall. Teachers may also deepen and monitor pupils' learning and involvement in the work by structured questioning in small-group work, scribing ideas, clarifying brainstorm sessions.
- *Observation*: of practical work, including rehearsal; devising; small-group discussions. This may be helped by using strategies which slow down or frame the dramatic action, such as audio or video recording, digital cameras, script-writing.
- *Reflection:* structured reflection on specific dramatic images, moments, roles; inviting pupils to evaluate their own learning and remark on each other's work both during and at the end of a lesson.

Drama on paper

Not all aspects of drama, however, are assessed through practical work. Many drama teachers also encourage pupils to use working notebooks to plan and reflect on ideas represented in drama. They may write scripts, draw storyboards, record in diagrams and note form what they are working on in lessons and sketch designs. As pupils progress in the subject, they are likely to be required to write reflectively about their own work, review plays seen and present structured analytical essays as well as engaging in creative practice. Some of this work will be undertaken in lessons, but it may also be given as homework. These elements of the drama curriculum provide valuable insights into the progress of individual pupils. Reading, commenting on and marking such work complements the formative assessments of practice and similarly contributes to the process of learning.

Formative assessments

- Clarify to the pupils what they are trying to achieve and their progress.
- Recognize that learning in drama may be observed in the processes or making and performing as well as in responding.
- Provide support to pupils in the process of learning by identifying achievements and reflecting on next steps.
- Enable pupils to discuss and negotiate how they are progressing in drama.
- Relate reflection to the context of practical drama and so deepen the learning process.
- Support teachers in their own planning and evaluation by focusing on the relationship between learning objectives, drama activities and assessment criteria.

Summative assessment

The term summative assessment can be a little misleading. Most obviously, summative assessment summarizes pupils' achievements at the end of a given period. However, such a period may be a unit of work, a term, a school year, a Key Stage or an examination course. In this sense, a summative assessment may be formative in that it contributes to pupils' understanding of their progress and informs future work in the subject. On the other hand, summative assessment can be more controversial than formative assessment because the effects on the learning process are not always so evident. It is the form of assessment most usually associated with public examinations and national tests, where issues of validity, reliability and consistency are often debated along with the justification and fairness of putting young people under pressure to perform in this way.

The importance of collaborative group work in drama and the involvement of the teacher in the work poses particular educational and pragmatic questions:

- How can the contribution individuals make to group work be assessed? While it is sometimes obvious who in a group is coming up with the ideas and doing the lion's share of the preparation this is certainly not always the case.
- What are the practicalities of trying to monitor the process a group goes through in devising and rehearsing work? Clearly, while a teacher is watching and listening to one group he or she may miss important turning points in another. It is possible that pupils are affected when their teachers are monitoring their process in this way. Even if the teacher says nothing, will their body language influence the group's decisions?
- How might the different ingredients of the process be assessed fairly? In drama it is often the case that the whole is greater than the sum of the parts. While one pupil may contribute a lot of useful ideas to a group, another may drop in just one, the value of which outweighs all others. It is sometimes extremely difficult, perhaps impossible, to find tangible evidence of exactly who did what in a successful collaboration.
- What is the role of external examiners in the assessment of drama practice? The duration of a piece of drama presented as a part of an examination will be constrained in some way. For example, the group size may be specified as between four and nine and the presentation limited to a maximum of 20 minutes. Is it really possible that examiners will be able to fairly assess pupils given such constraints? How will visiting examiners be able to detect individual contributions to the process by observing the product?
- How can teachers' assessment of practical drama work be externally moderated when they may have been integral to the group's work?

Finding the evidence for summative assessments

Find out from your drama mentor what evidence is used for summative assessment in drama at different Key Stages. What part does continuously assessed coursework play in end-of-year or end-of-course examinations? How do the following elements of drama contribute evidence towards summative assessment?

* improvisation * rehearsal * performance as actors, directors, designers and technicians * working notebooks * written tests * scriptwriting * play reviews * essays * group discussions and vivas * pupils' self-assessments.

Summative assessment at Key Stage 3

At Key Stage 3 the limited amount of time available for drama means that many teachers feel that tacking a task on to the end of a unit of work purely for the purposes of summative assessment is neither tenable nor desirable. However, where drama appears in the curriculum as a separate subject, there will most likely be an expectation (and it is certainly deemed good practice) that pupils' achievements are reported on. This may make it imperative that some form of summative assessment is undertaken. By the end of the Key Stage when pupils will be required to make their options for examination courses, both they and their teachers may also need something by which to judge their aptitude for the subject.

In order to address these issues drama teachers have developed ways of assessing pupils which are both productive and economical in time. Some schools provide no more than a brief generalized comment or an impressionistic 'effort/ achievement' grade. A more comprehensive and rather more useful approach to assessment in drama at Key Stage 3 which has gained considerable currency in recent years is the use of *level descriptors*.[7] In practice, level descriptors are formulated by considering what sort of evidence a teacher would use to establish the degree to which a pupil was meeting the assessment criteria. Level descriptors should always correspond to assessment criteria.

Sample level descriptors

Assessment criteria	To be able to interpret and portray a character in performance
Level	Descriptor
3	Maintains a role throughout a short devised scene that is being shared in the course of classwork
4	Communicates character through consistent use of voice, movement and gesture
5	Uses a range of vocal and physical skills to portray different characters including those from scripted plays
6	Employs a range of performance skills to convincingly create dramatic characters in short devised scenes and imaginatively interprets scripted roles

At Key Stage 3, pupils would normally be expected to fall between levels 3 and 6. Level descriptors such as these may be plotted on to a kind of chart which indicates the different aspects of making, performing and responding that pupils will be assessed on at any given stage. Summative assessment is made by plotting the 'best fit picture' for each individual pupil and aggregating the different levels. At this stage it is just not possible for teachers to notice every contribution pupils make to group work but, by monitoring their work over a period of time, patterns of learning and achievement may well begin to emerge. For example, a pupil may consistently offer thoughtful ideas for movement or use of space in small-group work, but may be less confident in spontaneous improvisation. By focusing units of work on different elements of the subject, employing a range of teaching methods and using a variety of assessment strategies throughout the academic year, drama teachers are able, with diligent monitoring, to formulate an overall profile of each individual pupil. Pupils should be able to recognize themselves in such a profile and, in many schools, they have the opportunity of adding their own comments.

Research and development

Find out what sort of summative assessments are made on Key Stage 3 pupils in your placement school. How is the assessment arrived at? Are level descriptors used or is the assessment just a general impression?

Discuss the validity and practicality of writing and using grade descriptors with your mentor.

Select one of the following strands of drama that might be taught at Key Stage 3 and write level descriptors for the strand:

- working supportively and creatively with others;
- working in a range of different genres and styles;
- using the language and vocabulary of drama when reflecting on their own and other people's work.

Summative assessment and examination specifications

Many student-teachers become understandably worried about how to grade pupils' work so that it complies with the assessment criteria of examination specifications. The teachers with whom they work will almost certainly be equally if not more concerned to ensure that the pupils are assessed in a fair, consistent and reliable way. A major safeguard in the process involves teachers working together and sharing their interpretation of criteria and standards. This invaluable collaboration may occur through:

- *standardization meetings*, where a group of teachers will mark samples of work to agree grades in advance of the examination process (in drama this may involve watching a group perform live or on video as well as marking written papers);
- *moderation*, where work is marked internally, by the teacher, but standards are scrutinized by a moderator appointed by the examination board (some schools have a policy of internal moderation whereby teachers regularly moderate each other's marking).

Other safeguards in place include:

- *external examiners*, who visit in order to assess objectively the performance of practical work;
- *external assessment* of written examinations, where scripts are marked against detailed mark schemes by professional markers who have no knowledge of the candidates.

Assessing at this level clearly requires a familiarity with the language of the specification. Teacher assessments in externally set and moderated examination courses have two audiences, the pupils and the examination board. For example, pupils often use working notebooks to explore and reflect on ideas, plans, designs and rehearsals when they are creating a piece of devised drama. The drama teacher may assess the work formatively and make suggestions for the development of the drama. The same notebook may then be read by an external examiner or moderator, who will use it as evidence for summative assessment.

Compare and contrast

- Study the grade descriptors of two different drama specifications for examination at 15 + . Pick just one grade band and look carefully at exactly what is required by each specification to achieve that grade. How similar are the requirements? What particular aspects of knowledge, skill and understanding are deemed representative of the grade in each?
- Compare the grade descriptors of a 15 + examination to those of an A2 level or Higher Still specification. To what extent is the progression from one level to another apparent in the descriptors?
- Consider carefully the language used in level descriptors, especially adjectives, and discuss with your mentor how they interpret this. How do they identify where the boundaries are between a student having 'an excellent grasp' , 'a grasp' or 'some grasp' of a subject? How does internal and external moderation help overcome these problems of interpretation?

The need to be fair to pupils, and to ensure consistent standards both within schools and between them, has led to assessment practices in drama which can seem complex, time-consuming and costly. However, summative assessment and grading of pupils' work in drama is an inevitable consequence of a public examination system. Because of the multi-faceted nature of drama as a subject, drama teachers have fought hard to have a range of assessment and moderation strategies built into specifications for examinations.

Summative assessment

- Measures standards of achievement.
- Summarizes pupils' learning, usually at the end of a scheme of work or course.
- Relates to assessment criteria and level descriptors.

Questioning, feedback and reflection

At some time or other we have probably all been mystified by the way a piece of our work has been graded. What does it mean when, at the end of a piece of creative dramatic writing or the review of a play, the teacher simply writes B-? Underpinning the discussions of assessment in this chapter is the idea that learning is only positively affected when assessment is offered as a way of helping pupils reflect on their progress and achievements. For student-teachers this means learning how to give constructive feedback.

131

In the course of drama lessons, student-teachers will doubtless observe their subject mentors:

- watching groups rehearse, then questioning the pupils and commenting on how things seem to be going;
- 'spotlighting' particular dramatic moments by, for example, stopping the work of the class as a whole to draw their attention to what some pupils are doing;
- inviting pupils to show their work in progress and using this as an opportunity to point out a particular aspect such as the use of a particular element of form;
- creating a forum for work in which the whole class are invited to help a group shape and develop a piece of work;
- drawing the class's attention to examples of particularly successful homework or journal writing in order to encourage the authors and model the standard.

All of these actions exemplify how assessment may be integrated into the learning process. The learning potential in each instance is increased when the teacher is able to facilitate a dialogue with the pupils rather than just providing a judgement. Asking questions and inviting the pupils to comment helps them to develop their ability to critically appreciate their own and each other's work. By prompting responses in this way teachers are able to assess the pupils' work in this important aspect of drama.

When student-teachers are learning to teach drama, one of their first contributions to the drama lesson may be providing feedback to small groups of pupils. In order to do this constructively they will need to know what the learning objectives are so that their questions and comments may be consistent with them. For example, if the pupils are working on a spontaneous improvisation, it may well be appropriate to comment on how they developed ideas in role or how new characters were accepted or introduced, but it would be unlikely that feedback on the finer points of voice projection would be so helpful at that stage. Some student-teachers find it useful to compile a 'comment bank' which reflects the learning objectives of the lesson. This may seem a little mechanistic but it can provide a positive start from which to build, and may prevent feelings of panic when the teacher suddenly turns to the student-teacher and asks, 'What would you like to say about that piece, Ms Taylor?'!

Finding ways of encouraging pupils to comment constructively on each other's work also depends on making sure that they work within well-defined parameters; that they know what they are being asked to reflect on and why. In turn this is dependent on asking carefully phrased, tightly focused questions. Having watched a small group share an emotionally charged piece of role-play about leaving home or a death in the family, for instance, the question 'So, how could they have made that better?' may only elicit comments such as: 'Well, when Jenny came in she mimed opening and closing a door but then Chris just walked straight through it.' The pupil offering this criticism may think that it is entirely justified. However, if the brief was to explore how people break and react to bad news then the performers may find such a comment trivial and irrelevant. Once again, student-teachers can avoid this sort of unproductive incident by preparing suitable questions when planning. Some teachers would argue that good teaching depends upon skilful questioning more than anything else. It is certainly worth spending time observing this aspect of teachers' work and discussing their questioning strategies with them.

Questioning for reflection

Consider the following tasks. Imagine that groups have worked on them and shared their work with the rest of the class. Write three questions that you could ask the rest of the class which would help them reflect on the work seen and contribute to their own learning.

Year 7:
Learning Objective: To communicate a simple story (taken from Aesop's fables) in a linear dramatic narrative showing how characters change.
Task: In groups of four, turn the story you have been given into a short play. When you show the play the audience must understand who you are, what happens in the story and how one of the characters is different at the end from how they were at the beginning.

Year 10
Learning objective: To combine the physical characteristics of different characters from *commedia dell'arte* in a comic scene appropriate to the genre.
Task: In groups, devise and present a *lazzi*. Each member of the group must play a different *commedia* character which the audience must be able to recognize. The scene must demonstrate some other features of the genre.

As student-teachers become more experienced, of course, they will be able to be increasingly spontaneous in their feedback and better able to focus the learning through judicial use of questions. Questioning itself needs to progress and explore different aspects of the work. It becomes extremely tedious and increasingly unproductive to ask the same questions about every group's work. Whilst they are developing the skill of finding different and increasingly probing questions to ask the class, a useful strategy for the student-teacher to adopt is creating 'expert panels'. This is a simple technique but very valuable in helping pupils focus their critical comments. All it involves is dividing the audience into sections and giving each something in particular to watch out for and prepare a comment on. For example, while watching a *lazzi* devised in response to the task above, different groups may be asked to prepare a few comments on:

- what *commedia* characters were shown and how did we know?
- what other features of the genre did the group use?
- how did the *lazzi* try to make us laugh?
- how did the performers engage with the audience?

It is always a good idea to allow pupils a minute or two to talk to each other about their responses before asking them to 'go public'. Affording them a few moments to check out their ideas with each other will result in them feeling more prepared and more confident in speaking aloud. Having offered a number of comments on their given 'areas of expertise' the class as a whole are in a much stronger position to move on, where it is appropriate, to speculate on how a piece of work may be developed.

Involving pupils in reflecting and commenting on each other's work is a prelude to self-assessment. There is considerable research evidence to suggest that when pupils are involved in the assessment of their own work, their sense of pride and ownership in the work increases.[8] In drama, self-assessment is one way in which pupils can capture significant dramatic moments and reflect on work which may otherwise appear ephemeral. By encouraging pupils to assess their own contributions to drama, they become increasingly informed practitioners and reflective thinkers.

Feedback

- Is focused, economical and reflects the learning objectives of the lesson.
- Productively invites pupils to reflect on aspects of their own and each other's work.
- Involves asking questions which are appropriate to the task set and help give pupils an ever-increasing range of new insights.
- Enhances the development of pupils' own critical appreciation and helps them assess themselves.

Evaluation, monitoring and planning

Baseline, formative, summative and self-assessments may all be used productively to record pupils' achievements and enhance learning. While there is justifiable unease about the way in which examination and test results are used to compare the quality of teaching within and between schools, monitoring pupils' progress can have a real impact on how teachers plan and teach their lessons. Taking account of the way pupils respond in different lessons and noting what they do well and what they struggle with does not usually require teachers to completely rewrite units of work or alter the content of lessons. Rather, monitoring may highlight the need to adjust the way something is explained, how a task is set or how feedback needs to be more focused. However, if assessment reveals that pupils have consistent difficulties in particular areas, the drama curriculum and teaching styles will need to be reviewed more comprehensively. By monitoring pupils' responses and levels of achievement teachers are thus better able to evaluate their own part in the learning process and adjust their planning and praxis accordingly. Inevitably, monitoring requires a systematic way of recording observations and assessments.

- Is used to measure standards of attainment within and between schools.
- Can reveal pupils' consistent strengths and areas of difficulty.
- Can provide teachers with concrete evidence with which to praise pupils' work.
- Enables pupils to participate in target setting and self-assessment.
- Facilitates planning to meet the needs of individual pupils or groups of pupils.

Recording and reporting

The business of recording and reporting pupils' achievements is in part an administrative responsibility though, as this chapter stresses, it is integral to the link between learning, evaluation and planning. Raffan and Ruthven define 'recording' in the following terms: 'Recording means keeping up-to-date records of the classroom experience and achievement of individual pupils, relating these systematically to the agreed curriculum and assessment framework laid down by the National Curriculum, or the corresponding requirements of upper secondary courses and qualifications.'[9] Seen in this light, there are particular issues related to record keeping for drama teachers, particularly in the 11–14 age-range. Not only is drama in an ambiguous position in the National Curriculum, there are also practical issues about how to keep track of individual pupils' progress if the teacher sees a whole year group for one drama lesson once a week. Although both these issues tend to be resolved by the time the pupils reach the age of public examinations, many drama teachers find that using ICT provides a relatively swift way of recording pupils' progress.[10]

The distinction between what is recorded and what is reported depends on the intended audience for the work; the style and form of the records and reports of pupils' work very often differ according to the purpose of the assessment. Raffan and Ruthven provide a clear summary of the nature and purpose of reporting:

> Reporting means preparing a summary overview of the performance of individual pupils. Intended both for official purposes and to advise pupils and their parents, pupil reports must relate achievement to the standards defined by national frameworks for curriculum and assessment, and must convey this and broader information about the pupils' learning in a way in which pupils and parents can understand.[11]

When student-teachers arrive in their placement schools, they will find it useful to have access to the drama records kept on the classes they will teach or observe. This will help them to plan work which is appropriate to the class, for example by ensuring that topics and skills are not revisited unnecessarily. The records should also indicate what individual needs may have to be taken into account. Obviously this is a lot to take in, particularly when student-teachers are relatively inexperienced, but it is nonetheless a useful start.

Keeping records: pupil profiles

Because drama provision can vary considerably from school to school, the nature of the records kept will also differ. At its most detailed, each individual pupil will have a drama profile or 'portfolio' in which information about their progress, achievements and learning in drama is built up from their entry into secondary education. This enables pupils and teachers to refer to the evidence amassed over a period of time and to reflect on long-term learning.

In practical terms, the profile keeps information about pupils' progress in drama together. If pupils are photographed at the beginning of Year 7, it can help teachers to learn names (as well as providing a source of amusement and bribery by the time they reach Year 9!). In some schools files may be entirely electronic and kept on disk. A comprehensive drama profile is likely to include the following information:

- self-evaluation and audit of experiences in drama in primary schools;
- summary of baseline assessment;
- self-assessment and teacher-assessment profiling forms for each unit of work;
- working notebooks;
- records of extra-curricular participation in drama;
- copies of yearly reports to parents.

In drama, however, written profiles are usually concerned with either the process of working or final evaluations and do not record the practical work itself. Teachers may use ICT to record group work or final performances of pupils' work in the form of video, digital, photographic or audio recordings, and this is a formal requirement of some examination specifications. Regularly recording practical work can lead to productive discussions with pupils and form a part of their work on appreciating and appraising drama. It is not practical to store hours of video, but some drama teachers have found that asking groups of pupils to edit a short tape which shows different aspects of their work over a term or a year is a valuable way of encouraging reflection.

Writing reports

It is a legal requirement that carers or parents will receive written reports regarding the pupils' academic progress once a year on each subject taught as a part of the curriculum.[12] Written reports, which will of course also form part of pupils' overall drama portfolios, have a particular audience in mind. Ascribing a grade to a pupil's work or making a generalized comment about their effort and attitude is unlikely to help them understand what it is they have achieved and how they might progress. Report forms such as the one shown here are more successful in informing all of the relevant parties what work has been undertaken and what the pupil has learnt. Moreover, by involving the pupil the reporting process becomes a part of their learning.

Sample progress report form for drama

Student's name: _____

Year/Group: _____ Teacher: _____

Work undertaken this year
The work this year has introduced the pupils to the way dramatic symbols are created. This has involved learning how to use stage lights, sound effects and props in their own devised work. We have also explored extracts from the play 'Anansi' and discovered how dramatic characters can symbolize other things. This led on to using movement and space to represent objects and ideas.

Student's comment on what they came to know, understand and be able to do:

_____

_____

_____

_____

_____

Self-assessment: 1   2   3   4
(1 indicates little progress over the year, 4 indicates excellent progress)

Teacher's comment on student's contribution to and development through the work:

_____

_____

_____

_____

_____

Teacher's assessment: 1   2   3   4
(1 indicates little progress over the year, 4 indicates excellent progress)

Teacher's signature _____ Date _____

Researching reports

How are pupils' achievements in drama recorded and formally reported on in your placement school? Discuss with your mentor the school's requirements and the way they go about meeting these. How often are reports sent home? Are the pupils involved in the process?

In addition to writing reports for parents/carers, does your mentor have to write any other kind of profiles for an external audience? What different types of information are conveyed and how?

Consultation evenings for parents and carers

Facing a consultation evening for the first time is a daunting experience. It is unusual for student-teachers to conduct a consultation evening alone, but attending the meeting and making contributions to the discussions is an invaluable part of the process of learning to teach drama. Ideally, such events should be a positive experience for everyone; teachers gain new insights into the pupils whilst parents and carers are offered information about their children's progress. Ideally, the net result is that the pupils themselves feel supported in their endeavours. In practice, however, it does not always feel so easy; teachers may be concerned about parental attitudes, parents may feel anxious about what they will hear and pupils will almost certainly worry about what will be said. It is a situation that requires teachers to exercise considerable diplomacy and skill. It is often said (perhaps ironically) that teachers are good talkers. In order to assess pupils and build a productive relationship with them and the adults who care for them, they also need to be very good listeners. Parents' evenings are not a platform for drama teachers to practise their skills in monologue; they are a forum for discussion.

Not all student-teachers will have worked with families before, and some may hold strong views about the environments in which children are brought up. As inductees into one of the so-called 'caring professions', however, student-teachers need to remain open minded and deal with any personal prejudices that may impede their work. The generic term 'parents' often includes carers as well as blood relatives. There are multiple versions of family life, and family structures other than the assumed norm of mum, dad and 2.4 children may be happy and successful. Equally, 'conventional' families may mask considerable unhappiness and tension which can affect children's learning and achievement. Parents or carers may well want to talk about their home life during consultations, especially if they feel it is impacting on their child's progress and learning in particular ways. By listening to them, teachers learn a great deal about how to re-assess their own approach to these pupils. The fact is, that despite the perception among some teachers that they are undervalued in society, a great many parents/carers hold their own children's teachers in high esteem and are sometimes in awe of them (the comment, sincerely made, 'I couldn't do what you do' is likely to be heard several times in a teacher's career).

The basis of a smooth-running consultation evening is thorough preparation. Most importantly, student-teachers should discuss it with their drama mentor and work out what they need to bring with them to the evening. It is always important to remember that the focus of the discussion should be on the pupils' learning in drama. Parents and carers may wish to go on to discuss other issues concerning their children's development, attitude, behaviour, habits, aptitude for mimicking television personalities, and so on. It is a real skill trying to keep a consultation to the point without offending, belittling or keeping a queue of other parents waiting. Experienced teachers recognize that they need to earn the parents' trust, and keeping a tight rein on the conversation is not necessarily at odds with this. It is helpful to open with constructive comments about how their son or daughter is progressing in drama. Referring them to other colleagues where necessary, for example pastoral tutors, is not fobbing them off but signalling the professional boundaries within which you are working. It is also useful to remember that some teenagers can be remarkably reluctant to discuss their school work at home. While some parents will have heard a lot about the work in drama, others may have little knowledge of the curriculum content. The discussion between parents and teachers should enable them to work together to offer positive support for pupils by giving clear and consistent messages about expectations, targets and achievements. Consultation evenings provide an excellent opportunity to explain the aims of the drama curriculum or scheme of work. Parents are unlikely to want a detailed account of the latest research into drama education but they will want to clarify what the long-term aims of the curriculum are, and how the work that pupils are currently undertaking will be extended and developed in future years. In particular, parents may be interested in examination courses in drama and how the subject is regarded by employers or higher education institutions. Both parents' and teachers' time is at a premium in consultation evenings; student-teachers should avoid holding court on issues that may be dear to them but are of little relevance or interest to parents.

Preparing for consultation evenings

Divide into groups of four. One pair should prepare some questions as if they were parents asking the drama teacher about the curriculum at a particular key stage. You may also like to construct a family history which influences the discussion, but which you may or may not divulge to the teachers.

Another pair should summarize the aims of a year group's work in drama, and consider the kind of things they would say about pupils' progress and learning in drama.

Role-play the parents' evening, and discuss the issues it raised for you.

139

Recording and reporting

- Records of pupils' progress are built up over a period of time. They reflect the aims of the curriculum and the pupils' contribution to and development in the subject.
- Reports are written according to the audience.
- Records and reports provide evidence of progression and learning in drama. They may be related to grades or level descriptors and can usefully contain pupils' self-assessment.
- Records provide teachers with solid foundation for discussion at consultation evenings.

Accountability

One of the biggest changes in education in the last ten years has been the increased emphasis on accountability. Whilst there are continuing debates about the fairness and validity of different inspection methods and league tables of examination results, on the whole there is a general agreement that there is a need for teachers to be accountable. Accepting this need, and learning how to comply with the structures set up by the department, school and national initiatives is part of the process of learning to teach drama.

Primarily, student-teachers are accountable to their mentors who, as well as supporting them, have the greater responsibility of ensuring that pupils progress in drama because they are, in turn, accountable to the school's senior management, governors, parents and inspectors. This means that student-teachers will be very carefully monitored and observed, not only for their own benefit, but so that pupils are in no way hindered by their lack of experience. This is perhaps the first lesson in accountability, which Raffan and Ruthven describe as 'the important part that formal assessment plays in evaluating the performance not just of pupils but of their teachers and schools'.[13]

Accountability and collaborative practices

For student-teachers, a great deal is to be gained from sharing and discussing lesson plans, units of work and assessment strategies with mentors. This is also a form of accountability, in which student-teachers learn to work within departmental frameworks and to accept advice about the quality of teaching and learning in their lessons. In many ways this balance between accountability and professional development reflects the best practice in schools, where teachers are supported by a positive staff development programme. Indeed, it is now common practice for senior members of staff to observe teaching and to provide constructive and negotiated advice to *all* teachers about how the standards of pupils' learning might improve in their lessons, and to share examples of good practice with other members of staff.

An education culture in which experienced teachers openly discuss their work and share ideas provides student-teachers with an opportunity to question and challenge. This way of working also highlights particular local issues which confront drama teachers and which may influence pupils' learning and achievement in the school. For example, there may be a large number of pupils for whom English is an additional language or a significant number of pupils who have special educational needs. In terms of accountability within a national context, these local issues need to be acknowledged.

Accountability, in many ways, involves being able to supply evidence of pupils' progress and learning readily. At present, there is still debate about how to find ways to account for the success of a school fairly and maintain a steady commitment to ensuring high standards of teaching and learning in all schools. Whilst this issue is unlikely to be resolved to the satisfaction of all teachers and politicians, it is always worth reconsidering and re-negotiating how methods of accountability can be made increasingly fair and just. It may seem a little clichéd to say so but, beyond any outside agencies, many teachers feel themselves to be, first and foremost, accountable to the pupils. It is for this reason, if no other, that drama lessons need to be well prepared, well resourced, well taught and carefully evaluated.

Accountability

- Aims to provide information to parents and official education bodies about the standards of teaching and learning in the school.
- Should take account of local issues as well as national standards.
- Depends on good professional development for teachers and student-teachers.
- Should help inform and improve teaching and learning rather than being a bureaucratic irrelevance.

Standards, monitoring and accountability

In England and Wales schools are regularly inspected by OFSTED. Whilst OFSTED inspectors must undergo special training and teams are led by qualified Registered Inspectors, they do not necessarily have a background in education or any first-hand experience of teaching. In Scotland and Northern Ireland a more flexible system of visiting is undertaken by Her Majesty's Inspectors for Education (HMIs). Inspections of schools represent one of the ways of ensuring that the education service is accountable to parents and the wider community.

The regular or periodic inspection of schools by outside agencies is intended to ensure a parity of standards across the country in much the same way that moderators appointed by examination boards seek to ensure that specifications and assessment criteria are being interpreted in broadly equitable ways in different schools. Arguably, the key difference is that whereas visiting moderators focus on what the pupils are achieving, inspectors are there to assess the quality of the teaching that leads to pupil achievement.

The results of an inspection can have a profound effect on a school's standing in the community. Knowing this can result in teachers having to deal with considerable stress in preparing for an inspection. Student-teachers will be well aware of how the effect of inspections on individual teachers and whole schools have been portrayed in the national media. It is of course inevitable that some student-teachers will be on placement in school while an inspection is being prepared for or is under way. It is essential therefore that they form a clear and rational view of the purpose and procedure involved.

Student-teachers of drama in England and Wales should understand that OFSTED sees drama as a part of the National Curriculum for English but also as a practical arts subject in its own right in which the emphasis lies in making, performing and responding. As such, although drama is inspected as a part of English, headteachers can ask for the work of the drama department to be inspected separately. Inspections may also seek evidence of how drama contributes to the pupils' personal, social, moral and spiritual development both as a part of a taught curriculum and as an extra-curricular activity.

OFSTED judge pupils' standards of attainment in drama in terms of 'making and presenting drama' and 'appreciating and appraising it'. Inspectors review the extent to which the pupils:

- use imagination with belief and feeling;
- create drama with conviction and concentration;
- respond sensitively to their own work and that of others;
- use a range of dramatic skills, techniques, forms and conventions to express ideas and feelings effectively;
- grasp and use dramatic concepts effectively, recalling, recording and evaluating their own work and that of others.

In the context of lessons, inspectors expect to see evidence of:

- co-operation in creating and communicating effective drama;
- the use of drama to widen experience of English, especially through the use of speaking and listening and purposeful reading;
- the integration of language skills for a creative purpose;
- the contribution of drama to the students' social and moral development and understanding.[14]

There is no reason why a school inspection should interfere with a student-teacher's training programme. Inspectors do have the right to attend lessons taught by student-teachers and will report on the way they address the criteria described above on this understanding. Their remit is to inspect the way drama is being taught in the school and the learning that results from this, not how good or bad the student-teacher is. However, should there be any notable problems or successes with the student-teacher's classroom practice inspectors are likely to want to speak with the subject mentor or professional tutor about them and, where appropriate, to satisfy themselves that appropriate support mechanisms are in place.

Reviewing the evidence

Find out when your placement school was last inspected and look up the report on the OFSTED website at www.ofsted.gov.uk

Discuss the contents of the report with your mentor and find out how the school has responded to what it said about drama.

NOTES

1 See J. Bruner (1986) *Actual Minds, Possible Worlds* (Cambridge, MA: Harvard University Press).

2 M. Fleming (1994) *Starting Drama Teaching* (London: David Fulton Publishers), pp. 50–1.

3 Ibid., p. 50.

4 Adapted from A. Kempe and M. Ashwell (2000) *Progression in Secondary Drama* (Oxford: Heinemann).

5 J. Raffan and K. Ruthven (2000) 'Monitoring, Assessment, Recording, Reporting and Accountability' in J. Beck and M. Earl (eds) *Key Issues in Secondary Education* (London: Continuum), p. 23.

6 For further discussion and practical advice on setting and recording baseline assessment in drama, see Kempe and Ashwell, *Progression in Secondary Drama*, pp. 45–8.

7 Detailed examples of level descriptors and how to use them may be found in Kempe and Ashwell, *Progression in Secondary Drama*, pp. 58–63.

8 See Raffan and Ruthven, 'Monitoring', p. 26.

9 Ibid., p. 23.

10 For examples and exemplification of this practice see Kempe and Ashwell, *Progression in Secondary Drama*, pp. 50–5.

11 Raffan and Ruthven, 'Monitoring', p. 24.

12 Croner (2000) *The Head's Legal Guide* (London: Croner Publishing), pp. 450–4.

13 Raffan and Ruthven, 'Monitoring', p. 24.

14 OFSTED (1999) *Inspecting Subjects and Aspects* (London: HMSO), pp. 11–18.

6 Working in Context: Professional Responsibilities

Professionalism

On the face of it, it would seem perfectly reasonable to expect new teachers to demonstrate professionalism. The fact that they are paid for doing the job means, after all, that they are professional and teaching is considered a profession.

But exactly how do these three concepts relate to each other? Does 'professional' mean the opposite of 'amateur' (as in 'professional actor')? Or does it imply that 'professionals' hold appropriate specialist qualifications, or that they feel a special kind of calling to a particular career? Perhaps it suggests how the job is done. What is meant by a professional 'level of service' or a 'professional attitude'? Would these be similarly defined for all jobs? And what about the 'oldest profession'? These questions show the complexity of the concept and, significantly, the very different assumptions suggested by the term.

In a 'profession' such as teaching, 'professionalism' is, in many ways, an abstract ideal that becomes most noticeable when it lapses. The term thus implies a set of attitudes and qualities which should be consistent in the thinking and practice of those who teach. While many of these attitudes and qualities are implicit and form a kind of unwritten code, there are definitions of 'professional conduct' which are inscribed in law. While student-teachers do not need to be able to cite such laws, they certainly need to know which laws have particular relevance to their work and understand why this is so. Professionalism is perhaps most fully demonstrated through student-teachers' attitudes and behaviour in school, the commitment and aspirations they bring to their work and how they relate to pupils, colleagues and parents. In other words, it is impossible to discuss professionalism without also discussing values.

Values, attributes and abilities

The Scottish Office's *Guidelines for Initial Teacher Education Courses* offers a particularly helpful description of what professionalism entails within a set of competences relating to the 'values, attributes and abilities *integral* to professionalism' (our italics).[1] The word 'integral' is important here. No description of the actions associated with professionalism can ever be fully complete, nor may the constituent elements of professionalism be separated from the overall picture. Professionalism incorporates all those attitudes to teaching which guide and inform daily judgements. Seen in this light, it suggests more than an easily identifiable and readily measurable level of competence or skill in teaching.

What makes a professional?

Standards of professionalism are dependent on a consensus between those who work in a particular context. At times, people may find that their own values are at odds with this consensus.

Consider the following list of competences taken from the *Guidelines for Initial Teacher Education Courses in Scotland.* To what extent do you agree that a teacher should be able to demonstrate these attributes? Are there any that you feel uncomfortable with or would worry about being able to meet? How might drama teachers find themselves especially able to demonstrate such attitudes and abilities?

List of competences

To qualify as a professional, a student-teacher must:

4.1   be committed to and enthusiastic about teaching as a profession and encouraging pupils to become learners

4.2   be committed to promoting pupils' achievements and raising their expectations of themselves and others, in collaboration with colleagues, parents and other members of the community

4.3   value and promote the moral and spiritual well-being of pupils

4.4   be able to self-evaluate the quality of his or her own teaching, and set and achieve targets for professional development

4.5   demonstrate the abilities associated with analysing situations and problems, seeking solutions and exercising sound judgement in making decisions

4.6   demonstrate effective interpersonal skills and the ability to develop them further, in order to respond appropriately in relating to pupils, colleagues, other professionals, parents and members of the community

4.7   value and promote equality of opportunity and fairness and adopt non-discriminatory practices, in respect of age, gender, race or religion

4.8   be committed to promoting and responding to partnerships within the community

4.9 demonstrate that he or she knows about and is able to contribute to education for sustainable development in a school and the wider community

4.10 demonstrate a commitment to undertaking continuing professional development to keep up-to-date in his or her subject area(s) and be ready to respond to changes in education[2]

Student-teachers will almost inevitably observe that professionalism is variously described and interpreted by different schools. In some schools, for example, it would be considered extremely unprofessional to turn up for work informally dressed. The expectation may be that men wear ties, that women don't wear short skirts and anyone wearing a nose stud is regarded as a serious threat to moral order. In other schools, calling pupils 'the kids' is deemed to be unacceptably patronizing and thus unprofessional. Right from the beginning of the training process, student-teachers will need to observe the codes of the school community in which they are working. As we pointed out in Chapter 1, student-teachers need to develop 'professional antennae', that is, the ability to detect what codes are at work and matching those against their own considered values. Some codes may be invisible and only really obvious when acceptable boundaries are transgressed. Whilst individual student-teachers may disagree with a school's interpretation of professionalism, they must also ask themselves if the training year is the most appropriate time and place to challenge it.

For student-teachers of drama, there are particular issues concerning professionalism. It is a subject that may make a very special contribution to the life of the school and may influence the perceptions of the school in the wider community. Drama education also deals with difficult and sometimes sensitive issues, uses potentially dangerous equipment and often requires bonds of trust which are physical and emotional as well as intellectual. All these aspects of the subject raise issues about how drama teachers negotiate various roles and appropriate professional boundaries.

For the purposes of this chapter, the concept of professionalism has been categorised into five areas of practice. These broad categories take account of professional requirements which are generic to all teachers and consider those which particularly pertain to the teaching of drama. In this context, the professional requirements of teaching drama have been defined in terms of:

- principles of equal opportunities and attitudes to pupils and learning;
- the legal obligations to which teachers must comply and which they should know;
- promoting partnerships with the wider community;
- collaboration with colleagues and contribution to the school as community;
- commitment to continuing professional development.

In many ways, these broad categories represent the rewards of teaching drama which transcend basic requirements of competence. Perhaps it is more productive to see the categories as a basis for good practice rather than rules with which student-teachers must comply. However, there are also local codes of conduct which may need to be observed; drama teachers need to acknowledge that schools operate as communities, and to recognize that particular ways of working have evolved in response to the individual context and the community's needs.

Equal opportunities in drama

Striving to create an environment and a curriculum in which all pupils thrive academically, physically and spiritually involves student-teachers in developing a practical methodology which reflects equal opportunities principles. In other words, it is not just a question of learning a number of 'dos and don'ts' or employing the odd tokenistic gesture, but of understanding the complexities of equality and diversity and responding positively towards them. Practice which promotes equal opportunity is far more than the antithesis of that which discriminates. Student-teachers of drama will need to be aware of what might constitute discrimination and learn how to adopt anti-discriminatory practices (this is discussed below), but, arguably, equal opportunity principles should underpin all teaching and learning in the drama curriculum.[3] In order to think critically and constructively about patterns which concern gender, ethnicity, (dis)ability and class, student-teachers will need to examine statistical evidence of pupils' achievement as well as research into attitudes to teaching and learning.

Research task: lies, damned lies and statistics

If you are working in a mixed school, find out how many girls and boys opt to take drama at examination level. Interview Year 10 or 11 pupils about influences which governed their choices.

Read the examination results of the school as a whole. Examine the statistical evidence about the success of girls and boys, and pupils from different ethnic backgrounds. What emerging patterns are you able to identify?

Drama is usually taught in mixed ability groups. If this is not the case throughout the school, read class lists for two subjects in which there are sets (English and Maths, for example). Are there equal numbers of boys and girls in the top sets? To what extent are pupils of different ethnic backgrounds equally represented?

Find out if there are any whole-school policies in place which relate particularly to equal opportunities and achievement.

An equal opportunities curriculum recognizes the injustice of social inequality and values cultural difference. It does not aim to treat all pupils the same, but is more fully differentiated. On one level, this means that teaching is structured to take account of the needs of individual pupils, by providing additional support for pupils with special needs or those with learning difficulties. However, this is only part of the picture, and to individualize equal opportunities in this way is likely to ignore the multiple social, personal and cultural perspectives and identities young people bring to the drama classroom. In order to create a drama curriculum which is informed by, in James Tully's words, 'the politics of cultural recognition', there is a need to take account of both the content of the curriculum and the way it is taught.[4]

In many ways, drama is very well placed to encourage young people to explore the interface between individual and collective identities. Drama, in common with other art forms, symbolizes cultural values and beliefs, as well as representing personal experiences. As we have pointed out elsewhere, drama provides a forum for inspecting attitudes and investigating social and moral issues. In terms of the content of the drama curriculum, student-teachers may wish to consider the following questions:

- does the drama curriculum include texts from a range of cultures and traditions?
- does the drama curriculum acknowledge the importance of non-Western dramatic practices and popular culture?
- do the pupils read plays by women as well as by men?
- taken as a whole, do the themes, issues and stories chosen for exploration in drama reflect a variety of social experiences and cultural perspectives?

Seen in this light, the challenge for drama teachers is to create a curriculum which values diversity *and* provides opportunities for interesting drama. This does not mean presenting pupils with ideas, texts and stories which represent only those attitudes which appear politically correct at the time. On the contrary, a robust equal opportunities drama curriculum will challenge established norms by, for example, interrogating the assumptions implicit in 'universal truths' and questioning the values of canonical drama.[5]

While drama teachers obviously do not set out deliberately to discriminate against any individual or social group, sometimes the ways in which the drama is taught or assessed may do just that. Some examination specifications, for example, especially their moderation procedures and mark schemes, may reveal an institutional element to discrimination. For example, it is sometimes specified that pupils must work in the English language for assessment purposes or that cross-gender casting should be avoided. This raises particular issues for pupils who express their ideas and feelings most fluently in other languages (British Sign Language or Urdu, for example), or where drama is taught in single-sex groups.[6] In other contexts, student-teachers may wish to focus on how they structure drama in their lessons and consider the implications of the following questions:

- are there opportunities for pupils to explore ideas in their home languages as well as the official language of the school?
- does the drama offer a range of challenging roles for both boys and girls?
- what provision has been made for pupils learning English as an additional language?
- is it assumed that pupils know particular cultural reference points (Western fairy stories, for example)?
- is there provision for a range of physical abilities in the work?

In a pluralist democracy, what constitutes equal opportunities in drama education (as elsewhere) is contested terrain, and rightly so. In some schools equal opportunities policies and practices are well established, but elsewhere student-teachers may find provision more limited. There are, however, a number of statutory obligations that teachers are expected to fulfil in order to ensure that the pupils are, as far as is possible, afforded equal opportunities. Student-teachers need to know what these particular obligations are, but perhaps more importantly they need to consider what their own values and aspirations are for an equitable society.

Legal obligations and responsibilities

In order to achieve Qualified Teacher Status, student-teachers need to have a working knowledge and understanding of their legal responsibilities and liabilities. In England and Wales student-teachers are required to demonstrate that they know about a number of specified statutes.[7] In Scotland and Northern Ireland the requirements are not so prescriptive but the need for an awareness of professional responsibilities is clearly signalled. In Scotland, for example, newly qualified teachers must be able to 'demonstrate an understanding of international, national and local guidelines on child protection and teachers' roles and responsibilities in this area'.[8] Student-teachers are most likely to be introduced to the details of different legal responsibilities as part of their professional studies programme. The purpose of this section is to discuss the particular relevance these legal responsibilities have to drama teachers.

School teachers' pay and conditions

Teachers' pay and conditions vary in different parts of the UK. In England they are set out by the DfEE, whereas in Scotland local education authorities have traditionally had responsibility for issuing contracts of employment which apply conditions negotiated with the General Teaching Council of Scotland. In addition to setting out the general duties that teachers are expected to perform, contracts stipulate how many days they must be available for work. Not all of these days will involve classroom teaching. For example, *The School Teachers' Pay and Conditions Document 1997* which applied to teachers in all maintained schools in England and Wales stated that they must be available for 195 days in any school year, of which they may be required to teach for 190 days. Following this document, teachers must be available for 1265 hours in any school year to 'perform such duties as may be specified by the head teacher'. These hours are usually referred to as 'directed time'. The headteacher must allocate these hours reasonably throughout the days on which the teacher is required to be available for work. The document also notes that teachers may be required to work 'such additional hours as may be needed to enable him to discharge effectively his professional duties'.[9]

Whilst these regulations do not apply throughout the UK their basic tenor raises some interesting questions for student-teachers of drama. For example, what is the implication of phrases such as 'such additional hours as may be needed to enable him to discharge effectively his professional duties'? Would time spent rehearsing extra-curricular drama productions or clubs be included in this? Perhaps these activities are accepted beyond directed time. But what about time spent supervising rehearsals for examination work, or accompanying examination groups to the theatre in order for them to write reviews as required in some examination specifications?

The division of teachers' hours between teaching and other duties is determined by headteachers, often in negotiation with individual members of staff, local trade unions and professional organizations. In principle, headteachers could insist that drama teachers produce school plays or run drama clubs. However, good headteachers value the judgements of staff members and will understand that although drama productions are worthwhile they are only one part of the drama provision in a school.

Anti-discrimination legislation

In legal terms, *direct discrimination* is deemed to have occurred when one person is treated less favourably than another in the same circumstances because of their sex, race or physical or mental disability. The Acts define discrimination as 'direct' or 'indirect'. *Indirect discrimination* is held to occur when individuals are treated equally but the *effect* of this treatment is that one person or group is favoured over the other.

Specific regulations which have implications for and apply to all schools in the UK are:

The Sex Discrimination Act 1975
The Race Relations Act 1976
The Disability Discrimination Act 1995

In England and Wales student-teachers are required to have a working knowledge and understanding of the first two of these as part of their work towards achieving the *Standards for the Award of Qualified Teacher Status.* They are not legally required to know the third.

It is expected that student-teachers are in agreement with the purpose and parameters of anti-discrimination legislation, but they should also be aware of the practical implications. As we have already noted, drama education has long been concerned with exploring the social consequences of actions and events. Framing and containing the exploration and expression of potentially contentious ideas or sensitive issues through drama as an art form requires good subject-knowledge and classroom-management skills. It also requires a sound knowledge of the pupils not only as individuals, but as members of social groups. It may be, for example, that there are religious reasons why some pupils are unable to participate actively in some drama activities. Student-teachers should be aware that adolescent boys and girls may frequently feel uncomfortable doing things that draw attention to their gender or sexuality. While introducing activities that do this is not necessarily discriminatory in itself, forcing pupils to undertake tasks that they are unhappy about for this reason, and downgrading them for refusing to do them, could well be seen as discriminatory.

Where pupils have physical disabilities provision will need to be made for supporting them within drama lessons. It is the responsibility of the school governors to publish details of how the school prevents pupils with disabilities from being treated less favourably than other pupils. Schools must state what provision there is to assist access to the school and 'join in the everyday activities of the school as far as is practical'.[10] In some ways, discrimination against pupils with physical disabilities can be avoided by ensuring access to the same rooms and equipment as other pupils and that teachers know how to use available technology appropriately. Where they are used in school, student-teachers will need training in how to employ, for example, radio audio aids and loop systems to assist hearing-impaired pupils, and concept and Braille keyboards for the partially sighted. There is, however, an element of attitude in discrimination which rests on deficit; that is to say, a belief that, for whatever reason, a person or group 'can't' do something rather than the acceptance that they can or at least might be able to given appropriate support. As the work of theatre companies such as *CandoCo* or *Chicken Shed* show, there are many different ways that people can express themselves in drama and through which they can learn.

Child protection

A phrase that is often used to describe the basis of teachers' role and respon-sibilities regarding the care of pupils, is that they are held to be *in loco parentis.*

This means that they are seen to be in place of the parent and so expected to protect children in much the same way as parents would. However, while this is accepted as 'common law', exactly what it entails is not defined. In practice, judgments regarding what constitutes abuse or negligence often depend on a body of case law. From student-teachers' point of view the two salient points to consider are:

- Some children are abused. Not only will this impact on their general behaviour and personality, its effects may well become particularly noticeable in the context of drama.
- Children can be damaged physically and emotionally very easily. Once again, because of the nature of the subject and the activities it sometimes involves, student-teachers need to be acutely aware of how this damage may occur.

Relevant UK legislation which applies to these aspects of a teacher's work include the *Children Act 1989*, the *Health and Safety at Work Act 1974* and the *Young Persons' Safety Act 1995*. What is under discussion here is the principles that lie behind these laws and why they must be considered by student-teachers training to teach drama.

Drama is one of the areas of the curriculum where, because of the physical and emotional content of the work, it sometimes becomes apparent that a pupil may be suffering some kind of abuse. It is essential that student-teachers understand that they are not responsible for investigating such cases. Questioning the pupil about what is happening to them and how they feel about it can affect the evidence in any subsequent legal proceedings. Sometimes pupils will seek to confide in student-teachers because they seem friendly, supportive, accessible and perhaps closer to the pupil in age than other teachers. Maybe the content of the drama lessons leads pupils to assume that the student-teacher is an ideal person to talk to as they will understand and not rebuke. For student-teachers, it may feel quite flattering to have a pupil wishing to confide in them. Once revealed, however, they may find the nature of the confidence very difficult to cope with. In fact, all teachers must make it clear to pupils who request that information given is kept secret that they can not guarantee absolute confidentiality because, in some matters, there is a legal responsibility to share the information with other agencies.

Physical contact

It is a commonly held misconception that all physical contact with children is unlawful.

In the normal course of teaching a subject which has a physical element it may quite often be necessary to make physical contact with pupils in order to demonstrate or help them develop particular physical skills. In the drama curriculum there will be many occasions when the physical nature of the work will require this. For example, teaching pupils the rudiments of stage fighting by demonstrating with a pupil who is clear on what to expect and how to react may be a useful, relevant and enjoyable part of the curriculum.

It is also recognized in law that it is sometimes appropriate to use physical contact to reassure children. The riders on this acceptance are clear: teachers should never touch pupils in ways or on parts of the body that may be considered indecent and any use of physical contact must be appropriate to the situation. Teachers must always bear in mind that innocent actions can be misconstrued, particularly in contacts between members of the opposite sex. Gently placing a hand on a child's shoulder may, on the face of it and in front of witnesses, appear to be a perfectly natural action intended to comfort rather than cause further distress. Drama students, with their incisive understanding of body language, may be particularly aware that the manner in which the contact is made can radically alter its meaning. Making any kind of physical contact in a one-to-one situation is extremely ill advised. (As a general point, student-teachers should avoid any situation in which they are alone with a pupil.)

Restraint is another aspect of physical contact about which student-teachers must be clear. Specific laws directly concerned with education vary across the UK, but the principle in each region is the same: there are sometimes justifiable reasons for teachers to physically restrain children. Such situations would include those in which the child is:

- committing a criminal offence;
- injuring themselves or others;
- damaging property;
- behaving in a manner that threatens the maintenance of good order.

Underlying each of these scenarios is a concern for children's welfare and an understanding that any physical force used must be in proportion to the circumstances. Given the 'common law' principle of *in loco parentis,* rulings such as these apply at any time when teachers have lawful charge of pupils, including trips out of school. Student-teachers should be aware that this provision covers only qualified teachers and others authorized by the headteacher. However, there is also a common law duty of care that accepts that it is reasonable for adults caring for children to act in a way that a 'reasonable parent' would. Because the drama room may present particular hazards, student-teachers must be satisfied that they understand the implications of these rulings. Except in extreme circumstances where there is a grave and immediate danger of a child being seriously hurt, student-teachers should avoid physically restraining pupils.

There are some individual children and groups of pupils for whom any physical contact with teachers may create discomfort or represent a particular problem. In some cases this relates to ethnic or religious backgrounds; in others

153

it may be an issue relating to the pupil's personal history. Even experienced teachers can, and frequently do, make mistakes in matters of conduct such as these. Some mistakes can be avoided by checking out the situation with colleagues one would expect to know about pupils' circumstances, but even this is no absolute guarantee. When mistakes are made it is important to discuss them with someone else. Certainly, student-teachers should discuss this issue and any incidents with their mentors both by way of protecting themselves and as a means of learning from the situation.

Heightening awareness

- Which aspects of the drama curriculum in your placement school do you feel would warrant special consideration of child protection issues because of their emotional, moral or physical content? Discuss with your mentor how safeguards are put in place when these units are being taught.
- Consider situations in your own drama career when it has been necessary for a drama teacher or director to make physical contact with you. How did you feel about it? Was it appropriate and necessary? If you felt uncomfortable, try to identify why and think about how the teacher/director might have avoided this outcome.
- Discuss with your subject-mentor situations in drama in which physical contact may be either unavoidable or in fact desirable.
- What sort of issues often covered in drama do you think should warrant a special awareness of pupils' backgrounds and responses?
- Discuss with your mentor incidents that they have personally encountered in which child protection has been an issue (for example, occasions in which they have felt it necessary to physically reassure or restrain pupils).

Health and safety

Embedded in professional considerations of child protection are issues concerning health and safety. As we have already noted, there may be times when teachers must intervene physically in order to protect children but these incidents are, in practice, few and far between. By and large schools are very safe environments although teachers of some subjects, and drama is one of them, do have to pay particular attention to health and safety matters because of the nature of the subject and the space in which it may be taught. In fact, among the first things that need to be addressed when student-teachers of drama visit their placement school are the rules and routines that are in place to ensure the safety of the pupils.

The health and safety of staff and pupils is ultimately the responsibility of the school's governing body and, where appropriate, the LEA. Schools must have their own policy for health and safety which shows how statutory requirements are managed. (The relevant act which applies throughout the

UK is the *Health and Safety at Work Act 1974.)* Some matters, such as fire regulations and procedures in case of fire or bomb alert, will be common to the whole school and drills will regularly take place. What is of particular importance to student-teachers of drama beyond these matters is how the health and safety policy has been translated by drama teachers in order to ensure that drama spaces are safe working environments.

A number of health and safety issues are largely a matter of classroom management and dealt with by introducing pupils to a number of ground rules. Sometimes these are clearly displayed in the drama classroom. They might cover, for example, rules such as bringing appropriate footwear to drama. However, even this seemingly straightforward attempt to serve pupils' interests needs interpretation at a local level. Wearing inappropriate outdoor shoes can lead to sprained ankles for the wearer and bruises for their classmates (they can also leave a terrible mess in wet weather!). Wearing only socks or tights on a polished hall floor is dangerous if the class are going to be running around. Wearing no shoes at all can risk spreading verrucas and some pupils may justifiably complain about how cold the drama room gets in winter.

Before they start teaching, student-teachers will want to know the usual practices of the department in order to maintain consistency and standards. Both timetabled drama lessons and extra-curricular activities pose a number of health and safety issues which student-teachers will need to discuss with their mentors:

- Exactly what is the procedure in case of fire? Where is the assembly point for the drama room? What are the teachers' responsibilities in the event of the alarm being raised? Is the fire exit always kept clear of scenery, rostra and other clutter? Where are the fire extinguishers? How and when should they be used? (It should not be assumed that all extinguishers do the same thing. Using a water-based extinguisher on an electrical fire can be a very big mistake!)
- What are the regulations for pupils handling electrical equipment? Are they allowed to set lights for themselves? Is there a requirement to wear hard hats? Are they allowed to change fuses and plugs? Do drama teachers take the opportunity to work with, for example, physics teachers in order to teach pupils about ratios for wattage, voltage and amperage or the hazardous effects of coiling live cables? Do drama teachers themselves receive any kind of training in this? Some schools and LEAs have strict guidelines regarding what teachers are allowed to do when it comes to handling electrical equipment.
- If the school has a scaffolding tower, are pupils allowed to erect it themselves? Are any of them allowed up the tower? What is the minimum amount of supervision expected?
- Are pupils allowed to move rostra on their own? Some types of rostra must be moved in a particular way to avoid the risk of them falling on to pupils. Are pupils made explicitly aware of the manufacturer's guidelines? (Are teachers aware of them?)
- What, exactly, are the procedures if a child is hurt in the drama studio? While electrocution sounds (and is) pretty serious, a simple flesh wound may appear to be easier to deal with. But given an appropriate and sensitive awareness to diseases such as AIDS and hepatitis, is this really so straightforward?

Although this list of questions may appear quite daunting there should be no cause for student-teachers to be alarmed by them. Section 7 of the *Health and Safety at Work Act 1974* makes it a duty of all employees to take reasonable care for their own safety and the safety of anyone who may be affected by their 'acts or omissions'.[11] Such legal liabilities clearly have implications for drama teachers who might reasonably expect, as part of their professional duties, to work with a range of electrical and staging equipment which, if mishandled, could present a considerable threat to their own safety and that of other people – including, of course, the pupils *and* student-teachers for whom they are responsible. In other words, while it is in the interests of student-teachers to find out about health and safety procedures it is also in the interests of their mentors to ensure that such issues are fully covered in the training programme.

Drama and the community

A lively and flourishing drama curriculum can make a significant difference to the life of a school as a community. Drama may complement the school's pastoral programme, and offer opportunities for pupils to share their work with others through performance and presentations. The process of working collaboratively in drama may have a very positive influence on the culture and atmosphere of the school. As such, drama may play a significant part in creating a sense of community.

Because drama enables pupils to explore ideas and issues which are important to them, it inevitably draws on the local community of which the school is a part. Furthermore, productions and other artistic events provide one of the few ways in which members of the wider community can participate in the life of the school. A thriving drama curriculum also provides opportunities for pupils to work with artists and theatre companies, and pupils' education is undoubtedly enriched by experience of the arts. As such, drama can both reflect and enrich the community that exists beyond the school gates.

Drama in the school community

Schools thrive when there is a shared ethos but creating a community in which there are shared aims and values is a complex process. Pupils and teachers come from a diversity of community contexts which can mean that they have very different experiences and expectations. This means that shared values and codes of conduct cannot be assumed, but need to be negotiated and discussed. In some schools, the process of establishing a school community has led staff and pupils to draw up mission statements, which identify the aims, aspirations and

156

expectations which guide the school. Such statements are often displayed around the school, replacing old grammar-school-style mottoes, so that teachers and pupils are reminded of the principles on which the school community is built.

In many schools, drama plays a very active role in inducting new pupils into the ethos of the school and reinforcing the values of the school community as they progress through it. This is achieved by, for example:

- *Incorporating into the drama curriculum units of work that explicitly tackle issues related to the school community.* A common example of this is an exploration in drama of bullying. This may be tackled in a 'head-on' sort of way through role-playing situations in the school context and using strategies such as forum theatre to help pupils recognize and change the situation. Alternatively, the power of metaphor in drama may be employed by studying extracts from playscripts such as *Lord of the Flies* or *The Terrible Fate of Humpty Dumpty*. Student-teachers are very likely to come across other issues important to the maintenance of the school ethos being dealt with in drama.
- *Regularly playing a part in whole-school, class or year/house group assemblies.* There is a considerable amount of very liberal interpretation of the requirement, set down in the 1944 Education Act, that the school day should include an act of collective worship. A very common hybrid derived from this stipulation is that pupils attend and sometimes contribute to assemblies which address some sort of issue. Student-teachers may well find themselves becoming involved in this aspect of school life through their work with a tutor group or because they are drama specialists and therefore worth consulting about ways of presenting ideas.
- *Organizing a programme of drama presentations by pupils, visiting artists and teachers themselves.* The practicalities, benefits and challenges of this aspect of a drama teacher's work are discussed below. Suffice to say here, though, that the choice of what is performed, how such performances are managed and who they involve provide insights into the values espoused by the school.

As members of a community, teachers need to form positive relationships with colleagues as well as pupils. This relies on effective interpersonal skills. As in the classroom, so in the staffroom; drama teachers need to be good listeners as well as accomplished talkers. Although many drama teachers may see themselves as sensitive, warm-hearted and popular members of the staffroom, the truth may be that they scare the living daylights out of some colleagues or simply annoy and frustrate others. As one newly qualified teacher emphatically commented when asked how well she had been served by her training course: 'nothing can prepare you for the staffroom politics!'

Not all teachers understand or respect what drama education involves and some are perplexed by the enjoyment the pupils seem to take from it and the value they place on it. Some teachers may feel jealous or threatened and intimidated by the apparent popularity of a gregarious and energetic drama teacher. The perceptions and prejudices of colleagues are not always easy to deal with. Lecturing them about the wonders and validity of drama education is unlikely to help and flaunting one's popularity amongst the pupils is certainly unlikely to generate much respect in the staffroom. However, to be regarded as 'professional' by colleagues is to be recognized as a member of a team which is working together towards similar objectives.

Drama and the wider community

Schools are a significant presence in any local community. On a purely physical level they are often notable landmarks. On the commercial front they are not only big employers themselves but provide various local businesses and suppliers with work. The quality of life for local residents is inevitably affected by the presence of a school. Student-teachers need to understand that learning takes place outside as well as inside the school gates. A really successful drama curriculum will not only recognize this fact but seek ways of using it.

Developing productive links with the local community obviously includes forging good relationships with individual parents and carers. In addition to consultation evenings, some drama teachers run practical workshops and open evenings for parents, organize theatre trips for them or help groups establish their own drama clubs and performing companies.

The link between the management of the school and the wider community is through the governing body which represents the different interests of the school and the local community. There are, however, other ways in which teachers promote positive links with the community. In the curriculum, work experience and work placements form an important part of pupils' learning, and qualifications such as GNVQs require teachers and pupils to build strong working partnerships with specific employers and industries. Furthermore, extra-curricular activities provide an important link between the school and the wider community. As an art form which, as John Arden famously suggested, is a 'public art' which should 'appeal to more than a minority if it is to remain healthy', drama has a particularly significant role to play in developing links with the wider community.[12] In order to realize this potential, student-teachers in drama will need to recognize how to extend links with the wider community through these three main areas: the management of the school, the drama curriculum and extra-curricular activities.

Managing drama in the school: the role of the governors

The nature of schools' governing bodies has undergone a huge sea-change in the last decade. In contemporary maintained schools at least, stereotypical visions of crusty, dusty old fogies whose sole purpose is to be wheeled out for prize-giving ceremonies may now be consigned to history along with the Ealing comedies that spawned them. Governing bodies now have a tremendously important part to play in the running of schools. More often than not governors are people who have a genuine interest in making things happen; when they are asked for advice and support they will generally respond with commitment and hard work. Knowing who the governors are and what they do can be of inestimable worth to the drama teacher, some of whose work provides a direct interface with the local community represented in the school by the governing body.

The governing body of a school maintained by a local education authority will be made up of parents, people appointed by the local education authority, teachers and (usually but not necessarily) the headteacher and a number of co-optees who will help to provide a bridge between the school and the local community. In the case of schools controlled by other bodies such as a church or voluntary organization, a number of these co-opted positions will be taken by people appointed by the controlling foundation.

First and foremost, it is the responsibility of the governing body to ensure that the school provides good quality education by serving national and local requirements and the aspirations and expectations of the stakeholders themselves, that is, the pupils and their parents. Although the governors are not involved in the day-to-day running of the school, they have a right to discuss, question and refine proposals that will affect how the school is run. This will include, for example, the decision to become a partnership school or offer any kind of training experience to student-teachers. Governors might also be involved in discussing the provision of extra-curricular activities such as plays, theatre trips or visits to the school by professional artists.

Governors do not have an automatic right to visit schools but do need to visit from time to time in order to develop their understanding of how the schools work. Governing bodies usually organize themselves so that each governor takes a responsibility for finding out about and monitoring the work in a particular subject. In this sense the governors can be useful 'critical friends', undertaking the scrutiny of policy documents and providing feedback to curriculum leaders on their appropriateness. Given that their function is to act as a link with the community, governors can also be instrumental in supporting the work of the drama department by raising funds and supporting events such as productions. They may have useful contacts with local business and industry that can be tapped when, for example, special equipment is needed for a production. It is probably quite unlikely that student-teachers will have any direct contact with the governors. If they do, it is important for them to remember that governors do not have the right to intervene in lessons or comment on their work. However, they do have a responsibility to report anything they feel is unsatisfactory or likely to damage the good standing of the school to the governing body as a whole.

Enquiry task

Find out if there is a governor with special responsibility for drama in your placement school and discuss with the subject-mentor how the contact the department has had with them has been organized to the benefit of the drama in the school.

The drama curriculum and the local community

The content of the drama curriculum may play a significant part in helping pupils understand the nature of the community in which they live along with the opportunity of actively contributing to the cultural enrichment of that community. The local community offers drama teachers a priceless resource on which to draw for stories and issues that lend themselves to exploration in drama throughout the secondary school. Examinations in the subject require pupils to consider how drama anticipates and relates to different audiences. Identifying the different needs and attitudes of the subgroups that make up the local community is an essential part of studying drama at this level.

It is difficult to conceive of a drama curriculum that sets out to promote pupils' progression in understanding the role of drama in the society that does not have the establishment of actual and conceptual links between drama and the community as a strand. In practice, student-teachers may most readily identify how notions of community inform the curriculum by investigating the following:

- *Themes and issues in the taught curriculum.* Many drama teachers use elements of local history or traditions as the focus of exploration or investigation in drama. For example, a unit of work at Key Stage 3 might involve role-playing the effect of a battle, the coming of the railways or the arrival of evacuees on the lives of local people in the past. Contemporary issues such as the closing of a local industry, the building of a new road or the changing nature of the community itself can be investigated through a structured drama or used as the basis for a devised piece of theatre. There are obvious opportunities here for drama teachers to work collaboratively with colleagues in other subject disciplines both to inform the work and ensure that, from the pupils' point of view, the same issues are not being 'done to death' ('But miss, we already did the by-pass in Geography!') Sometimes, there are opportunities to bring local people into the drama class to talk about personal experiences of interesting events or give some new insight into a current issue.
- *Subject-specific studies.* There is a wealth of drama in the local community which drama teachers may encourage their pupils to enjoy. Examination-level students and those pursuing vocational courses often wish to make a study of the work of local theatres and companies. Beyond the study of performance, local theatres and other venues can offer pupils insights into and practical experience of a number of areas such as arts administration, design and technical support. Spreading the net wider and investigating local radio and television stations along with film and video production companies is a valuable way of acknowledging the breadth of the subject and perhaps providing pupils with work-experience in related fields.

- *Special projects.* Beyond writing the investigation of different aspects concerning the community into the set drama curriculum, there are many ways in which links can be made through special projects involving or centred around drama. For example, examination groups or extra-curricular drama groups may take pieces of theatre-in-education into local schools, hospitals or old people's homes or contribute to local festivals and carnivals. Similarly, they might devise interactive workshops for specified groups. While incorporating this sort of activity into the drama curriculum may well be laudable and valuable to all concerned, it is essential that the quality of such work is of the highest order and the educational purpose clear. Some examination specifications offer the chance to be assessed on 'outreach' work such as this. Others rightly assume that candidates will have considered how successful drama takes account of its audience as a part of their course.

- *Artists in residence.* Many schools see it as an inalienable right of pupils to have the opportunity of working with artists at first hand. Certainly, local and regional arts councils along with education authorities and central government all support this notion in principle and, to a greater or lesser degree, financially. Using the support offered by arts and education organizations to bring artists into school on a regular basis can clearly raise the profile of the school locally, especially if ways are found to share the work and its outcomes with the community. Rather more importantly, giving pupils direct access to artists provides stimulating new models for their own creative and exploratory work as well as valuable knowledge about how and why art is made and its place in society.

- *Platform for performance.* In many local communities the school may well represent the largest and best-equipped venue for a public event. This being the case, there is an ideal opportunity to offer all members of the community the chance to see a wide range of dramatic events. The school may, for example, invite professional companies or groups from a variety of other cultures to perform there. School can apply for support for such programmes from their Regional Arts Board, who will almost certainly respond warmly to the request for assistance in setting the programme up by offering sound advice if not actual financial backing. Local councils should also be approached; employing the service of school governors can also be particularly productive. In any event, schools need to establish the quality and reliability of any group invited to perform by using these authorities in an advisory capacity and checking that the appropriate performance licences and safety facilities are in place.

Research

- Discuss with your subject-mentor how the drama curriculum and the work of the department generally draws from and contributes to the local community.
- Find out about the role and function of the local Arts Association by contacting the Education Officer. How much support are they able to give schools who ask for it? How often do schools ask? Do they have an eclectic and well-used artists-in-residence scheme?
- What drama and performance groups are at work in the area? What funding is there available to use such groups as a resource? What facility is there to give such groups access to the school as a performance venue?

Extra-curricular drama

Extra-curricular drama plays an important part in the life of most schools. For student-teachers, exploring and contributing to the drama programme that exists beyond the taught curriculum offers opportunities to come to know the pupils, the school and the local community much better. Experienced drama mentors will appreciate that student-teachers have a number of calls on their time and energy which must take precedence over extra-curricular events and will understand that they cannot insist on student-teachers being involved or taking a particular responsibility for any extra work of this kind. On the other hand, many student-teachers will recall how their own experience of extra-curricular work positively affected their relationships with teachers in the classroom. Even if it is impossible to commit fully to an extra-curricular project, student-teachers in drama should, at least, endeavour to find out at first hand what the project entails.

Drama activities that take place outside timetabled lessons might include:

- *Drama clubs.* These could be organized for certain year or key stage groups or open to all comers. Sometimes the purpose of the club is to work towards some kind of presentation. At other times the focus may be on playing 'drama games' or activities set up to encourage pupils to work co-operatively in enjoyable environments.
- *Theatre trips.* Visits to the theatre may be specifically linked to examination syllabuses or organized to offer the pupils new experiences in drama. In addition to organizing trips for the pupils, some schools offer an impressive range of excursions open to staff and parents. This policy can cater both for curricular demands and eclectic tastes in entertainment while generating a lot of goodwill towards the teacher who organizes such events.
- *Production work.* Perhaps this is the most obvious aspect of extra-curricular work in drama. It is certainly the most public and most likely to have an impact on the time and resources of the school and indeed the local community's perception of drama there. Many schools regularly produce plays of which they are proud and productions often play a vital role in the life of the school.

For student-teachers, involvement in these kinds of activities can be highly beneficial. For example, contributing to the organization and running of a Key Stage 3 drama club can give student-teachers extra chances to develop their repertoire of games and exercises and hone the skills required to explain and demonstrate them. However, the activities undertaken in the drama club will also need preparing and student-teachers will need to watch out for the pitfall of using up all their lesson material in extra-curricular sessions.

Experiencing drama out of school

Taking pupils out of school to experience drama can be a productive event for them and the teachers. When trips to the theatre or performance tours are organized well they are a huge amount of fun, a great way of getting to know and appreciate pupils better and a genuinely rich learning experience for all involved.

At some point during the period of initial teacher training it will be very useful for student-teachers in drama to go through the process of organizing a visit out of school. Most obviously this will be to the theatre. The purpose of such a trip may be simply to see a play that the pupils will enjoy and be able to discuss afterwards or review more formally as a part of their examination work. Some theatres offer special day-long events or courses which might be of particular benefit to certain teaching groups.

Organizing any activity outside school demands attention to a number of legal and professional conditions that relate to principles of equal opportunities and the protection of children. For example, parents can only be *required* to pay for activities happening outside school hours when the activities are not a necessary part of the National Curriculum. No charge can be imposed on activities that are an essential part of an examination syllabus. Schools can, and of course do, invite parents to make voluntary contributions in order to stop school funds being drained too rapidly by providing these experiences, but pupils cannot be excluded from events if they are in fact regarded as an essential part of the curriculum any more than they can be denied use of books and equipment integral to fulfilling syllabus demands.[13]

Such rulings have notable implications for planning and teaching in drama. For example, it is not justifiable to 'demand' that candidates attend the performance of a particular production for the sake of writing a review if some of them have an opportunity to see a different production that would serve the same purpose. Even when the financial constraints have been dealt with there will always be other circumstances to accommodate. Some of these may concern the nature of the play being reviewed or a clash of time commitments for some pupils. In order to avoid putting undue pressure on pupils (and their parents) and risking embarrassment or confrontation drama teachers need to be absolutely clear about the difference between what is necessary and what is desirable and be prepared to convey their judgement honestly.

Having established that, for whatever reason, a trip is worth organizing, there are a number of practical considerations and student-teachers should certainly discuss with their mentors the following checklist:

- *Ensure that pupils and parents are aware of the visit, its purpose and what it will involve*. Details of time of departure and return, cost, location, contact names and telephone numbers and the member of staff responsible for the trip must be made clear. This is best done through a letter where what is committed to print is unequivocal and unambiguous.
- *Cover the financing of the trip*. It is illegal for the school to make any profit on such trips, though it is acceptable to cover the out-of-pocket expenses incurred by staff accompanying the pupils. In the case of theatre trips, the overall cost that pupils are asked

to contribute to may therefore include the theatre ticket, a proportion of the cost of hiring a coach and a proportion of the cost of theatre tickets for the staff. Schools may ask parents to make a voluntary contribution to costs but if it is deemed essential that pupils have the experience the school is obliged to pay for them in full if parents are unable or unwilling to contribute.

- *Negotiate with the theatre or venue to be visited and organize transport.* It sounds obvious, but theatres and coach companies do need to realize that it is a school party that is making a booking. It may well be that school groups are entitled to a discount that has gone unnoticed. For coach companies, knowing the age and number of pupils will very probably affect their choice of driver.
- *Ensure that pupils wishing to join the trip have written permission from the adult(s) responsible for them.* The easiest way of doing this is to provide a tear-off-and-return slip along with the letter outlining the other details. Along with verifying that the pupil is allowed to join the trip, it is a very good idea to ask for verification that arrangements have been made to collect the pupil from school on their return to school. Teachers should not be expected to personally provide lifts home for pupils; in fact, doing so is not advisable given issues of insurance and professional integrity and liability.
- *Arrange to collect money and record this.* There is an obvious need for diligence here. The figures will have to add up. It is a good idea to tick pupils' names off the list before their eyes when they pay. Some schools may have a policy of issuing a written receipt; in others, giving a cloakroom ticket can serve the purpose (if teachers write the pupil's name on the stub as they tear it off).

Practical task

Discuss with your subject-mentor what would constitute a suitable out-of-school visit for a drama group. Investigate what the procedures are for organizing such a trip in the placement school. If possible, under the supervision of your mentor, undertake to liaise with a theatre, coach company, pupils and parents in order to facilitate such a visit. If it is impossible to actually arrange a visit, write a letter to parents/guardians as an exercise.

The school play

Drama, along with music and dance, is one of the most public of all the subjects taught in the secondary school. While the finer details of the taught curriculum in drama may not be so apparent, the regular or periodic production of plays to which members of the school and the local community are welcomed will give an insight into its values and outcomes. Many of the performances open to a wider school and community audience will be linked to examination work.

It is highly likely that student-teachers will possess knowledge and skills invaluable to any production team. For directors, simply having another adult around to help coach young actors and technicians is extremely useful. When a production is in the air some drama teachers can become, understandably, somewhat preoccupied with the project. If they seem to forget that they have

The school play

The benefits of the school play	. . . and its costs
• Pupils become involved in a positive school-based experience of their own volition.	• Productions make considerable demands on the time and energy of the staff.
• They may find a sense of belonging and identity.	• They can distract staff and pupils mostly closely involved from the more important aspects of everyday teaching and learning.
• Involvement can constitute one of the most memorable events in a school career.	
• Gives the chance for pupils and teachers to work together in new ways.	• Other staff may be aggravated by pupils being distracted from their subjects or by drama staff being allowed time away from teaching in order to manage the production.
• Teachers can gain considerable respect from pupils who appreciate the time and effort they give to the project.	
• Teachers discover new things about the pupils.	• Productions can be financially draining. Performance rights must be paid. There may be a need to hire costumes and technical equipment or pay overtime to caretaking staff.
• Involvement in a production can contribute to the drama teacher's assessment of a pupil's progress.	
• The production can raise the profile of drama within the school. Involving other staff can help them appreciate what drama does for the pupils.	• Pupils may experience transport problems, meaning some are unable to take part or parents are pressurized into making special arrangements.
• The play can serve as a bridge between the school and the local community.	
• Productions enrich the cultural and spiritual life of the school.	
• They can make a good deal of money that may in turn be fed back into drama resources.	
• The production may be used to contribute to the drama curriculum. Its subject may be explored in drama lessons or classes can learn from demonstrations of the design and technical features.	

specialist student-teachers who might like to be involved then it is really up to the student-teachers to use their own initiative and see how they can contribute without getting in the way and adding to the tension.

Most drama teachers will welcome an extra hand with the thousands of jobs that need tackling in a production or helping to monitor and organize excitable drama clubs. They will be especially appreciative of the student-teacher who can spot what needs to be done and volunteers to do it. They will be less appreciative of student-teachers who:

• meddle or contradict what they have said to the cast or club members;
• hang around like a bad smell doing nothing apart from getting in the way;
• look bored and distract the pupils with idle chatter;
• 'tut' a lot and proclaim that they 'wouldn't do it like that'.

While on school placements, some students' involvement in extra-curricular events may be hampered by transport arrangements or personal commitments. Mentors should respect these but the onus is on student-teachers to ensure that they understand the situation. Student-teachers who show no interest in finding out about the extra-curricular programme or observing a few rehearsals regardless of their personal situations may find themselves being received in an increasingly cool manner in the drama department.

Some of the advantages and challenges of producing plays in schools are tabulated on p. 165 in order to illustrate both why so many drama teachers are keen to work on them and why they can become wrapped up in the project.

Productions in school can take many forms. A public performance may be, for example:

- a full-blown performance of a scripted play or piece of music theatre;
- a devised piece;
- a montage of scripted and devised scenes around a given theme.

The production may involve:

- everybody across the school who wishes to take part;
- a particular class;
- examination candidates;
- a particular age-group;
- the members of a drama club;
- 'invited' pupils;
- other teaching staff;
- members of the community.

Before opening any kind of presentation to a public audience, including parents and friends, a number of questions need to be satisfied:

- *Is the performance space licensed appropriately?* Most school halls are licensed for certain types of public events. The licence will have details of what is allowed in terms of activities. In secondary schools the licence will normally be looked after by the bursar or school secretary.
- *What is the audience capacity?* Cramming extra seats in to either collect more money or satisfy demand is both dangerous and can limit the enjoyment of the audience because of the discomfort. The capacity of a licensed space will be specified on the licence.
- *What are the fire and safety regulations?* In addition to ensuring that exits are clearly marked and open, it may be necessary to alert the audience to the use of stroboscopes, loud noises, smoke machines, and so on. All electrical equipment must be carefully checked, cables secured in line with regulations and lanterns held with safety chains. Secondary schools should have a member of staff nominated as the fire and safety officer and the school governors will have a sub-committee responsible for the premises who can inform and assist when there are questions concerning responsibilities and liabilities.

- *Do performance rights have to be paid on any of the material?* Heavy fines can be (and have been) imposed for failing to check and pay rights. Agents may forbid the performance of plays and musicals if there is a professional production running concurrently, so it is always prudent to enquire about the cost and availability of performance rights *before* starting rehearsals.
- *How much budget is available?* Some schools have a special 'production account' where the profits made on one show can be held to finance setting up the next one and, if necessary, offset any loss.
- *Are there opportunities for an appropriate gender balance?* This is a crucial question. Insisting that the cast of every single play produced in a co-educational school has a gender balance might well be difficult to justify on educational and ideological grounds. Ensuring that the programme of productions overall offers equal opportunities is an entirely different matter.
- *What other staff might usefully be involved?* Some drama teachers do find it very hard to delegate. The fact is that in any staffroom there will be a wealth of talent and experience and a tremendous willingness on the part of some colleagues to make a contribution. Teachers other than drama specialists will enjoy working with pupils outside the taught curriculum and many will have had their own positive experiences of drama; consistently denying them the chance to be involved is to waste a resource and risk becoming isolated.
- *How aware are the headteacher and the governors of the nature and content of the piece? Do they fully approve?* Drama teachers are fully justified in refusing to build a programme of productions around the tastes and predilections of headteachers and governors, but the dangers of blatantly ignoring any concerns they may have about the content of a proposed project can be grave. It is prudent to enlist their support.
- *How much time and energy is this thing really going to take?* Abandoning a project half-way through because the reality of the workload hits home will leave pupils feeling disgruntled and demoralized.

In a flush of enthusiasm and a desire to impress pupils and colleagues, student-teachers working in drama may well be tempted to mount some kind of presentation while on their school placement. It is possible to do this and can be an invaluable and highly enjoyable experience. However, tensions and difficulties can arise when insufficient attention is paid to the quality of the production and the choice of play. Furthermore, while it is appropriate to demand commitment of the cast and production team to any such venture, placing the play above everything else can put a great deal of pressure on pupils who may become torn between the production and other work and commitments. For student-teachers themselves, there is similarly a danger that the production will completely take over their lives with the effect that it impedes their progress towards qualifying as a teacher.

The most appropriate ethos for a school production is to see it as complementing both the drama curriculum and the work of the school as a whole. The school play has been described by David Hargreaves as 'an exemplar of differentiated teamwork'.[14] Such a description implies an ensemble in which the teacher in charge is more of a 'team manager' who encourages, cares, leads by example and sometimes cajoles rather than dictating, lecturing and demoralizing those of lesser status. Similarly, pupils are encouraged to see their contribution as being a part of the whole and warned off seeing themselves as being indispensable. (Neither fellow pupils nor teaching colleagues tend to have much patience and warmth for teenage prima donnas – encouraging 'stardom' will not help the individual pupil in the long run.)

Casting a play demands diplomacy, sensitivity and the acceptance that some pupils will be disappointed. Enthusiasm and reliability may well be more important criteria than talent. Offering some sort of a part to everyone interested in being involved may seem a good solution at the time but can lead to problems later on. It's not much fun for pupils to spend most of a performance crushed in a crowd at the back of the stage, or imprisoned in an adjacent hall being told to keep their noise down!

Publicly presenting drama work, whether through the auspices of the all-singing, all-dancing, flash-bang-wallop school play, or as part of the pupils' preparations for an examination, provides an opportunity to share and give something back to the community. It also affords an opportunity to instil high personal, social and professional standards in the pupils. Although things may go wrong on the night, the whole team needs to trust that everyone has prepared as best as they are able. It is useful to set and strictly abide by some basic rules regarding punctuality, preparedness and conduct on and off stage. A measure of success for many drama teachers and pupils alike is when the audience leave talking about the play and its effect on them, whilst the remark that 'they did really well for kids', however well meant, is considered the most damning of criticisms.

Research

- Find out what sort of productions have been mounted in your placement school. Who were they open to and how were they organized?
- Discuss with your mentor what criteria were used in selecting the text or theme? How was the budget handled? To what extent was the local community involved or informed about the production?
- Ask a range of teachers and pupils about how the production was received and what was the overall effect on the school community.
- Consider for yourself what sort of contributions you could usefully make to a production in your placement school. Be honest with yourself and your mentor regarding anything that worries you about becoming involved.

Continuing professional development

Underlying all that has been discussed so far is the recognition that professionalism is as much about values and attitudes as it is about knowledge and action. Sitting hand-in-hand with the view that teachers should be committed to instilling a desire to learn in their pupils, is the standpoint that teachers should also see themselves as learners. To qualify as a teacher, student-teachers must demonstrate that they understand that successfully completing their initial training is, in effect, just the first step along a path of professional and personal development.

Strands of professional development

For drama teachers, there will always be new things to learn because drama is constantly evolving in response to new social circumstances and artistic practices and visions. New content, new form; the job of drama teachers is to stay abreast of these developments and find ways of sharing them with pupils so that they might learn to create, interpret, use and develop drama for themselves.

In parallel to developments in drama and theatre practice, the educational climate is also in a constant state of flux. Teachers need to be ready and able to respond to these changes in the educational context by interpreting them with critical eyes and weighing them against existing beliefs and practice. In turn, this involves drama teachers constantly re-evaluating and adjusting their praxis in order to achieve a balance between new knowledge, new methods and new demands that will satisfy their own conception of professional integrity.

'Professionalism' in the context of drama teaching may be seen as two intertwining strands: developments in the art form and developments in education. Educational change comes about when teachers reflect on and respond to both aspects of their work. This is the core of the drama teacher's praxis.

In pursuit of professional development

In the analysis of professional development given above, three factors were identified. For the newly qualified teacher, what might covering these factors actually involve?

- The subject of drama. Keeping up to date with developments in the field of drama will probably be far from an onerous task for drama specialists. Visiting the theatre, watching drama on film and television, reading new plays, reading reviews and finding out about the works of theatre companies, playwrights, directors, performers and designers is not generally a question of motivation for drama teachers. However, beyond the constraints of time, money and, realistically, energy, drama teachers' interests in all of these pursuits will transcend the level of passing interest or hobby. Using new experiences to nurture classroom practice inevitably means appraising their usefulness to educational contexts. Some theatres and various other agencies offer workshops for teachers to help them see the potential of particular plays and productions along with approaches to the study of drama in general. These may be just as valuable to experienced teachers who are in search of new perspectives and stimulation as they are to newly qualified teachers trying to find footholds in teaching drama. Some drama teachers move on to take a higher degree in drama, theatre studies or related fields on either a part-time or full-time basis as much for their personal development as their professional interest (not that the two can be or should be completely separated).

- *The educational context.* At one level, professionalism involves knowing about and accommodating new initiatives, opportunities and requirements. For drama teachers, this will involve understanding amendments and changes to national, local and examination specifications and guidelines in the subject. Updating and upgrading this kind of knowledge can be partially achieved by attending courses and conferences offered by the LEA, professional associations and examination boards. Newly qualified teachers often find moderation meetings organized as part of the examination procedure an especially useful forum for meeting colleagues from other schools and learning from their experience.

  Another form of development involves nurturing a broader interest in education. There is a huge amount of valuable research into things that are very relevant to drama teachers. Pastoral care and the role of the tutor, the sociology and psychology of education, curriculum management and development, mentoring and professional development are a few of these areas. While drama teachers may not become expert in any one specific area of education theory, maintaining an active interest in reading and education debates has an impact on both the drama curriculum and classroom practice.

- *Praxis.* Effective teaching results from carefully planned and executed decisions. Good teachers know what they want to do and how they are going to do it. In the context of drama, however, teachers also need to be able to encourage creativity. In terms of professional development, student-teachers and newly qualified teachers should be under no illusions; this kind of highly evolved and effective practice does not come about by accident or as a reward for a number of years' service. Rather it is acquired through professional development – through reading, attending courses, talking with colleagues and pursuing further qualifications.

NOTES

1 The Scottish Office (1998) *Guidelines for Initial Teacher Education Courses* (Edinburgh: SOED), p. 13.

2 Ibid., pp.13–14.

3 See M. Arnot (2000) 'Equal Opportunities and Educational Performance: Gender, Race and Class' in J. Beck and M. Earl (eds) *Key Issues in Secondary Education* (London: Continuum), pp. 77–85.

4 For an account of the politics of pluralism, see J. Tully (1995) *Strange Multiplicity: Constitutionalism in an Age of Diversity* (Cambridge: Cambridge University Press).

5 For an account of the relationship between feminist theory and drama education, see H. Nicholson (1995) 'Performative Acts: Drama, Education and Gender', *NADIE Journal*, vol. 19, no. 1, pp. 27–38.

6 For a discussion of how this impacts on a single-sex school, see L. Warner and A. Parr (2000) 'Cross Gender Drama', *Drama,* vol. 7 no. 2, pp. 35–40.

7 See as a part of their compliance to the *Standards for the Award of Qualified Teacher Status.*

8 The Scottish Office (1998) *Guidelines for Initial Teacher Education Courses* (Edinburgh: SOED), p. 13.

9 *School Teachers' Pay and Conditions Document 1997* – see *The Law of Education, 9th Edition* (2000) (London: Butterworth).

10 DfEE (1997) *School Governors: A Guide to the Law* (London: DfEE), p. 34.

11 *Health and Safety at Work Act 1974* – see *The Law of Education, 9th Edition.*

12 J. Arden (1960) 'A Thoroughly Romantic View', *London Magazine,* vol. 7, no. 7, (July), p. 14.

13 DfEE, *School Governors,* p. 94.

14 D. Hargreaves (1982) *The Challenge of the Comprehensive School* (London: Routledge and Kegan Paul), p. 152.

Working in Partnership: Mentors and Student-teachers

Models of partnership

One of the biggest changes that has happened in initial teacher training in the last ten years is the enhanced responsibility given to experienced teachers in the training process. Student-teachers who choose to follow a training programme at a university will find that there are close links between teachers in schools and university lecturers, usually referred to as a 'partnership'. Partnership schools are invited to be involved in all levels of decision-making about the course structure and outline, and this is a positive way of ensuring that the initial teacher training year is a coherent experience for student-teachers.

Within a partnership arrangement, there are plenty of opportunities for professional dialogue between experienced teachers (usually referred to as mentors) and subject-lecturers about the process of initial teacher training. The work undertaken by student-teachers in the university and in school is intended to be complementary, with a clearly structured programme for student-teachers' learning and progression.

It has become widely accepted that school-based training, particularly when it is combined with a university course, has many positive benefits. Student-teachers need access to different forms of professional knowledge. It would be misleading, however, to suggest that there is a sharp division between theory and practice, with university lecturers primarily concerned with theoretical issues and mentors concerning themselves solely with practical matters. On the contrary, many university lecturers continue to develop their own skills as classroom practitioners, and most drama teachers engage in theoretical readings which inform their teaching. Nonetheless, in terms of the division of labour on initial teacher training courses, it is probably fair to say that because mentors work with individual student-teachers on a day-to-day basis, their role is primarily concerned with enabling student-teachers to develop their practical classroom knowledge. However, as Donald McIntyre and Hazel Hagger have argued, learning to become competent in the classroom is also dependent on theoretically based knowledge and this dual focus is most successfully achieved when different aspects of professional knowledge are used to inform and interrogate each other.[1]

Because drama is a subject rooted in practical work, there are particularly complex relationships between practical classroom knowledge and subject-knowledge. Student-teachers entering partnership schools can expect their mentors to be familiar with how they will learn to facilitate practical drama and where in the course they will be taught to integrate theoretical understandings with practical classroom knowledge. Many schools have a long history of working in partnership with initial teacher training programmes. They will not only know the structure of the drama course very well, but will also have developed a culture and an ethos in which working with student-teachers is integral to the whole-school staff development programme. Across the UK, however, different models of partnership have evolved in which the roles and responsibilities of mentors and subject-lecturers (or, on some school-based training programmes, LEA advisors) have been variously defined.

On some ITT programmes mentors and subject-lecturers are regarded as equal partners in the training process, albeit with different roles, whilst on other courses subject-lecturers are regarded as the specialists in ITT issues and practices. These two models lead to slightly different practices.

Collaborative partnerships follow the former ethos and involve subject-lecturers and mentors working together in the design of the whole course, including university- and school-based elements of the programme. Mentors and lecturers will expect each other to work within an agreed framework for student-teachers' progression. In this model, mentors' experience *as* mentors is integral to the whole course. Experienced mentors will be involved in training new drama mentors and, whilst the subject-lecturer may be charged with monitoring the quality of mentoring across the partnership, they will only actively participate in the school-based training programmes where student-teachers are experiencing difficulties or where mentors need additional support. Reciprocally, whilst mentors may be welcome in university training programmes, they are not usually expected to participate in the subject-lecturer's teaching.

In *complementary partnerships*, subject-lecturers are regarded as specialists in ITT in drama; they may consult mentors about different elements of the training programme but will continue to be directly involved in the school-based training of all individual student-teachers. Mentors thus have an important supportive role in the process, but the major responsibility for student-teachers' progress lies with the university drama lecturer.

Both models can be highly successful, provided that the roles and respon-sibilities of those involved in the partnership are clearly defined and communicated to student-teachers.[2]

In this chapter we shall focus on the key relationship between mentors and student-teachers, and discuss the role of the mentor in student-teachers' professional development. Before we look at the practical implications of how mentors and student-teachers might work together, it is important to consider different approaches to mentoring in order to reach a principled understanding and a clear rationale for the mentor's role.

Discussion activity: models of partnership

Consider the implications of these roles and responsibilities for student-teachers.

The drama lecturer's responsibilities include:

- Devising the training programme with subject-mentors; discussing with subject-mentors targets and progression expected for student-teachers.
- Teaching the drama courses in the training institution.
- Research related to drama education; providing a link between research and national developments in drama and drama taught in partnership schools.
- Facilitating liaison between other university staff and mentors in different schools, and disseminating good practice across the partnership.
- Appraisal and assessment; offering mentors support in their assessment of student-teachers' practical competence; assessing student-teachers' written assignments.
- Offering advice and support to student-teachers experiencing difficulties; assisting mentors in organizing conferences and training opportunities to discuss approaches to mentoring.
- Overview and management of course content, structure and policies.
- Selection and admission of student-teachers.

The drama mentor's responsibilities include:

- Devising the training programme with other subject-mentors and subject-lecturers; discussing targets and progression expected for student-teachers.
- Providing models of good practice and access to a range of teaching styles.
- Responsibility for student-teachers' learning; identifying strengths and needs on entry to the school; observing lessons regularly; meeting student-teachers at regular weekly meetings to provide critical feedback; monitoring and reviewing student-teachers' progress and setting targets.
- Developing student-teachers' craft knowledge of teaching; using model of structured progression agreed with subject-lecturer and other mentors; devising a developmental programme for student-teachers on placements.
- Providing advice and support; providing professional and pastoral support for the student-teacher; offering advice to other members of staff working with student-teacher.
- Evaluation and assessment; keeping appropriate records of the student-teacher's performance, progress and progression; writing reports at agreed intervals; working with internal and external examiners where appropriate.
- Liaison with professional tutor about student-teacher's progress; liaison with subject-lecturer about course content and mentor development programmes; liaison with other drama mentors to ensure consistent experience for student-teachers.
- Selection and admission of student-teachers when requested.

The role of the mentor

In most partnership schemes, the mentor's role is to take responsibility for all aspects of student-teachers' learning throughout their professional placements. Although there is usually a particular focus on helping them to develop practical classroom skills and knowledge, this process cannot be divorced from intellectual and theoretical issues in drama education. Many mentors find that one of the rewards of the job is the opportunity to discuss different theoretical perspectives with student-teachers in the context of classroom practice. As such, mentors are uniquely placed to encourage student-teachers to explore a range of alternative ways of working in drama and to help them to interpret what they observe. As we pointed out in Chapter 2, student-teachers are not empty vessels, but bring with them a range of skills and experiences, values and attitudes which will be explored, questioned, challenged and tested as the year progresses. This can be an unsettling process for some student-teachers. Mentors have a key role in supporting student-teachers by giving them practical advice, reassurance and new challenges. They will recognize that it is far more difficult to try out new creative ideas with a class, and take some risks, than it is to follow tried-and-tested activities but that trying out new ideas is an essential element in student-teachers' development.

In acknowledging that student-teachers need to be both challenged and supported, McIntyre and Hagger suggest that there are four interrelated strategies which define the role of the mentor.[3]

- *Managing student-teachers' learning opportunities*. Mentors have a clear responsibility to encourage student-teachers to use the resources available in a particular school. As well as ensuring that there is a structured programme for progression, they provide information about the drama curriculum and organization for student-teachers. They may also work collaboratively with colleagues in the drama department and cognate disciplines to ensure that student-teachers have a range of experiences on their placements.
- *Collaborative teaching*. This is where mentors and student-teachers plan and teach lessons together. It is a process in which student-teachers begin by observing, then move to small-group work and teaching part of the mentor's lesson. As the year proceeds, the roles will be reversed and student-teachers will take the lead in planning and teaching lessons.
- *Access to mentor's knowledge of the craft of teaching*. This involves student-teachers and mentors in reflective conversation, where student-teachers and mentors are able to engage in focused discussion of lessons they have taught and observed.
- *Discussing student-teachers' ideas*. As student-teachers progress, their ideas will be challenged, and they should be inspired to try out new ideas they have learnt through observation, reading, seminars and workshops. Mentors can help by supporting student-teachers in their experimentation and by anticipating the practical implications of their ideas in the drama classroom or studio.

Within each of these four strategies, all of which are useful during the training process, there are particular roles which mentors undertake. In the next section, we will discuss different models of mentoring, before returning to consider how these four strategies affect student-teachers when they are learning to teach drama.

Discussion task: the roles of the mentor

In most partnership schemes, the mentor will undertake the following roles:

- modelling or demonstrating different approaches to teaching and a variety of teaching styles;
- organizing weekly mentor meetings and devising a developmental programme for student-teacher's progression;
- acting as a role-model for student-teachers;
- engaging in theoretical debate;
- observing lessons on a regular basis and providing constructive written feedback;
- negotiating and setting appropriate targets and giving precise strategies for meeting them;
- offering pastoral and professional support for student-teachers;
- planning lessons and team teaching with student-teachers;
- providing drama syllabuses, schemes of work and assessment policies;
- assisting in interpretation of drama documentation;
- assisting student-teachers to integrate whole-school policies into their teaching;
- providing a balanced timetable which offers student-teachers a range of teaching opportunities;
- reading and discussing the student-teacher's teaching file at regular intervals;
- encouraging student-teachers to reflect on their own lessons and on those they observe;
- negotiating and discussing student-teachers' progress towards qualified teacher status, including written reports on them;
- writing reports at specified intervals on student-teachers.

Models of mentoring

Implicit in the four strategies McIntyre and Hagger identified lies a model of mentoring which values the knowledge, skills and expertise of both student-teachers and mentors. The collaboration between mentors and student-teachers is often very productive, and mentors frequently find that their own practice is enhanced by working closely with people who are learning to teach drama. However, not only are mentors called upon to perform different roles, there are also different models of mentoring upon which to draw. Trisha Maynard and John Furlong have distinguished three models of mentoring, all of which may have a part to play in student-teachers' development: the apprenticeship model; the competency model and the reflective practitioner model.[4]

In the *apprenticeship* model, student-teachers work alongside more experienced teachers and learn particular skills from them. When the apprenticeship model was first devised, its advocates expected that student-teachers would be encouraged to emulate more experienced teachers, but this was found to be an intellectually impoverished way of working because student-teachers were only trained to reproduce the practice they observed, however good or bad that was. Such an apprenticeship would do little to encourage drama student-teachers to become creative, thoughtful and independent practitioners and educators. However, the model has now been adapted and can enable mentors to assist student-teachers by working collaboratively alongside them in the classroom. This form of apprenticeship is further supported when mentors help student-teachers interpret the learning pupils have achieved in lessons in which they have both participated.

The *competency* model is currently much in favour with government agencies, where there are prescribed areas of competence which student-teachers are required to meet in order to achieve qualified teacher status. In this model, mentors adopt a systematic approach to the training process, offering targets for development which lead towards clearly defined learning outcomes and identifiable levels of competence for student-teachers. One of the disadvantages of this model, for drama in particular, is that it can discourage student-teachers from taking creative risks; once they have reached a level of competence, they may be reluctant to experiment with alternative ways of working. Furthermore, it can mitigate against discussion of teaching and learning if evidence for competence is given by ticking boxes. Some student-teachers, particularly if they are very insecure, may find that a competency model in which they are told what to do makes them feel safe. Although this may offer some temporary reassurance, arguably this approach does little to address their feelings of inadequacy and encourage independence in the long term.

In the *reflective practitioner* model, mentors encourage student-teachers to reflect on their teaching, focusing particularly on the relationship between their own teaching and the pupils' learning. This leads student-teachers to examine their own practice critically, and to consider how pupils learn and the effectiveness of different ways of working in drama. This process invites student-teachers to confront their own values and beliefs, and share ideas openly with mentors. It is often suggested that this model is the most difficult to define and, whilst it is widely supported in drama education, it has sometimes been argued that it is difficult to be precise about what mentoring activities best promote this way of thinking. In relation to teaching drama, Donald Schon's model of 'reflection-in-action' may be particularly apposite. Schon suggested that reflective teachers use modes of enquiry based on improvisation, in which they draw on what he calls an 'intuitive' knowledge base. For student-teachers, however, this model has its limitations; the kind of 'professional' intuition Schon identifies is based on knowledge and experience which student-teachers have often yet to acquire.[5]

In defining these models of mentoring, all of which student-teachers are likely to encounter during their training year, Furlong and Maynard suggest that they work best in sequence.[6] They argue that an apprenticeship model should precede a competency model and that reflective practice is only really appropriate when a level of competence has already been achieved. In theory, this sounds reasonable, and many student-teachers and mentors find it useful to focus on one model at particular times in the training process. In practice, though, there are problems with trying to adhere rigidly to this pattern. Student-teachers learn at different rates, and learning to teach drama, with all its complexities and diverse practices, is not a linear process. Many student-teachers will be able to reflect thoughtfully on some aspects of their practice early in the training process, particularly when they are working collaboratively with their mentors. Furthermore, whilst student-teachers obviously need to be able to lead drama lessons by the end of the training process, to suggest that collaborative teaching is an easier model for less experienced teachers underestimates the very real challenges and varied opportunities presented by team teaching. To continue to work collaboratively for some classes, or to undertake a period of observation later in the year, need not be a retrograde step. In fact, it often deepens the student-teachers' understanding of how pupils learn in drama. In practice, therefore, different models of mentoring may be used concurrently for different purposes and in ways that encourage student-teachers to progress at times when they are most ready to learn.

Planning and structuring progression

One of the challenges facing mentors is how to achieve a balance between the individual needs of the student-teacher and the prescribed levels of professional competence required for qualified teacher status. In practice, many partnership schemes have addressed this issue by providing a clear, structured progression for student-teachers. Such frameworks use the competency model of mentoring in such a way that it gives student-teachers a clear idea about how they should progress, but they should also allow for a degree of flexibility which enables student-teachers to consolidate their learning at different rates during the training period. A structure for progression is important even when student-teachers already have considerable classroom experience; they need time to look at approaches to *learning* in drama by gradually building up their classroom experience in this way.

A model of structured progression

In this model, student-teachers on a PGCE course attend their placement schools two days a week. The student-teachers' timetable remains the same throughout the term, although the activities undertaken follow the agreed model of structured progression. Consider what further examples of drama activities might be included in such a programme.

Stage	Progression	Exemplar Activities
1 (weeks 1–4)	*Observation*: student-teachers start by working with individuals and small groups, learning names, procedures and practical work.	Observe Year 7 story-telling project, noting different opportunities for speaking and listening. Help Year 12 with devised work.
2 (weeks 5 and 6)	*Small-group work and micro-teaching*: with the guidance, team teaching but with responsibility for planning and teaching small-group work or part of lessons.	Take role in Year 8 evacuees' project. Video part of Year 10 lesson for assessment.
3 (weeks 7 and 8)	*Development*: take greater responsibility for planning and evaluating some specified lessons each week.	Lead Year 8 lesson – drama teacher's role is killed off!
4 (weeks 11–13)	*Whole-class, whole-lesson teaching*: lessons planned jointly with the drama teacher; student-teacher takes full responsibility for delivery. Teacher provides written feedback.	Movement session for Year 10 on devising.

Readiness to learn

However useful a model of structured progression may be in outlining appropriate progress towards prescribed levels of competency, the process of learning to teach drama cannot always be described so crudely. In drama, where teachers are actively involved in the lessons, often as creative participants in the learning process, student-teachers often find it helpful to work alongside more experienced members of staff, experimenting with new dramatic practices, even when they are reasonably competent at teaching a whole class. This means that student-teachers are not only learning to teach; they are also learning new practical skills as drama practitioners. Complex social interactions are both inherent in good drama teaching and integral to the subject; as a physical, interactive and creative art form, learning to teach drama requires more than a competent ability to manage a classroom.

Student-teachers in drama acquire confidence and competence in the classroom at different rates. They may also demonstrate different qualities in the classroom according to the context in which they are working and the challenges presented. Given this, it is helpful to consider research into how student-teachers move from novice to independent teacher. Furlong and Maynard, for example, have usefully described five stages of development which characterize student-teachers' experiences on their professional placements. These stages might be summarized as:

- 'early idealism', where drama student-teachers have high expectations and may be critical of the practice they observe;
- 'personal survival', where their biggest concern is that they have some credibility in the classroom;
- 'dealing with difficulties', where they experiment with practical solutions to problems they have identified;
- 'hitting a plateau', where a level of competence has been reached;
- 'moving on', a period in which student-teachers may be particularly receptive to thinking about learning.

Furlong and Maynard stress that these stages of progression are not 'a narrow linear pathway, moving smoothly from stage to stage'.[7] On the contrary, their research suggests that the successful development of student-teachers is dependent on their ability to actively engage in professional dialogue with fellow student-teachers, university lecturers and mentors in school.

In drama, the ability to explore and interrogate practice is integral to the subject itself. Unlike graduates from many other disciplines, student-teachers in drama are likely to have worked collaboratively as practitioners and many will have developed an ability to reflect on the success of their practical work. Indeed, in his work on reflective practitioners in drama, Philip Taylor draws attention to the similarities between reflective practice in education and the artistic process. Invoking Schon, he argues that reflection in action is a form of improvisation that is also intrinsic to working as drama practitioners.[8] This observation may have notable implications for those learning to teach drama. Whilst student-teachers may indeed follow the stages of development identified by Furlong and Maynard, they may also find that their previous experiences of reflecting on their own practice as drama practitioners and interpreting live performative events will assist them in raising questions about how their lessons have worked and help them to 'read' a classroom through observation. However, despite these skills of critical enquiry, student-teachers in drama may need particular guidance in how to reflect on their work as *teachers* of drama and move the focus of their reflection away from their own skills as performers to what and how the pupils are learning. To ensure that pupils are given ample opportunity to develop a range of skills, student-teachers may wish to frame their teaching around the interrelated practices of making, performing and responding to drama.

During the training year, student-teachers will become ready to integrate their theoretical knowledge into their classroom practice at different rates. As we have already identified, there is a school of thought which argues that student-teachers are able to reflect on what pupils have learnt only after a level of competency has been reached in the classroom. Such an approach leads mentors to concentrate first on classroom management and progress to considering the effectiveness of their teaching on learning later. Other researchers, particularly those who advocate McIntyre's model of collaborative teaching, argue that student-teachers are best supported when they are invited and prompted to reflect on the pupil's learning from the very start of the training process. Whatever approach is adopted a coherent structure that integrates theory and practice is needed. Even so, learning to teach drama can still be a frustrating process, where student-teachers almost always want to be able to integrate their thinking into their practice rather more quickly than their practical skills allow.

Recognizing progress

Acquiring a repertoire of teaching skills in drama takes time and patience, and student-teachers will undoubtedly experience set-backs where things do not go as well as they have hoped. Mentors have a crucial role to play here in helping student-teachers to recognize why their teaching seemed to go well or badly, and giving them constructive advice about how to address areas of difficulty and build on success. This may well enable student-teachers to move on from the more impoverished stages of 'personal survival' Furlong and Maynard discussed. Interestingly, whilst their five stages of development continue to be a recognizable element of student-teachers' experiences, their description is based on studies conducted in the 1980s, well before a clear model of mentoring was established in schools. Experienced mentors have developed highly complex ways of working and have a huge part to play in enabling student-teachers to move forward without loss of the idealism which first informed their decision to learn to teach drama.

Mentors and student-teachers working together

Part of the process of encouraging student-teachers to maintain their idealism, despite occasional bruising encounters with the day-to-day business of teaching drama, is to continue to encourage them to keep a clear focus on why drama is an important aspect of education, and what pupils are expected to learn in their drama lessons. It is a question of how to encourage student-teachers to balance realistic and practical approaches to teaching and learning with an emergent vision of the qualities and opportunities presented by drama education. This section focuses on the practical issues faced by student-teachers and their mentors when they work together.

Working relations

Mentoring is a complex role, not only because it requires teachers to use a wide range of skills and strategies in addition to their expertise as teachers of drama, but also because it demands specific personal qualities and skills. Mentors work very closely with their student-teachers, and ideally develop very good professional relationships and mutual respect. Sometimes, for whatever reason, mentors and student-teachers have to try hard to find ways of working together, and in drama uneasy relationships can be problematic if there are only one or two drama teachers in the school. However, as with all professional roles, knowing what knowledge and skills are required – in this case for the effective mentoring of drama student-teachers – forms the basis of a productive learning partnership. In addition to the various strategies mentors and student-teachers employ to enhance their practice, it is helpful if there is a climate of openness and a culture of communication. Achieving this is facilitated when:

- both student-teacher and mentor actively listen to each other;
- they share ideas both in the formal context of regular mentor meetings and in the more informal context of the staffroom or drama office;
- there is an active programme of staff development in the drama team;
- the drama curriculum and ways of working are continually discussed and under frequent review.

Because mentors and student-teachers have contact on a daily basis during full-time professional placements, mentors have a particular overview of individual student-teachers' development, which is an important part of both the learning and assessment processes. Furthermore, student-teachers are also integrated into the life of the school and many quickly become involved in the life of the school as a community. As such, mentors are in a position to offer student-teachers unique insights into the particular context in which they are working, providing clear information about the pupils, the aims and ethos of the drama curriculum, resources, pastoral systems, special needs provision, and so on. This way of working, which takes account of the specific context of the school, enables all concerned to focus on the content of mentoring rather than overwhelmingly on personal relations. In other words, effective mentoring which encourages student-teachers to reach and go beyond the levels of competency required for qualified teacher status combines three key elements:

- appropriate practical strategies for mentoring;
- an informed understanding of the training programme and the school context;
- a knowledge of the individual student-teacher's strengths, ideas and progression.

Visits from subject-lecturers

As part of the training process, mentors are supported in their work by visits from subject-lecturers. The nature and purpose of these visits vary enormously from course to course, and this is where the different models of partnership are shown most acutely. In all cases, however, it is probably fair to say that visits from representatives of the training institution have changed considerably in character since the role of the mentor has been consolidated. It is now relatively rare that lecturers' visits are designed to make judgements about the progress of individual student-teachers. Assessment, pastoral support and student-teachers' progress is now more usually regarded as the responsibility of the mentors. Where subject-lecturers do make such visits to individual student-teachers, the drama mentors probably have quite a small role in the training process and, as such, are not expected to have the expertise to support student-teachers' development adequately on their own.`

As McIntyre and Hagger have noted, there is something of a risk that when mentors work alone with student-teachers they may offer only one approach to teaching a subject.[9] In this context, drama lecturers can offer additional perspectives which encourage student-teachers to extend their teaching repertoires. However, recognizing this risk enables mentors to explore the issue explicitly, and mentor-training programmes can ensure that they know how to avoid this pitfall. The drama lecturer's visit may also give student-teachers and mentors opportunities to discuss target setting and progress and to explore a range of strategies which might facilitate student-teachers' learning. As the nature of visits vary, student-teachers and mentors will need to know which of the following purposes it is designed to fulfil:

- to discuss the student-teacher's progress with the mentor;
- to provide school-based training by observing individual lessons, give feedback, set targets and monitor progress;
- to discuss the mentors' school-based training;
- to compare standards of practical teaching between student-teachers;
- to monitor consistency of mentoring across a partnership;
- to disseminate good mentoring practice gathered from other partnership schools to ensure equality of practice and opportunity within the course as a whole.

Respecting roles and responsibilities

Whatever the benefits of partnership and models of mentorship, it remains the case that drama teachers have very busy professional lives. Student-teachers have to learn to be sensitive and tactful, and to offer support to their mentors as well as the other way round. The primary responsibility of mentors is to teach the pupils drama. Although their role in initial teacher training should be structured into their workloads, there can sometimes be conflicting demands on their time. Student-teachers can support mentors by anticipating their requests for resources, by storing up questions and asking them at a time when their mentors are less busy. Queries which seem burning at the time can often be resolved if student-teachers take a little time to reflect on the situation.

In the following sections, the framework of four different strategies used by mentors and offered by McIntyre and Hagger has been applied to drama education. This framework, which was outlined earlier, can be used to explore how mentors manage the training, how they work collaboratively with student-teachers and how they engage in reflective conversation and discuss ideas. The advantage of this for drama teachers is that whilst the framework identifies different strategies they are not regarded as hierarchical; it enables student-teachers to reflect the qualities of drama as a subject by integrating reflective and creative thought with practical expertise throughout the training period.

Managing student-teachers' learning opportunities

In order for student-teachers and mentors to work successfully together, the school-based training needs to be organized and managed. In many schools the professional tutor will oversee the placements of student-teachers, but subject-mentors will have the responsibility of ensuring that student-teachers in drama have enough information about the context of the particular school to make a positive contribution to the drama curriculum. Drama mentors will need to organize a programme of school-based training which coheres with student-teachers' training elsewhere. They will also need to manage student-teachers' teaching experience by, for example, providing an appropriate timetable and ensuring that all colleagues working with the student-teacher are well prepared. Understandably, student-teachers frequently feel very pressured during the training period; the knowledge that they are working with well-informed colleagues who have clear ideas about how to structure their progress helps them to be more receptive to ideas and ready to learn.

Whilst in many ways it is the mentor's responsibility to organize opportunities for student-teachers' learning, there is much that student-teachers can do to facilitate the process. In order to develop an appropriate mentoring programme, drama mentors will need information about the student-teachers' previous experiences. Student-teachers can assist this process by preparing a brief biographical portfolio which draws from the following information:

- short curriculum vitae;
- opening statement;
- subject-knowledge audits, with targets for addressing omissions and a record of progress made;
- ICT audit and log of progress;
- copies of minutes of mentor meetings and reports on their progress from previous professional placements (where relevant);
- copies of assignments already completed.

Most importantly, student-teachers will need to show mentors their teaching files. The process of preparing such material encourages student-teachers to reflect on themselves as learners, and gives mentors valuable insights, not just into what student-teachers have done, but into how they think, their values, motivations and ideals. Stanislavsky would approve!

Sharing information

Drama mentors who work with student-teachers regularly often find it useful to provide a handbook specially written for them. The contents may be culled from drama handbooks, guidelines, syllabuses and units of work provided by, for example, staff, inspectors and, indeed, former student-teachers. This gives student-teachers all the information they need about the context in which they are working. Although it is initially time consuming to produce, it does mean that student-teachers can read it independently rather than having to rely on asking their mentors a lot of questions. The chart on p. 186 lists the kind of written information which is helpful for student-teachers to know when they first embark on a school placement.

Becoming familiar with this information is the student-teachers' responsibility. However, at the beginning of the course student-teachers may find it hard to interpret, and finding the right questions to ask can be difficult for many. Mentors can anticipate this by asking student-teachers to prepare questions for discussion, particularly about how the drama curriculum is taught. Useful questions to ask early on in the training process would include:

- How do pupils progress in drama?
- How much of classroom practice is based on improvisation?
- How is ICT integrated into the drama curriculum?
- At what point do pupils work with technical equipment such as lighting and sound?
- Is the curriculum organized thematically, or is it based on drama skills, or both?

Background information for student-teachers

About the drama curriculum:	About the whole-school context:
• names, roles and responsibilities of all drama teachers	• policies for literacy learning
• the drama syllabus and summary of schemes of work for Key Stage 3	• the role of Learning Support Assistants
• copies of drama syllabuses for examination classes	• policies for language diversity and English as an additional language
• how the drama elements of the National Curriculum are interpreted in the school	• the pastoral curriculum
• departmental guidelines for planning where appropriate	• personal, social and health education
• marking, homework and assessment policies	• citizenship education
• pupil groupings and provision for children with special needs	• links with the community
• policies and practices for discipline and rewards	• the purpose of parents' evenings
• lists of available play texts, resources and specialist equipment	
• how access to ICT equipment is organized	
• health and safety policy and practices	

Whilst these questions are quite general they are effective in opening up a dialogue. As student-teachers recognize in more detail what is going on in drama in the school, their questions should become more focused on specific aspects of how the subject is taught and what is being learnt. Many mentors report that answering student-teachers' questions about their own documentation and schemes of work helps them to clarify their own aims and values. Student-teachers need the policies of the drama department to be explicit – even if they do not agree with everything. Indeed, whilst it is important that they learn to question ideas presented to them, student-teachers also appreciate clear curriculum guidelines which they can interpret creatively in their own practical work.

Not all the information that will eventually be needed by student-teachers is immediately relevant to them when they first arrive in school. Mentors may wish to consider the time-span of the professional placement and anticipate student-teachers' needs by planning to discuss these issues when they need to use the information in a practical context. It can also avoid misunderstandings between mentors and student-teachers if the school's expectations are made very clear from the outset. To fulfil both these aims, providing student-teachers with the following information has proved invaluable:

• purpose, place and nature of mentor meetings;
• the role of the mentor;
• dress code, paying for coffee, lunch, etc.;

- who to contact and how to set work in the event of absence;
- the system for accountability: planning, record keeping, marking and assessment.

Managing teaching

Organizing everything that student-teachers need in order to prepare their lessons requires quite a lot of planning. It all hinges on the timetable which, if there are several student-teachers in the school, is usually co-ordinated by a professional tutor to ensure that they do not all end up teaching the same class. In addition to this, student-teachers are entitled to expect a range of classes from different age-ranges and a really balanced timetable should also include different aspects of the drama curriculum. When mentors plan the timetable, they will need to take account of student-teachers' previous teaching experiences on the course and their targets for development. For example, a student-teacher who has already taught scenes from *Romeo and Juliet* in one school should not simply repeat the same work in her second placement, and if her target for development is to use video or sound technology in drama lessons she should be given the opportunity to do so. In full-time professional placements, or on employment-based routes into teaching, it is important that student-teachers know which classes they will teach collaboratively with another member of staff and those for which they will take full responsibility for planning and delivering the lessons.

Discussion task:

Scrutinize the example of a timetable overleaf and consider the learning opportunities offered to the student-teacher. Look, for example, at the balance of age-groups and range of drama that it proposes. In an ideal world (and it must be remembered of course that there are many factors affecting what timetable student-teachers are offered) what else might be included?

In addition to information about policies and syllabuses, student-teachers also need practical information which they should use to organize their own teaching. Such information might include:

- discipline, sanctions, rewards and 'ground rules' for drama (detention slips and merits);
- their mentor's timetable;
- a register or planner;
- set lists for the classes they will be teaching;
- records of previous work undertaken by each class they will teach;
- access to records of individual pupil progress and achievement in drama for their classes;
- key dates for student-teachers' diaries' such as parents' consultation evenings, examination moderation, drama meetings, staff meetings.

Sample timetable

Period	Monday	Tuesday	Wednesday	Thursday	Friday
1	Year 10 Devising: team teach with JAB			Year 10 Devising: team teach with JAB	
2	Year 10	Year 7 Ca Myths and legends role-play			
3				Year 7 Jo Mask and movement	PHSE with Year 9 tutor group
4	Year 7 Ne Myths and legends role-play		Year 9 T *Macbeth*: key scene		
5		Year 9 N Media project with JAB	Mentor period		Year 13 Performance analysis

Most drama teachers collaborate with colleagues in related subjects, and this means that student-teachers in drama will need to be introduced to other members of staff and find out how their work has an impact on the drama curriculum. Many drama specialists also find it useful to observe English or other arts teachers on a regular basis and become involved in their lessons. This is often extremely enlightening, although unless they have received specialist training in the subject they should not be assessed as teachers in the curriculum area. In addition it is helpful if all members of staff who work with drama student-teachers are kept informed about their progress and targets for development.

Outlining support: mentor meetings

Effective mentoring can only take place when sufficient time is allocated for it. Mentoring is a rewarding experience, but it is also time consuming, and designated weekly mentor meetings are essential. Mentors should have one period a week allocated for meeting with student-teachers. In this protected time they undertake a structured programme designed to focus on the individual student-teacher's development. Student-teachers and mentors should prepare for these meetings carefully. Meetings are most productive when they address particular issues affecting student-teachers' development rather than chatting in general terms or giving feedback on individual lessons. It is at these regular mentor meetings that student-teachers should have an opportunity to review their own progress, discuss strategies

188

for development and negotiate new short-term targets. In these meetings, many mentors combine competency and reflective practice models of mentoring, where they both keep an eye on the standards needed to reach qualified teacher status, and encourage student-teachers to reflect in depth on their learning. This can be a very productive combination. In practice, mentor meetings can be most productive where there is an ongoing agenda which both addresses the individual student-teacher's targets and development, and introduces new approaches and additional ways of working. While there is always a need for some flexibility in order to deal with burning issues, compiling an outline of what the meeting will primarily focus on will help ensure that everything is covered and that both parties can organize their preparation. Such an outline establishes a structure for progression which both the mentor and student-teacher can follow.

Sample agenda for mentor meetings: second professional placement (6 weeks, full time)

Week One
Focus: Subject-knowledge
Review subject-knowledge and ICT audits; discuss school's drama syllabus.
Student-teacher's progression
Review progress on first placement; first report; targets for current placement

Week Two
Focus: Planning issues
Student-teacher to bring in short- and medium-term plans for Year 7 and Year 10 classes. Discuss range of opportunities presented by plans for pupils' learning.

Week Three: Class management
Discuss video of student-teacher teaching Year 8 lesson. Look for: use of verbal and body language; how tasks were set; how transitions managed.

Week Four: Differentiation and special needs
Look at this issue with learning support assistant present. Discuss how issues of SEN need to be integrated into both planning and classroom management. Consider what is meant by ability in drama. Student-teacher to bring something they have read on this area to meeting for critical review.

Week Five: Assessment and moderation of examination work
Watch video of Year 11 devised work and discuss possible marks/grades in light of published criteria. Review Year 11 working notebooks and consider how they support practical work.

Week Six: Preparing for Year 9 parents' evening
Discuss what evidence is needed to report on pupils' progress. Also, how to prepare what to say; what questions to expect; what to say about drama in Year 10. Discuss individual pupils and their reports.

Target setting

Managing opportunities for student-teachers' learning means that mentors are involved in both planning a structured progression in the practical knowledge that teachers of drama require and diagnosing their particular strengths and areas of difficulty. Each element of practical teaching discussed in mentor meetings may result in negotiating new targets. Progress towards addressing these can then be monitored the following week. Brief records of mentor meetings should be made and kept by student-teachers; they provide interesting insights into their progress, and aid continuity and progression from week to week and across the whole training period. Such records should be written for personal use. Student-teachers may wish to share them with mentors and tutors as evidence of their reflective practice, but their main function is to help the student-teacher consolidate their own learning and establish what they think they need to do next.

Sample of student-teacher's record of mentor meeting: week six

Week's training focus: recording and reporting (Year 9 parents' evening)
- Asked about how Year 9 drama leads to Year 10
- Reviewed how knowledge, skills and understanding in Year 9 units of work related to my teaching
- Considered what I would say to questions like: Why should my son do drama GCSE? What has my daughter learnt in drama this year? Will you be doing a school play? Is he doing his homework?
- Looked at evidence on individual pupils from reports, self-assessment sheet

Weekly review of targets
- Have now marked GCSE coursework and related this to published criteria. Jo double marked a sample and agreed my grades
- Observed moderation of Year 11 practical work
- Asked Rob to observe how I give explanations in Year 8 lesson. Am still not quite there with this. He suggested I script what I want to say as I waste time rambling

New targets
- Be more economical in my explanations
- Effective liaison with parents
- Consider pupils' progression in drama

Strategies to meet targets and training activities
- Script my explanations, prepare wall-display of key drama terms, observe how Jo and Rob explain things in Year 10 and Year 8 lessons
- Prepare and conduct Year 9 parents' evening
- Read drama reports and records of three or four pupils from different years.

Collaboration and teaching

One of the biggest issues which concerns both student-teachers and mentors is how to ensure that the pupils are receiving a high standard of drama education while student-teachers are learning their craft. It is a legitimate concern. Student-teachers spend the majority of their initial training period on professional placements. Drama teachers who work with training institutions on an annual basis can expect student-teachers in the drama classroom for much of the year, every year. In order to maintain a firm grip on the curriculum and their pupils' progress, many drama mentors expect student-teachers to teach collaboratively with them or other experienced teachers of drama. This way of working integrates a structure of progression into a model which suits teaching and learning in drama. Student-teachers are encouraged to take an active part in drama lessons and undertake specific tasks when they are observing, working with small groups or team teaching. This has benefits for the pupils, who can draw on the expertise of two adults in the classroom. It also provides student-teachers with an opportunity to target particular aspects of their own drama teaching with the immediate support of an experienced teacher and without having to cope with the kind of discipline problems which inexperienced student-teachers can face, particularly when they are working in an empty space.

In collaborative teaching, the experienced teacher focuses on the pupils' learning and takes account of the student-teachers' needs and progress. As both adults are actively involved in the lesson, they have a shared experience to discuss. Mentors can give student-teachers a very clear lens through which they can interpret lessons. In many ways, the model of collaboration is particularly appropriate to drama teaching as it can be a highly creative way of working, in which pupils are given a lively dramatic experience.

There are important considerations to be taken into account in collaborative teaching though. Planning can certainly take up a lot of time. Once in the classroom, there is a need for mentors and student-teacher to check frequently with each other how they are interpreting what is going on and what needs to happen next. There can be a danger, without adequate planning or on-the-spot consultation, of one teacher compromising the other by making a unilateral decision. Neither the student-teacher nor mentor will appreciate their teaching partner suddenly announcing to the class that 'Ms Fletcher is going to take over now . . .' if Ms Fletcher is not ready to take over.

Gaining independence

As student-teachers become more experienced, their mentors will wish to take an increasingly low profile in the lessons. Student-teachers do need to become independent teachers of drama by the end of the training period, although they may find that there are different views about when they are ready to be left alone with a class. Some argue that there are distinct benefits of having two adults in the classroom throughout much of the training process, albeit that the experienced teacher's role changes as student-teachers become increasingly competent. Others argue that student-teachers need to spend time without overt supervision in order to establish independent relationships with the class and learning support assistants. In practice, mentors usually negotiate with student-teachers and find a way of working which is appropriate to the context. Whatever is agreed, many mentors and student-teachers are encouraged to work collaboratively right to the end of the training process. Active and focused observation of pupils' learning, as opposed to observations which comment primarily on the student-teachers' teaching, is part of the process. In this form of observation the mentor's presence in the classroom is often fairly unobtrusive, not least because the pupils know they are primarily interested in their progress rather than the student-teacher's. Such observations provide fascinating insights for the class teachers, who are able to look at the pupils in new ways, and for the student-teachers themselves, who may know little about the individual profiles of the pupils.

Strategies for collaboration

The following ideas can all provide a good basis for discussion about different teaching strategies as well as highlighting what pupils are learning and how they are learning it:

- mentor teaches student-teacher's lesson plan, which he or she observes, and vice versa;
- mentor observes an individual pupil in the class and takes detailed notes on his or her progress and activity;
- mentor assesses small groups in relation to criteria specified in advance by the student-teacher;
- mentor videos pupils' devising process for later analysis;
- mentor and student-teacher work together to demonstrate a particular skill to the class;
- mentor and student-teacher take opposite sides in a debate about a play;
- mentor takes small role in drama, or vice versa.

Reflecting on the craft of teaching

Access to the mentor's knowledge of the craft of teaching is gained not only from within the practical context of the lessons themselves, but from the discussions and conversations between mentors and student-teachers. As part of creating a climate of openness and exchange, student-teachers often welcome the invitation to ask mentors about how their own ideas about drama teaching are reflected in the drama curriculum they have shaped and work with. When student-teachers are in the stages of early idealism at the beginning of the course, they may have lively views about how drama should be taught, but little experience of how to locate these ideas in the practical context they see. By sharing their own craft knowledge, mentors enable student-teachers to make connections between classroom practice and theoretical principles. In this section we will look at ways of encouraging such reflective conversations and how mentors might share their knowledge of the craft of teaching drama.

Observation and feedback

During the training process, student-teachers can expect their mentors and other colleagues to observe their teaching and give them regular feedback. This form of observation differs from that described earlier in this chapter which is focused on the pupils' learning in collaboratively taught lessons. Student-teachers are also entitled to receive written feedback on their own teaching which, as formative assessments, are explicitly focused on their own developing competence and skills. Such monitoring is now a part of school culture where the most experienced teachers are regularly observed as part of the procedure of appraisal and professional development.

During the training process, student-teachers should receive written feedback on different aspects of their teaching. Although classroom management issues are often the most obvious aspects of the lesson, and these are certainly skills student-teachers need to develop, to focus solely, or even primarily, on this is to neglect how the student-teachers' subject-knowledge, planning, assessment and other areas of professional competence are influencing their teaching.

In broad terms, there are two types of lesson observation: a general commentary on the lesson or specific comments on one or two aspects of teaching in depth. The first approach risks over-emphasis on the more obvious features of the lesson, but it can also enable experienced teachers to pick out a range of issues as they arise. The second method can be a little restrictive, but it also provides explicit feedback which can be related to the student-teachers' targets for progression. Both are useful, which is why it is important for whoever is observing the lesson to discuss with the student-teacher what their plan is, consult their teaching files and negotiate an appropriate focus for the observation.

Some student-teachers value having different teachers observe and give feedback in a variety of ways, whilst others prefer to ask all those observing the lessons to comment on particular aspects of classroom practice to help them reach targets set in mentor meetings. Either way, regular feedback on individual lessons should enable student-teachers to enter into dialogue with more than one teacher. In many schools some drama is taught by English teachers and, although the specialist knowledge of drama mentors is obviously invaluable, there is much to be gained from alternative perspectives. Feedback on individual lessons works best when it closely follows the lesson and when student-teachers are invited, by careful questioning, to deconstruct the lesson which has been observed. By shaping appropriate questions, experienced teachers can encourage student-teachers to reflect on their practice and recognize the implications of the decisions they made in their planning and in the lesson itself. Comment and discussion on individual lessons is obviously useful, but however expert this questioning is, unless it is part of an ongoing reflective dialogue which is clearly related to the student-teachers' progression and targets, it is unlikely to enable them to move forward very far.

Lesson observations

What kind of issues do you think might arise from this written record of a lesson observation? If you were the student-teacher who had been observed, what would you want clarified or discussed?

Year 7 drama: Macbeth *scheme*
Focus of observation: classroom management; subject-knowledge.

Classroom management
Excellent start. Ground rules clearly set out and excellent use of visual signs to gain attention instead of shouting. Efficient group management. Time limit for tasks set.

Excellent pace. Telling the story brought focus and attention after a hectic warm-up. Very mobile around class during written task. Able to challenge support here. Perhaps you can make use of the whiteboard to set out instructions – they can refer back to this during the lesson. How would this have helped?

Not all groups had finished – some needed more time than you allowed. Do you always need to stick to the time limit you originally set? How could you have given them more time?

Subject-knowledge
You were very clear from the opening of the lesson what it was going to be about, and told them. The warm-up used key words and emphasized drama skills important to this unit of work. You need to keep using dramatic vocabulary like 'dramatic atmosphere' until they get it.

You told story well, and spent time drawing their attention to how you used your voice to make a dramatic atmosphere. Do you think that they might have benefited from trying this out for themselves before they went into groups?

There were one or two moments when I wondered if you felt they really understood why they were doing an exercise. How did the sculpturing task fit in to the rest of the lesson? Only one group seemed to understand the relationship between the sculpture and the bit of text they were working on in groups. Again, I am sure you can answer any questions they may have about this, but do you want to spend your time explaining it? How can you make the *drama* in the lesson link together as well as the themes and ideas?

Showing some group-work helped consolidate. . . . whenever a group is an audience give them something to do. Maybe they should pick out something you suggested earlier to evaluate.

End allowed them to reflect on how the drama reflected their ideas. In terms of both subject-knowledge and classroom management I would say 'what have you learnt?' rather than 'what did you enjoy?'.

Reflecting on feedback

Even though mentors and visiting lecturers may try very hard to make their notes on observed lessons sound encouraging, there is often a tendency for student-teachers to focus on negative aspects. Questions designed to encourage further thought can easily be construed as criticisms. This being the case, it is vital that student-teachers have the chance to discuss written comments. Over the course of a week, student-teachers may be observed by a number of different people. It is the mentor's role to encourage student-teachers to make sense of the various insights and information by reflecting on their practice in regular mentor meetings. The process of becoming a reflective practitioner of teaching drama inevitably requires student-teachers recognizing their strengths and diagnosing the reasons for their difficulties.

Receiving praise for what went well is encouraging, but it is also very important for student-teachers to know why the teaching worked well so that they can repeat their successes in other contexts. Laying out evidence gleaned from videos of lessons and student-teachers' evaluations of individual lessons and lesson plans, as well as written observations, can lead to solving specific questions. For example, a student-teacher may have found that many of her lessons lack pace. It may be that she sees this as a classroom-management issue, whereas closer inspection of her teaching file reveals that it is because she is planning on a lesson-by-lesson basis rather than for the medium term. Knowing how the lessons will progress over a period of time may mean that lessons are paced to allow time for the pupils to learn. In other words, this kind of diagnosis leads to appropriate target setting.

In itself, target setting is of little use unless student-teachers are given specific strategies to meet them. This is where the mentor's craft-knowledge is particularly helpful. In order to turn abstract targets into practical classroom strategies mentors need to offer student-teachers concrete suggestions about how to proceed.

Target setting

Consider the following issues. Some solutions have been offered. You may like to consider alternative strategies.

Issue	Questions and target	Strategy
I have difficulty framing questions which enable pupils to evaluate their own work	Planning for learning: Do I know what they are learning in drama?	Script several alternative questions all focused on the learning objectives

The pupils' written work is usually poorly completed	Are you explaining it clearly? Are the tasks differentiated?	Use writing frames to focus their writing
Year 11 devised work is very unstructured	Have you given them adequate input? What are the elements of devising which would help?	Show examples of devised drama on video. Ask them to do 'storyboard' of devised drama

By their very definition, reflective conversations are retrospective but there is also a need to use mentor meetings to anticipate new experiences in the professional placement and to introduce new areas of learning. As has been pointed out already, planning on the part of the mentors should enable student-teachers to work independently and to ask useful and considered questions. Nonetheless, however successfully they are progressing, student-teachers will need different forms of encouragement, which means that mentors will at times need to offer both pastoral support and professional advice. In many ways, these roles are complementary; the term 'pastoral support' rather than 'friendship' implies a professional context and, as all teachers know, this sometimes entails giving tough advice. It involves the mentors in making assessments of student-teachers' progress and communicating this sensitively but unambiguously to student-teachers.

Assessing student-teachers' classroom practice

In most training programmes, drama mentors have a key role in the assessment of the practical skills of student-teachers. When this model was first introduced, there were some concerns that this would jeopardize the relationship of trust and openness that characterizes the best collaborations between mentors and student-teachers. However, in practice this has not proved to be the case. All assessments are monitored and moderated by the awarding body, and where there are difficulties or when student-teachers are at risk of failure additional support is offered by the training institution. In other words, no individual mentor is responsible for passing or failing a student-teacher.

In the best mentoring practice, student-teachers and mentors have developed ways of working in which regular monitoring, feedback and formative assessment are an accepted part of the process. Because the mentor meetings give student-teachers a regular opportunity to discuss their progress with their mentor, the formal reports should be integral to the process of reflective conversation. However, because of their formal status, writing the reports provides an opportunity to reflect on the level of competency reached, celebrate progress and negotiate new targets. It is a good time tc take stock and for student-teachers to receive very clear indications of their level of practical competence. Furthermore, if student-teachers are to accept responsibility for their learning, they will be very involved in the process, discussing draft reports and making suggestions for target setting. In many ways, it can be an opportunity for student-teachers to discuss how they will extend their practice by working in areas they have yet to experience – such as sixth-form teaching or working with pupils with special needs. It is a time to review both student-teachers' progress and the training provision.

It is likely that reports are written on student-teachers' progress at different times during the training period. They offer a form of benchmarking towards the levels of professional competence and, as such, they indicate progression in all aspects of teaching. Such reports are sent to the training institution and, if appropriate, to other mentors in partnership schools who will work with that student-teacher. They are used for assessment purposes, to ensure continuity for student-teachers within the programme, and they also provide useful information for reference writing.

Report forms

The following comments are taken from one student-teacher's reports from different reporting stages in the training year. These extracts focus on subject-knowledge and understanding.

First reporting stage: term 1
As well as demonstrating a good understanding of how to use drama effectively at Key Stage 3, Jane has made herself familiar with the GCSE syllabuses and inspection reports. She has worked particularly well with small groups and has facilitated the process of ideas into performance.
    Target for term 2: to gain wider experience of GCSE and A level; to become familiar with alternative approaches to how drama is taught at Key Stage 3.

Second reporting stage: half-term in term 2
Good knowledge of drama practices and the ways in which they may be used to explore issues, ideas, feelings and texts. Very good understanding of drama conventions and genres, and their use in performance drama. Good grasp of GCSE syllabuses, in particular Edexcel 1698 in drama. Effective use of ICT in classroom practice to support and develop pupils' learning and attainment.
    Target: Post-16 experience, especially integration of arts in Performing Arts course.

Third reporting stage: end of term 2
Very secure subject-knowledge for teaching drama in sixth-form college. Strong theoretical grasp of her subject, backed up by an instinctive understanding of the needs of the students and the demands of practice. She has effectively put into practice units of work which integrate music and dance in Performing Arts A/AS levels.
    Target: Build on subject-knowledge of contemporary theatre practitioners.

Developed detailed knowledge of A level syllabuses, including revised courses, and applied this to teaching. Made connections between new AS and A level and GCSE, and revised GCSE units of work to allow for this progression. Introduced elements of performance art to GCSE drama, and showed subject-knowledge by co-directing the school's summer production.

198

Discussing ideas

Throughout the training period, student-teachers will encounter new ideas about the teaching of drama from their reading, from fellow student-teachers, from university seminars and their professional placement. It is likely that they will discuss their emergent ideas about drama education with their mentors; there is much to be gained from articulating ideas to others in order to clarify them and explore them further. Mentors are particularly well placed to discuss the practical implications of implementing ideas in particular classrooms and will be able to suggest ways in which they might be adapted to suit the needs of the pupils they are teaching and the drama curriculum within which they are working. However, as student-teachers become more confident as drama practitioners in the classroom, they may find opportunities to discuss ideas in a more structured way particularly valuable.

Furlong and Maynard suggest that at one stage of student-teachers' development they reach a plateau, particularly after a level of competency has been achieved. This may be the case for some student-teachers, but many experience a crisis of confidence at this stage rather than a plateau. There is often a moment of crisis about half-way through the course or full-time professional placement when good student-teachers are reasonably well established in the classroom. At this point they often begin to realize how little they know about teaching and they become very concerned about the relationship between their teaching and the pupils' learning. This can be very painful for student-teachers, but if they re-focus their attention on the 'bigger picture' by discussing key ideas with their mentors they may well find that their early idealism is revisited. Moving on involves considering how ideals have been revised and integrated into classroom practice.

Of course not all student-teachers experience such doubts, but finding time to discuss ideas with mentors deepens student-teachers' understanding of why and how drama is taught. Structuring time to discuss ideas may also build on student-teachers' experiences in drama before the training began, and can help them to fill gaps in their subject-knowledge.

- Mentor and student-teacher both read new drama education publication and discuss in mentor meeting.
- Mentor reads student-teachers' written assignments.
- Student-teachers take part in a departmental or faculty meeting, introducing new plays or other resources suitable for particular key stages.
- Student-teachers lead practical workshop for sixth form and staff based on degree work.

Reaching professional competence and beyond

Not all experiences of professional placements are positive. Some student-teachers experience real difficulties in the classroom, and some decide to give up the idea of teaching drama altogether. Conversely, some student-teachers reach a satisfactory level of competence before the training period is completed, and these student-teachers will wish to challenge themselves further. The final section of this chapter addresses issues that surround both these situations.

When things go wrong

Teaching drama is often an inspiring and creative job, but when it is not going well it can be very depressing. Daily battles with pupils to get them to participate in practical work, followed by evenings of lesson planning and nights of worry can make it hard for student-teachers to work out exactly what is going wrong and how to sort it out. Mentors who are closely involved in this process are well placed to offer not only moral support, but practical advice. Quite often the problems are not as significant as they first appear.

Diagnosing what the difficulties are is the first stage in rectifying them. The problem when things go wrong is that it is often quite difficult for student-teachers to reflect productively on the situation; if they knew what was wrong and how to sort it out they probably would not be in such a muddle. This is where specific advice is important. It is likely that the realization that things are not progressing as well as they might is gradual, with student-teachers finding it increasingly difficult to meet targets for development. It can be frustrating for both student-teachers and mentors: student-teachers feel that all their best efforts fail, whilst mentors may think that they have not heeded their advice fully. If this is the case, it is important to remain open and ask for additional support. Discussion of the difficulties, as well as successes, can help diagnose precisely what the student-teacher and mentor can work on. Student-teachers who are experiencing extreme difficulties benefit from the support structures identified throughout this chapter. They may need more regular feedback and very precise target setting, but the principles for support are identical.

At this stage, many training institutions have procedures of support and clarification that are designed to make the situation absolutely transparent for everyone involved. Some issue student-teachers with learning contracts, which make the targets very explicit, whilst others will ensure that additional reports document exactly what issues need to be addressed. It is imperative that everything is documented at this stage; student-teachers have a right to know exactly what they can do to address their problems, what practical strategies they need to employ to get better and what support they will be given. Sometimes it is recommended that student-teachers change schools or undertake an extended professional placement; this will usually be decided by an examination board and student-teachers will be kept fully informed of the process.

Learning contract

The following learning contract is an example of the kind issued to student-teachers who are at risk of failing to reach qualified teacher status.

This contract was written after discussions between you, the drama mentor in your school, the professional tutor and course leader. It was agreed that:

- Your medium-term planning still lacks focus. This means that there is little sense of progression between one lesson and another, particularly at Key Stage 3. You will be given additional mentor periods to discuss medium-term planning and the drama mentor will work collaboratively with you to plan the outline of a series of six lessons. In return, it is expected that you take on this planning and translate it into individual lesson plans.
- You are still arriving late for school. In the last two weeks, you have arrived too late to take your tutor period on three occasions. No more lateness will be tolerated and, should this occur, you will be expected to make up time after the official ending of the course. You are advised to find out more about the school's tutorial system from the head of year.

Signed by _____(mentor, course leader, student-teacher)

If they find themselves in a position wherein they are likely to fail, student-teachers may seriously consider giving up training to be a drama teacher. At this point it is always worth discussing the situation fully with mentors in school and course tutors. It may be that everyone concerned has every confidence that the student-teacher will become a good teacher of drama in time. Not everyone progresses at the same rate. If they decide to stay on and persevere, they may need a lot of support to stay positive, but can help themselves by being hard working, well organized and showing how they have learnt from experience. Conversely, it may be that they decide that teaching drama is simply not what they want to do after all. This is often a brave decision to take, given the investment of time and energy that may already have been expended. However, not everyone is suited to drama teaching and some student-teachers may not find it satisfying.

Beyond competence

Towards the end of the training process, many student-teachers have reached a good level of competence and wish to undertake additional challenges. Most training programmes allow for this stage in development in their structures and student-teachers are often given the opportunity to work flexibly in school during the final weeks of the course. By this stage many student-teachers will have been appointed to their first teaching job, and they may wish to take this into account when consolidating areas of their practice and experimenting with new ways of working.

There are three key areas student-teachers in drama may wish to consider when extending their practice beyond competence. They may wish to:

- become more aware of the whole-school context of teaching and learning;
- bring sources of knowledge from outside the school into the drama curriculum;
- focus on particular aspects of their own teaching practice which they have not had a chance to consolidate or develop.

As this part of the training period often coincides with the end of the academic year, there are a variety of opportunities which may provide a context for this work, such as arts weeks, foreign exchanges or camps, literacy weeks and school plays. Some student-teachers find it useful to undertake a period of focused observation, perhaps revisiting experiences such as a pupil pursuit which they may have undertaken in the early part of their training course. The contrast with their perceptions in the light of experience can be very illuminating!

Some suggestions for school-based experiences beyond competence

In the school context

- Pupil pursuit; follow a pupil for the day in all lessons
- Planning drama components of literacy strategy (with English student-teacher)
- Contribute to arts week
- Performance project for pupils with special needs
- Work on school play
- Research place of boys in drama and the arts
- Contribute to careers' convention for sixth form

Outside school

- Develop drama unit of work based on visit to art gallery
- Write work pack for a theatre company's touring production to use in school
- Visit primary schools or middle schools
- Gather information about different drama degrees for 18+ progression

Consolidating practice

- Assess Year 9 practical work for summative report
- Use digital cameras in Year 10 devising project
- Write units of work for post-16 classes
- Write differentiated resources for unit of work

As student-teachers learn to become competent teachers, they will inevitably develop their own particular interests and strengths in drama. Some find that they are able to use their knowledge of dance and movement, whilst others may enjoy integrating text-based work into the practical curriculum. By the end of the training process, they should also know what kind of drama teacher they wish to become, and what kind of professional development they may wish to receive in their induction years. It is testament to a successful mentoring process when student-teachers have developed the practical craft of teaching in partnership with their mentors, when they have built on the advice they have received, but when they do not emulate all their mentors' practices.

NOTES

1 D. McIntyre (1990) 'The Oxford Internship and the Cambridge Analytical Framework: Models of Partnership in Initial Teacher Training' in M. Booth, J. Furlong and M. Wilkin (eds) *Partnership in Initial Teacher Training* (London: Cassell), pp. 78–84.

2 J. Furlong, L. Barton, S. Miles, C. Whiting and G. Whitty (2000) *Teacher Education in Transition* (Buckingham: Open University Press), pp. 77–9.

3 D. McIntyre and H. Hagger (1993) 'Teachers' Expertise and Models of Mentoring' in D. McIntyre, H. Hagger and M. Wilkin (eds) *Mentoring: Perspectives on School-Based Teacher Education* (London: Kogan Page), pp. 94–9.

4 T. Maynard and J. Furlong (1993) 'Learning to Teach and Models of Mentoring' in McIntyre et al., *Mentoring*, p. 81.

5 D. Schon (1983) *The Reflective Practitioner: How Professionals Think in Action* (New York: Basic Books).

6 J. Furlong and T. Maynard (1995) *Mentoring Student Teachers* (London: Routledge), pp. 70–3.

7 Ibid., p. 70.

8 P. Taylor (ed.) (1996) *Researching Drama and Arts Education* (London: Falmer Press), pp. 25–9.

9 D. McIntyre and H. Hagger, 'Teachers' Expertise and Models of Mentoring', p. 93.

Transition

Beyond initial teacher education

The term 'initial teacher education' suggests that there is something more extensive that might constitute 'teacher education'. At the end of Chapter 6 we suggested that successfully completing an initial teacher training course implied a commitment to further professional development and in recent years a number of initiatives have been launched to help newly qualified teachers embark on this journey. In effect, finishing training simply marks the start of a new phase of learning; as The Player in Tom Stoppard's *Rosencrantz and Guildenstern Are Dead* wryly observes, 'every exit is an entrance somewhere else'.[1]

Not everyone completing an initial teacher training course will go straight into teaching. Some newly qualified drama specialists may find work as education officers in theatres or join theatre-in-education companies. Others choose to take some time out travelling or to transfer the knowledge and skills they have acquired to the commercial world. This is their right; there is no obligation to move straight from initial training into teaching. At present there is no set period in which a newly qualified teacher must start their induction year. However, the vast majority of newly qualified drama teachers do move straight into employment as full-time teachers.[2]

Deciding to move into teaching is, for many, a perfectly logical thing to do, but the actual transition from being a student-teacher to becoming a fully qualified, paid professional is a big undertaking. In the first place they need to find, and obtain, a post which suits them. They then need to prepare for their professional development as a newly qualified teacher. This involves identifying what they already know and can do, and setting reasonable targets to consolidate their skills or develop new areas of learning. As one newly qualified teacher reflected: 'The methodology and training turned someone who thought he could teach into someone who had the tools to go into school and become a teacher.'

During their initial training, most student-teachers advanced from a position of early idealism, through survival and recognizing difficulties, to the point where they hit a plateau and finally moved on. One of the problems of accepting this model at face value is that it can suggest that professional development is sequential. In fact, it is far more complex. In the first years of teaching, teachers are likely to be better at some aspects of their job than others, and whilst they may be very competent in some areas they may need additional help elsewhere. If this is not recognized, and adequate support is not offered, the result is depressingly obvious: they either stagnate or leave teaching entirely. This has prompted teaching agencies to place a stronger emphasis on provision for induction and in-service training.

Applying for jobs

Most student-teachers start applying for jobs several months before they qualify and have usually been offered posts well before they receive qualified teacher status. Student-teachers who are familiar with standard procedures for applications and interviews tend to find success more rapidly than those who are not. Some people like to discuss their letter of application and interview preparation with mentors and tutors, who generally regard this as part of their role. However, they often wait to be approached rather than offering unsolicited advice.

Schools generally advertise vacant or new posts in the press. Applicants to some local authorities are required to apply direct to a 'pool' where, if successful, they will be offered a suitable post when it arises. Advertisements for teaching jobs sometimes appear in local papers but, more commonly, they will be put in *The Times Educational Supplement* (there is a separate Scottish edition). Other national papers such as the *Guardian* and the *Scotsman* also publish education sections on a weekly basis.

Published adverts only give very brief information about the post but invite prospective candidates to write for application forms and further details. Deadlines are set for applications and, following this closing date, a short-list is drawn up and references are usually, but not always, called for. While it was once usual for applicants to be invited for interview following receipt of references, it is now often the case that invitations to interview are sent out at the same time as requests for references. There is nothing sinister in this. Rather, it signals the determination of schools to appoint good candidates as quickly as they can. However, this situation can mean that there is a good deal of pressure on referees to respond to requests very quickly and for their references to arrive promptly. Student-teachers should, therefore, let their referees know when they are applying for jobs so that references can be prepared or updated.

In teaching, interviews usually last for a full day. By the end of the day it is likely that one candidate will be offered the job. For many people with experience of employment in fields other than teaching this system can appear very strange, if not brutal. Certainly, when they first hear about the procedure, most student-teachers are concerned that they will be unable to make up their minds about a school and a job on the day. This is a legitimate concern. However, in defence of the system, if applicants have done their homework, have thought through what they want from a post and have read all the available information on the school carefully, many of their questions will have been answered. It is quite possible to get a feel of a school in a day and, although it is not always a comfort to hear this, student-teachers do tend to get jobs that fit.

Task: find a job

- Log on to the *TES* website. This allows you to register your interests and specify areas you wish to work in and what sort of post you are seeking. You will then be e-mailed with information about suitable jobs as and when they come up.
- Look at the following two advertisements for drama posts. Draw up a list of things that would either attract or dissuade you from finding out more about these jobs. What sort of questions about the schools do these brief adverts raise for you?

Huntersbourne High School
Woodlands Avenue, Huntersbourne Marshall
Required immediately, an enthusiastic and committed teacher to teach Drama as part of the core curriculum in KS 3 and to GCSE in this split-site 11–18 comprehensive school. The school boasts excellent facilities for drama. The appointee will be expected to contribute to the school's highly regarded performing arts programme. The ability to offer a second subject is desirable.
   Candidates should telephone for further details and an application form.

Alderman Foggitt School
Conduit Street, Gastown
We are seeking to appoint a highly qualified and imaginative specialist teacher of drama to join our thriving arts faculty in this expanding 11–18 school. Drama is a compulsory subject at KS 3 where it is taught as part of the arts curriculum. The school is particularly proud of its pupils' achievements in Drama. There are currently 3 GCSE groups and a healthily sized A level group. You will join a team that is highly skilled and committed to working closely with the local community. Further details may be obtained by writing or telephone. The closing date for applications is 18 April.

The importance of thorough preparation in applying for teaching jobs cannot be stressed too highly. Student-teachers can avoid landing an unsuitable job or missing one they would have loved by taking the right steps. It is sensible for student-teachers to begin by considering the kind of school in which they wish to work. If they know they want to work in a school with a sixth form, for example, they should not waste time applying to 11–16 schools. They will need to consider the different challenges presented by rural, suburban or inner-city schools and be prepared to question stereotypical notions of each. Some people will be tied to a particular area and need to consider how far they are prepared to commute; for others, house prices may be a significant factor. Whatever the criteria, it is very important not to waste interviewers' time applying for a job which is clearly unsuitable. Although it is quite acceptable to withdraw an application while attending interview if there are good reasons, headteachers are very likely to be peeved with applicants whose criteria obviously do not match the post on offer. Student-teachers tempted to play this game need to remember that in many areas drama teachers form a close-knit community and they may find that rumours about their unreliability are circulated. Furthermore, heads of department who are offended in an interview may have to be faced again as colleagues at meetings and moderations.

Checklist

- Find out who it is best to cite as your referees. There are different systems here. Some universities request that the course director or principal is cited, whilst others name individual tutors. Referees should note that if they are named individually they may be, in law, personally liable for the contents of the reference. Before agreeing to write references they are advised to check their legal status.
- In school, you should ask the professional tutor or drama mentor who it is best to approach, and do not assume that they will write a reference for all jobs. Some teachers will not wish to write a reference for a post in the independent sector, for example.
- Ask your referee if they need to know when you are applying for jobs so that they can prepare a reference for you.
- If you are called for interview, you will need to request permission for absence from the appropriate members of staff.
- You may wish to seek advice from referees about the content of your letter of application and curriculum vitae. They may know the school to which you are applying and will be able to give you useful information.
- Let your referees know when you have been offered a job.

Deciding to apply

Finding a job that really suits may require applicants to look across a wide geographical area, and those who wish to stay in a particular area may have to wait for the right job to come up. Even so, it is always worth writing for details for a number of jobs in order to find out how schools present themselves. OFSTED reports and websites also provide very helpful introductions to schools, although league tables of examination results do not necessarily indicate lively educational environments. In order to decide whether or not to apply and perhaps subsequently complete an application form, applicants need to know about the ethos, structures and managerial style of a school, as well as about the drama curriculum. It is possible to glean a great deal by reading the written information the school sends out. At the very least, details should include:

- *Details of the school as a whole.* Applicants need to be able to get an idea of the context in which the school exists. Details about the catchment area and number of pupils on roll are helpful. The school's mission and philosophy should be clearly expressed in the details. It is useful to know about any education initiatives the school is involved in, for example if they have Community School or Arts College status. This sort of information may be far more useful to an applicant than examination scores or de-contextualized extracts from OFSTED reports.

- *Information about the drama department or faculty.* This may include details of the department such as how many staff teach drama, the drama facilities, how drama fits into the curriculum at Key Stage 3, what examination specifications are taught and how many candidates there usually are, what sort of extra-curricular work goes on and any special projects or links with the community. Some details will include statements about the methodology of the department or long-term aims for developing the work.
- *A job description* sent out to candidates should make it clear exactly what the position entails; what opportunities there may be for teaching different ages, ability groups and examination classes. If an ability and willingness to teach a second subject is preferred, the details should specify what subjects will be considered and how much teaching time they are likely to consume. Student-teachers of drama will also be interested to know what expectations there will be regarding extra-curricular work as they may justifiably be wary of taking on too much responsibility in the first year or so of full-time teaching.

Interpreting the details schools send out is quite a skilful task. If there is scant information, it begs questions about how the school is managed. Job details will obviously be trying to sell the school, but only to the right candidate. From the student-teacher's point of view it is important to consider whether or not it is a 'thinking' school which genuinely wants to develop its practice, or whether there is a suggestion of complacency.

Throughout the whole process of finding a teaching post there is a danger of being influenced by superficialities. For example, OFSTED reports on vibrant schools in difficult areas may be very misleading in that, by focusing on the challenges faced by the school, they can give readers with no first-hand experience of the situation a negative impression. Conversely, the school that sports a whizzo website and distributes glossy prospectuses might well be spending money on bolstering its image rather than supporting the curriculum. Writing letters of application and attending interviews consumes valuable time and energy in the training year. Critically appraising what a school says about itself and what other agencies say about it is worthwhile because it may ensure that student-teachers only make applications to appropriate schools.

There are two key questions for student-teachers to ask when deciding whether to pursue an application:

- Will this school support me as a newly qualified teacher in ways that will allow me to grow and develop in my career?

- What experiences am I likely to have gained in the first two or three years that will enable me to fulfil my longer-term aims?

The state education system in the UK includes an incredibly diverse mixture of different types of school: co-educational/single sex, comprehensive/selective, LEA, foundation and controlled, 11–18/12–16, rural/suburban/inner city. Any one may offer newly qualified teachers an exciting induction into teaching and excellent opportunities for professional development. Student-teachers may, of course, have preferences about the sort of school in which they wish to teach but harbouring prejudices can turn out to be to their own detriment.

Letters of application

Application forms must be completed very carefully. Applicants should read through the whole form before putting pen to paper. Some schools are strict and insist that applicants return only the form and nothing else. If this is not specified it is worth including a covering letter and a CV, even though this might mean a bit of repetition. The way the letter is presented is very important. It is now standard practice to word process a letter of application. A decent size font should be used (11 or 12 point), along with 1.5-line spacing. Just one side of A4 in this orientation will be too short to develop ideas, but presenting more than two sides runs the risk of waffling. Finding the right tone is difficult. Some jobs in industry or business may well expect applications to show some aggression and an overt confidence, but teachers tend to prefer a more modest tone which is based on substance and factual information rather than assertions. In a sense, the letter acts as an introduction in that, having read it, it encourages the selection panel to meet the candidates in order to ask about their experiences and ideas. It is more helpful for the interview panel to know what candidates think they have gained from the training programme than to be told bluntly that they have, for example, 'excellent interpersonal skills and a good sense of humour'. Interview panels usually prefer to ascertain this sort of thing for themselves.

The CV is a valuable way of giving the selection panel additional information from which they can formulate questions and establish the breadth and depth of the candidate's knowledge, experience and personal qualities. For student-teachers of drama the CV is likely to contain:

- subjects studied at examination level at school, college and university, and grades achieved (if they were particularly good);
- details of other qualifications related to education and the arts (this may include sports coaching or counselling qualifications, etc.);
- a list of significant productions undertaken, stating the applicant's role as director, actor, designer, etc.:
- a summary of research topics or dissertations undertaken at degree level and on subsequent courses;

- previous employment and voluntary experiences (including things like griddle chef at Burger King, bar work or youth summer camp attendant is fine; the purpose is to give people an idea of who you are and what you have done).

Letters and CVs must always be thoroughly checked for spelling and punctuation errors; headteachers and governors have remarkably sharp eyes and will notice the tiniest mistakes. Many student-teachers find it helpful to structure their letter of application around a template such as the one offered here.

Structuring a letter of application

Para. 1 Say something about what you find interesting about the school to which you are applying. While much of what you put in the letter will relate to all of your applications, it is important to show that you have considered the particular job advertised.

Para. 2 Describe the key features of the course you are on – what you are gaining from it and the ideas/experience you are finding most beneficial in shaping your ideas and practice.

Para. 3 Discuss the work you have undertaken in your professional placement. Make it clear where you think your strengths lie and hint at how these will be useful in the post for which you are applying.

Para. 4 Most important – talk about yourself and what your educational philosophy is. Why should they bother to meet you? What qualities and beliefs do you have that make you special?

Preparing for the interview

Before attending an interview applicants may wish to visit the school informally or visit the area to get a sense of the community context. It is always sensible to check how to get to the school and to prepare some questions to ask. The interview process is always two-way. Applicants will want to find out the principles and ethos which guide the school and what opportunities teaching drama there will offer. It is far more important that student-teachers prepare for an interview by balancing their ideas for teaching drama and educational principles with those of the school, rather than spending hours swotting up the examination specifications they use. A selection panel will be more interested in the applicants' ideas, intellect, creativity and analysis of their own professional development than in whether they can recite examination assessment criteria. They will want to know what kind of contribution candidates can make to the school in general and the drama curriculum in particular. It is an interview and not a test, although applicants need to be well informed.

Check:

- that you have familiarized yourself with the educational values in drama offered by the examination syllabuses being used in the school;
- that you know about National Curriculum requirements and guidelines in drama and can give practical examples of how to implement them in your teaching;
- that you can talk about the relationship between drama and citizenship, key skills and personal, social, moral and health education;
- that you have an example of a lesson and unit of work which worked well and are able to talk about how you would adapt it in the light of experience;
- that you know what areas of your teaching you wish to develop and what support you would be expecting from the school (modesty and integrity count for a lot).

On the day

Interview candidates should turn up on time looking smart, well presented and comfortable. Usually the day will begin with a tour of the school. This will often be followed by a short teaching exercise and/or small-group interviews, with a more formal interview in the afternoon. Candidates need to be open minded, and look particularly at the staff as well as the pupils. They need to assimilate and interpret what they see:

- Do rows of neat blazers indicate an orderly environment or regimentation?
- How easy is it to like and respect the head of drama? Does he or she appear to be able to challenge as well as support staff? Or do you detect a *laissez-faire* attitude?
- Are there other colleagues in the department or staffroom who have responsibility for facilitating your professional development?
- What seems to be the relationship between staff and pupils? How do the staff behave towards each other? How do the pupils appear to get on together?
- Are senior staff approachable?

Expensive drama facilities may be impressive, but how well used are they? Not all schools have the money for sophisticated hardware but might nevertheless offer pupils an exciting experience of drama. Candidates will want to ascertain if the drama curriculum really is as lively as perhaps it was portrayed in the details. Are there opportunities for working collaboratively within the arts, or with English teachers? It is particularly important to establish what sort of team new drama teachers will be working in. Perhaps they will be largely on their own, which will not suit all newly qualified teachers.

Even in the initial tour of the school, candidates can learn a great deal. Are there interesting, well-kept displays on classroom and corridor walls? Are notices given in a range of languages? Are the pupils' achievements and projects publicly celebrated? Writing notes while on the tour is not advisable, but it is very useful to notice things in order to talk or ask about them when the appropriate opportunity arises.

Throughout the day candidates will probably have the chance to speak to quite a lot of people and they may find themselves in different group situations. There may be a group discussion built into the formal interview process or they may be in groups over coffee or lunch. Candidates should be in no doubt that they are being observed all the time. It does not pay to be too pushy, but there is a need to find things out. In group discussions, it works well to take a little time in answering questions and to be generous when others want to speak. Candidates may also wish to observe how the interviewers listen to them. Do they seem to be treating everyone equally? Are they genuinely interested in the answers to their questions?

It is becoming standard procedure to ask interview candidates to teach a lesson to a whole class or small group. Schools should give prior warning of this and state how long the lesson will be and with which age-group. It is best for candidates not to try and plan anything too complex. Some members of interview panels may be primarily observing how quickly candidates make positive relationships with pupils by organizing and motivating them effectively. Others will be more interested in the relationship between teaching and learning. It is important to attend to both in the lesson. Candidates might take along a word-processed lesson plan, in which teaching and learning objectives are clearly stated, and give a copy to the panel. Using a well-prepared resource signals that candidates know how to integrate suitable stimulus material into their teaching. The lesson should certainly offer the pupils a chance not only to do some practical work but also to reflect on it. Good use of voice, command of the space and making eye contact with pupils is, as ever, vital. Finding out and using some of the pupils' names is also sensible. Overall, observers are likely to be more interested in the candidate's manner and approach to the task than in the showy contents of a lesson.

The panel for the formal interview will probably include the headteacher, the head of drama and a governor. There may be other senior teachers or the LEA inspector for drama, English or the arts present. Candidates need to communicate with them all, using an appropriately formal tone and avoiding colloquialisms (for example, referring to 'the pupils' or 'the students' rather than 'the kids'). It is essential to listen carefully to what has been asked and give succinct answers to questions. There is no reason why a parent-governor or the headteacher should know about forum theatre or semiotics, so care is needed in order not to mystify those on the panel who are not subject specialists in drama.

It may be appropriate to refer to things that have been seen and heard during the day; the panel may warm to compliments about their school, but not to sycophancy. They will want to hear how the candidate intends to contribute to the school's ethos and practice. So, for example, a candidate who is impressed by the quality of the artwork displayed in the school may also suggest how they would

introduce displays in their own drama studio as a way of furthering the pupils'
subject-knowledge. Above all else, candidates should articulate their own views
and beliefs, say what they want to say and not what they think members of the
interview panel want to hear. Not only are such candidates rarely appointed (as
Postman and Weingartner point out, experienced teachers have extraordinarily
well-developed crap detectors!)[3], it is far better not to get a job if it means
seriously compromising one's own values.

Preparing for an interview

- For some drama posts candidates are expected to teach some English. This should
  be specified in the job description. If you are unqualified in this area it is advisable
  not to apply; English teaching requires knowledge of grammar and linguistics as well
  as literary texts. If you do apply, candidates in England and Wales (in particular)
  should study the ITT National Curriculum for English, ensure they can fulfil many of
  its demands and know precisely in which areas they will need support.
- It is important not to make huge promises about undertaking school plays. Newly
  qualified teachers should prioritize their work in the curriculum first, and reasonable
  headteachers will regard this as a sensible decision. Furthermore, school plays are
  usually extra-curricular activities and, as such, are voluntary.
- Sometimes, candidates may find that they are asked personal questions. These may
  include how you balance work and home life, how you relax, what makes you happy
  and what your domestic arrangements and future family plans are. Candidates may
  justifiably consider questions such as these to be intrusive and inappropriate in an
  interview context. A very short polite answer, using humour, is the best solution.
- Look at the following table of interview questions. They are designed to assist your
  preparation. Interview candidates sometimes do not do themselves justice because
  they have not thought through what they know, understand and can do, and
  formulated their own standpoint on fundamental issues in education.

Interview questions

In general	Drama specific	Related fields
Why have you applied to this school in particular?	What would you expect pupils in Years 7–9 to be able to achieve in drama?	What importance do the performing arts have for young people?
What made you decide to become a teacher?	What sort of strategies would you use to differentiate work in drama?	What key skills are shared by the arts and why are the arts an important part of the whole curriculum?
Tell us about your own strengths and weaknesses as a teacher.	How is drama represented in the National Curriculum?	
How do you relax?		What sort of drama strategies could you use to assist in the teaching of the English National Curriculum?
What makes you angry?	How helpful do you, as a drama teacher, find the orders for English?	
What would you like to be doing in five years' time?		

Interview questions *continued*

In general	Drama specific	Related fields
What would you do if you found yourself disagreeing with your head of department or the headteacher?	What is more important in teaching drama for you: using it as a method to help engage pupils with topics, or focusing on its artistic and technical aspects?	Is there a difference between teaching plays in English and teaching them in drama?
What are your views on school uniform?	What special facilities and resources will you need in order to deliver drama the way you think it should be delivered?	Talk about some authors whose work you find lends itself to exploration through drama?
How do you see yourself contributing to the pastoral system here?	What does progression in drama imply for you?	What poems, novels and short stories have you found to be a rich resource for drama?
What can you offer the students here in terms of extra-curricular work?	How would you go about monitoring/recording progression in drama?	What do you think about the SATs in English, particularly the way they test a knowledge of Shakespeare?
How would you hope your students remember you once they have left?	Given the opportunity, what plays would you like to see produced in this school?	Do you think that a science teacher could use drama methods in their work? What sort of techniques might they employ in their classroom?
What initiatives could you take to develop closer links between this school and the community?	Tell us about a play that you have seen recently that you feel it would have been good to have taken a school group to see?	How will you be able to contribute to the National Literacy Strategy?
Can you tell us about a particularly successful/unsuccessful lesson you have taught and explain why it worked/failed?	How would you accommodate a non-sexist policy in the drama curriculum?	Do we need a separate drama department now that there is so much drama in the English National Curriculum?
If I were to drop into one of your lessons, what would impress me?	What can you tell us about GNVQs and do you see that drama might have a place in such a scheme?	What is the relationship between ICT and drama?
How has your thinking developed over the training year?	What special qualities do you have as a drama teacher?	What do you understand the demands of PSHE and Citizenship to be? How will you be able to contribute to these programmes?
What could be improved in this school?	How would you introduce Brecht in a practical way to a new group of sixth formers?	Recommend a title for the English Department's KS 3 book stock.
Can you change a plug? Should you ever?	If you had the opportunity to produce a school play, what would you choose to do and why?	What plays would you want to teach as part of the Year 7 English programme?
What do you suppose your mentor or university lecturer thinks of you?		

Protocol

Candidates who know, having gone round the school, that they do not want to work there should withdraw before the formal interview. Some people argue that it is worth staying for the experience but doing this is usually regarded as highly unprofessional. The formal interview is unlikely to alter candidates' impressions and it is quite acceptable at this stage to thank the interviewers for their time and decline the opportunity of proceeding. Those who decide to go forward to the formal interview may well be asked if they are still serious candidates or, more bluntly, if they would accept the job if it were offered to them. Candidates are expected to answer honestly and stick to their decision. If at this stage the candidate signals serious interest it will be deemed very bad form to withdraw later.

It may be that candidates are not sure at the end of the interview whether or not they want to accept the post. They may ask for a little time to think about it but they must be prepared for the headteacher to apply pressure in order to get an answer straightaway. Headteachers will want to make an appointment if possible, and may be reluctant to lose other good candidates while waiting for one person's decision. Asking for time may risk the loss of the job; it is up to the candidate to decide what to do in this situation. It is always worth remembering that no job (or timetable) is perfect from the outset. The main thing is to ascertain how far the position will provide new opportunities and support.

The Career Entry Profile

Since the late 1990s, the practice of profiling professional development has become an established part of teaching. Profiles play an increasingly important role in the appraisal of teachers. They are used to counsel teachers on how to progress in their careers and give new employers insights into their interests, skills and achievements. Towards the end of their period of initial teacher training, student-teachers need to consolidate what they have achieved and identify what they yet need to develop in order to become established as teachers. Committing these observations to paper is the first step towards creating a profile of professional development.

In England and Wales student-teachers will, at the end of their initial teacher training, complete a formalized Career Entry Profile (CEP) as part of the requirements for qualification. In Scotland and Northern Ireland a similar form of profiling is strongly recommended as good practice but it is not statutory. The principle which underlies all these systems is that student-teachers should make sure that what they state on this first important entry in their career profile is honest and accurate. The reason for this is neatly expressed by the DfEE where it is stated that a CEP 'supports new teachers as they make the transition from ITT to becoming established in the profession and helps schools to provide the support and monitoring which each individual NQT needs from the outset of their career'.[4]

At the end of their initial training there is no need for drama specialists to make decisions about whether they wish to become head of a drama department, head of faculty or pursue a career in the pastoral side of teaching. What is far more important is that they look forward to their induction period as a way of building on their achievements and drawing on the support systems available to address aspects of their practice in which they are not yet wholly confident. Compiling CEPs gives student-teachers an opportunity to set out clearly what they want and need from their first job.

Compiling a CEP

The CEP is an official document against which standards of professional competence achieved by NQTs may be measured. This means that, although induction programmes are intended to offer NQTs support, it is advisable to distinguish between professional development and personal needs. However, as a prelude to compiling their official CEP, student-teachers sometimes find it useful to think about their strengths and areas for development. For this, student-teachers may find a SWOT (Strengths, Weaknesses, Opportunities, Threats) activity useful. It is a device used in management training to help people think about their strengths and weaknesses. In this context, 'weakness' is an unhelpful term, but the exercise still has validity as one way of focusing on professional development.

- *Strengths*. In subject-knowledge, classroom practice, experience.
- *Weaknesses*. More usefully recognized as areas for further development. These may relate to a number of gaps in teaching experience, subject-knowledge or practice.
- *Opportunities*. How is the first year of teaching perceived in terms of new areas of learning? What openings do new teachers see for their professional development? Those that have already secured employment before completing their training course may wish to consider the role they will undertake.
- *Threats*. What is there at the philosophical, ideological, national and local levels that may make the first years of teaching difficult? This may involve clarifying aims and values, and some people may wish to consider personal issues here which might present particular challenges.

Over the course of ITT, student-teachers are likely to have assessed and re-assessed the ways in which they think, feel and operate. In all, student-teachers will have a huge amount of valuable experience and achievements on which to draw as a professional; the process of compiling a CEP will help them to fully recognize this.

Be aware, be a SWOT!

- Make a copy of the SWOT chart for yourself. Write bullet points in each section to indicate what you think and feel about the first year of teaching. Some things come up in more than one box. For example, being engrossed in the study of drama may be a strength in that it will inform a good deal of your work, but a weakness if it closes your mind to other things or consumes all of your time.
- Share what you have written on your chart with your mentor or with your peers. While they are in no position to disagree with what you have written (the chart shows what your *perception* is), they may be surprised and offer a different perspective. Perhaps, for example, you have identified that you need to be more confident. They may tell you that you already come across as being very confident. This mismatch could represent a threat in that others may assume that you are coping better than you actually are.

SWOT chart

Strengths	*Weaknesses*
Make a summary list here all of the things you are good at that will help you as a drama teacher. For example:	Summarize here what you feel your gaps are. For example:
• Bags of enthusiasm	• Tend to take on too much, then worry about inability to manage it all
• Extensive knowledge of theatre history, practitioners and plays	• Limited experience of technical skills in drama, e.g. lighting and sound recording
• Ability to enthuse young people	• Timing lessons – still try to cram too much in
• Setting clear and purposeful tasks which lead to progression	• Sometimes pitch lessons too high – lower-ability groups get bored
• Good personal organization and IT skills	

Opportunities	*Threats*
When considering the first year of full-time teaching, what sort of opportunities will you look forward to taking? For example:	When considering the first year of full-time teaching, what sort of pitfalls will you need to watch for? For example:
• Involvement in big school production (possibility of learning more technical stuff)	• Taking on too much – getting too tired to do things properly
• Planning progression for a whole year	• Professional support networks
• More work with sixth form on subject specialism	• Discipline problems with some groups

The SWOT awareness exercise is a personal process, and its audience should be limited to those outside the remit of the CEP. Compiling a CEP productively involves student-teachers trying to put themselves into the shoes of the people who will be responsible for their induction as newly qualified teachers. This involves helping NQTs fulfil their strengths while facilitating opportunities to address those areas in which they have identifiable gaps or omissions. Induction tutors will be concerned about the personal welfare of an NQT but, at the end of the induction year, it is the NQT's professional progress which must be assessed. This assessment will determine whether or not they may proceed with their teaching career. It is for this reason that it is best to separate out the more personal aspects of the SWOT chart from those that can be readily linked to published lists of standards and competences.

Swotting up on standards

- Look at the statements on the SWOT chart above. Identify those that are personal and keep them to yourself. Identify those that might usefully serve as a benchmark against which progression in the published standards and competences might be made.
- Now consider the statements you have made on your own chart. How might you re-phrase the statements you have made to make it clear how they link with the standards and competences with which you are required to comply?

Student-teachers may expect their placement schools and training institutions to scrutinize, agree upon and sign a copy of the CEP. The NQT's first school must be presented with a copy of the profile. Schools will then be able to keep the profiles on record and use them to inform the NQT's induction programme and serve as a baseline against which to judge progression in the first year of teaching.

In writing any kind of CEP a balance does need to be struck between the idealistic and the realistic. It is particularly crucial for student-teachers to identify as accurately as possible what areas there are for further development in terms of subject-knowledge, planning, classroom management and monitoring and assessment. However, student-teachers who have already secured a post before compiling an entry profile should consider the particular situation of their new school. Forwarding an extensive 'wish list' that includes everything the student-teacher would one day like to be good at may be unproductive and the school may not be able to satisfy all of the NQT's objectives. For example, stating a need for further support in working with A level groups in a school with no sixth form begs questions of why they accepted the job.

The induction programme

Induction programmes seek to support new teachers by establishing opportunities for them to develop their knowledge, skills, interests and areas of expertise. One of the ways it achieves this is by ensuring that they are given the time to work on areas needing special attention. The programme will be managed by an Induction Tutor who is likely to have undergone some training for the role. Many will have made a special study of mentoring and may be responsible for professional development throughout the school as well as having a role in the induction of NQTs.

In addition to the induction tutor, who will take an overview of their progress, new teachers can expect heads of drama to monitor and support their work as subject specialists. Some schools also provide NQTs with a personal mentor. The distinction between the three roles is neatly summarized by this NQT:

> There's never been a case where I've been left to my own devices and nobody's bothered to come over and see how I'm getting on. We have regular meetings. Jim is concerned mostly with the NQT programme which is not just going on courses and things that are subject specific but everything else – pastoral stuff, special needs, everything. Glynne, that's the head of the Arts faculty, focuses more on target setting and assessment and schemes of work, that type of thing. He's more subject specific whereas Jo is all the other little things. If I'm having a problem I can't deal with, like when I was worried that I couldn't do some reports because of time, I'll go to her and have a moan about it and she'll see what she can do.

Providing induction tutors with copies of the CEP in advance of the new school year allows them to collaborate with relevant colleagues in order to address NQTs' individual needs. There will also be a core programme which identifies particular aspects of teaching which will be discussed during the year. This programme should be sent to NQTs before they take up their post.

Moving into a first teaching appointment presents exciting prospects for learning more about the craft of teaching but there is a need for induction programmes to ensure that small procedural points are covered early on. This should ensure that NQTs do not worry unnecessarily, which may impede their progress. These comments are typical of NQTs just about to take up their first appointment:

NQT 1 I'm a bit concerned about the fact that on the first day when the kids come in we'll be busy marking the register having not had the register training session.

NQT 2 Yes, because that comes half-way through the first term doesn't it? It's a bit late then if you've been filling it in wrong all that time! That'll be fun!

The very first week I was there we were supposed to be doing break duty and just simple things like that were a worry. You know, what do I do? Where do I stand? What's the kind of approach to problems here?

Although there are, with regional variations, a number of prescribed obligations for schools regarding induction, individual schools will design a programme that suits their particular circumstances. From the NQTs' point of view, knowing what the induction period will involve helps them to formulate questions and make their own appropriate preparations. Outlined below are the parameters induction programmes follow. In England and Wales these are statutory requirements.

Some of the arrangements for induction noted here have a particular relevance to new drama teachers. For example, the requirement that they should not be burdened with responsibilities outside normal teaching suggests that it would be unfair to expect them to direct the school play or run extra-curricular drama activities. Caution needs to be exercised in interpreting guidelines and stated requirements. For example, headteachers may ask drama specialists to contribute to other parts of the curriculum. Drama specialists should be aware of this and ask, at the time of appointment, what other subjects they may be asked to teach and what additional support will be available to them in such work.

Not all of the induction programme will take place in the school itself. Most LEAs run training days especially designed for NQTs, and there are subject-specific INSET courses which are open to drama teachers. Attending these courses

Induction programmes

NQTs should be given opportunities to, for example:	NQTs should not be required to:
receive information about the school, their specific duties and the induction arrangements in advance of their first day in post;	teach more than 90% of a normal timetable;
receive information about their rights and responsibilities and those of others involved in induction;	teach outside the age/subject-range trained for;
take part in staff training at the school;	deal with demanding discipline problems on a daily basis;
find out about whole-school policies on child protection, behaviour management, health and safety, equal opportunities, etc.;	undertake additional non-teaching responsibilities without appropriate support.
spend time with the school's SENCO;	
observe experienced teachers in their own and other schools;	
regularly teach the same classes;	
be assisted in employing similar planning, teaching and assessment processes to other colleagues;	
receive training development and advice from professionals outside the school, e.g. LEAs, higher education institutions, professional bodies and subject associations;	
attend external training events that are relevant to identified individual needs.	

usually helps new teachers consolidate and further their subject-knowledge while making new professional contacts in the area. Examination syndicates, theatres, higher education institutions and training agencies also offer courses and support which will help NQTs address areas identified for further development. Details of these courses may be sent directly to the school. NQTs should also be given the opportunity to visit other schools in the area to observe good practice. It is always worth keeping a lookout for opportunities to broaden experience.

The sting in the tail

Induction programmes are primarily intended to set NQTs off on their professional development. Their progress will be monitored and, ultimately, assessed against a set of criteria or standards. NQTs should expect to have their lessons observed regularly and be given feedback by their mentor or induction tutor on their developing practice. To be of any real use, observations should occur regularly and one should certainly take place within the first four weeks of the NQT taking up a post in order to establish a baseline. Following their initial training most NQTs will be fairly comfortable with observing other teachers, being observed and receiving feedback, as these comments made after the first half-term of teaching illustrate:

> I'm used to having someone watch me teach. On my TP I had loads of time on my own but at every opportunity I'd go in and watch somebody else teach. I do find watching teachers teach and having them watch me is the most valuable thing.

> Yes, I could reach some conclusion but it would probably take six months or a year to realize 'Oh God! Maybe I could . . .' So, you definitely need someone there observing and giving pieces of advice.

> I think observation is a good idea because I don't want to start forming bad habits. Having someone come in and say 'Well, that wasn't . . . whatever . . . let's talk about that' makes you reflect more carefully.

During the induction period, NQTs should expect to have a number of formal meetings with the headteacher or the induction tutor to review evidence of progress towards predetermined targets. These meetings should be informed by written reports from observations of the NQT at work in the classroom and regular progress reviews with the head of drama or arts faculty. All these records will be added to the CEP to form the beginnings of a portfolio which, by tracing a teacher's development from the very start, can be used to appraise their achievements and guide further professional development.

As well as supporting professional development, monitoring a new teacher's progress is a means of identifying 'the small minority of teachers who, even with the additional support and guidance, may fall short of the standards we have a right to expect of those entering the profession'.[5] Cases of new teachers failing to achieve an acceptable level of competence at the end of the induction period are comparatively rare. An appeals procedure exists and people who suspect they may find themselves in such a position are well advised to consult with their union. In a very few cases there will be those who will be asked to leave the profession.

Seeing the whole picture

In order to provide a platform for further professional development, induction programmes should not be solely concerned with making sure that NQTs have adopted daily routines and can survive in the classroom. Over the course of a year, NQTs will be involved in more general discussions about curriculum development, pastoral issues and management of the school. In drama, the NQT can expect to be involved with:

- introducing new groups of pupils to the school and examination courses;
- talking to prospective pupils and parents about the work of the department;
- formally reporting on the achievements of pupils;
- advising pupils and parents about examination options;
- contributing to external moderating and examining procedures;
- public performances and presentations of drama work;
- liaising and collaborating with other subject-areas in the school;
- liaising with colleagues in other schools and local consortia;
- liaising with primary schools.

Trying to assimilate all of this in the first term as an NQT is unlikely to be beneficial. People have a tendency to block out information to which they cannot relate; they need to be ready to learn and have a good reason for learning. Look at the following compilation of what drama NQTs have found valuable in their first year of teaching ('Structuring induction'). It illustrates the need for subject-mentors to plan a programme for the whole year and so avoid over-burdening new teachers with too much information too quickly. The table also recognizes what is practical and possible; while there is much to be learnt from attending courses and conferences or visiting other schools, NQTs must be realistic about the financial burden this places on schools. There are many benefits in focusing on what the school itself has to offer in terms of learning experiences.

Some NQTs of drama soon find themselves in the position of mentoring student-teachers. Many will move on quickly to become head of drama with responsibility for the induction of NQTs. It is particularly helpful for induction programmes in drama to take account of this. Involving the NQT in the construction and monitoring of their own induction not only makes the programme relevant to them as new teachers; it contributes to their professional development by helping to prepare them for the next stage in their career. Effective drama teachers and mentors are not necessarily the ones who have been teaching the longest; they are the ones who have reflected the most and taken an active part in their own professional development and the development of others.

Structuring induction

Term	In school activities and discussions	Out of school
Prior to starting	Receive information about dept's policy for drama, drama curriculum, examples of schemes of work, timetable	
	Discuss unit plans for first term	
	Discuss subject-specific overall induction programme and CEP	
Autumn	Establishing classroom routines and using the dept's code of discipline	Meeting with other drama NQTs and local support group
	Locating and using resources including operating lighting, sound and audiovisual equipment	Attending local GCSE moderation meeting
	Baseline assessment	Attending course run by LEA/HEI for new teachers of drama
	Guidance on how to work with classroom support staff	
	Team teaching with subject-mentor	
	Observing subject-mentor and other teachers	
	Interviewing new pupils about their drama experience	
	Discussing and contributing to prospective parents' evening	
	Guidance on formative assessment in drama	
	Reflecting on personal targets in drama teaching	
Spring	Organizing and participating in GCSE and A level practical examinations	Attending a subject-specific INSET course, e.g. at a theatre or run by LEA/HEI or training service
	Liaising with other subject departments (e.g. English dept re Year 9 SATs)	
	Guidance on summative assessment in drama	Observing an experienced teacher at work in a different school
	Writing reports	
	Preparing for consultation evenings	
	Planning a production	
	Extending use of ICT in drama	
	Organizing a trip to the theatre	
	Observation and feedback from SENCO on tackling IEPs in drama	
	Reviewing development of subject-knowledge	
Summer	Planning an arts festival	Liaising with primary schools; teaching Year 6 groups
	Liaising with local arts organizations and theatre groups; arranging a visit to the school from a theatre company	Attending a course on literacy and primary/secondary transfer
	Collaborating with mentor on a project involving whole-year group	
	Reviewing the drama curriculum	Visiting another drama dept with contrasting organization
	Auditing department resources	
	Contributing to action planning for following year	
	Devising action plan	

NOTES

1 T. Stoppard (1967) *Rosencrantz and Guildenstern Are Dead* (London: Faber and Faber), p. 20.

2 This statistic is monitored annually. Similarly, financial inducements to stay in teaching are reviewed regularly.

3 N. Postman and C. Weingartner (1971) *Teaching as a Subversive Activity* (London: Penguin) pp. 15–27.

4 DfEE (1999) *Supporting Induction for Newly Qualified Teachers: Overview*. London: HMSO, p. 28.

3 In England and Wales there are statutory requirements regarding how much teaching may be expected of newly qualified teachers and what sort of opportunities they must be given. These are set out in DfEE Circular No. 5/99. In Scotland and Northern Ireland schools are strongly recommended to use the guidelines made available by the respective governing bodies. In all UK countries comprehensive support materials are available to schools to help establish induction programmes.

5 National Committee of Inquiry into Higher Education (1997) *Report 10: Teacher Education and Training: A Study* (The Sutherland Report) (London: HMSO).

Useful Websites

Examination Boards

ACCAC: www.accac.org.uk

AQA: www.aqa.org.uk

Edexcel: www.edexcel.org.uk

NCLN: www.cfbt.com

Government Agencies

CCEA: www.ccea.org.uk

DfEE: www.dfee.gov.uk

NC: www.nc.uk.net

OFSTED: www.ofsted.gov.uk

QCA: www.qca.org.uk

SQA: www.sqa.org.uk

TTA: www.canteach.gov.uk

Resources

BT Connections: www.connectionsplays.co.uk

National Theatre: www.nt-online.org

Edexcel: www.edexcel.org.uk

NCLN: www.cfbt.com

ND: www.dokumenta.co.uk

OCR: www.ocr.org.uk

WJEC: www.wjec.co.uk

Theatre Museum: www.londontheatre.co.uk

References

Arden, J. (1960) 'A Thoroughly Romantic View', *London Magazine*, vol. vii, no. 7 (July).

Arnot, M. (2000) 'Equal Opportunities and Educational Performance: Gender, Race and Class' in J. Beck and M. Earl (eds) *Key Issues in Secondary Education* (London: Continuum), pp. 77–85.

Bailin, S. (1998) 'Creativity in Context' in D. Hornbrook (ed.) *On the Subject of Drama* (London: Routledge), pp. 36–50.

Beats, J. and Barrett, P. (1996) in A. Kempe (ed.) *Drama Education and Special Needs* (Cheltenham: Stanley Thornes), pp. 130–54.

Bolton, G. (1998) *Acting in Classroom Drama* (London: Trentham Books).

Bourdieu, P. (1984) *Distinction: A Social Critique of the Judgement of Taste* (London: Routledge).

Bruner, J. (1986) *Actual Minds, Possible Worlds* (Cambridge, MA: Harvard University Press).

Cohen, B. (1969) *Educational Thought: An Introduction* (London: Macmillan).

Croner (2000) *The Head's Legal Guide* (London: Croner Publishing).

Curry, N. E. and Johnson, C. N. (1990) *Beyond Self-esteem: Developing a Genuine Sense of Human Value* (Washington, DC: National Association for the Education of Young Children).

Department of Education, Northern Ireland (1993) *Key Stage 4 Programmes of Study: Drama* (Belfast: DENI).

DES (1989) *English for Ages 5–16* (The Cox Report), paras 2.20–2.25 (London: DES).

DfEE (1997) *School Governors: A Guide to the Law* (London: DfEE).

DfEE (1998) *Initial Teacher Training National Curriculum for the Use of Information and Communications Technology in Subject Teaching* (London: HMSO).

DfEE (1999) *The National Curriculum: Citizenship* (London: HMSO).

DfEE (1999) *The National Curriculum: Promoting Skills across the National Curriculum* (London: HMSO).

DfEE (1999) *Supporting Induction for Newly Qualified Teachers: Overview*. London: HMSO.

Doyle, W. (1986) 'Classroom Organisation and Management' in M. C. Wittrock (ed.) *Handbook of Research on Teaching* (3rd edn) (New York: Macmillan), pp. 393–9.

Elsom, J. (1976) *Post-war British Theatre* (London: Routledge and Kegan Paul).

Fielding, M. (1996) 'How and Why Learning Styles Matter: Valuing Difference in Teachers and Learners' in S. Hart (ed.) *Differentiation and Equal Opportunities* (London: Routledge), pp. 81–103.

Fleming, M. (1994) *Starting Drama Teaching* (London: David Fulton).

Furlong, J., Barton, L., Miles, S., Whiting, C. and Whitty, G. (2000) *Teacher Education in Transition* (Buckingham: Open University Press).

Furlong, J., and Maynard, T. (1995) *Mentoring Student Teachers* (London: Routledge).

Gardner, P. (2000) 'The Secondary School' in J. Beck and M. Earl (eds) *Key Issues in Secondary Education* (London: Continuum), pp. 3–12.

Goodwyn, A. (1992) 'English Teachers and the Cox Models', *English and Education*, vol. 28, no. 3, pp. 4–10.

Grady, S. (2000) 'Languages of the Stage: A Critical Framework for Analysing *and* Creating Performance' in H. Nicholson (ed.) *Teaching Drama 11–18* (London: Continuum), pp. 144–59.

Hargreaves, D. (1982) *The Challenge of the Comprehensive School* (London: Routledge and Kegan Paul).

Health and Safety at Work Act 1974 in *The Law of Education 9th Edition (2000)* (London: Butterworths).

Hornbrook, D. (1985–6) 'Drama, Education and the Politics of Change', *New Theatre Quarterly*, no. 4 and no. 5.

Hornbook, D. (1998) *Education and Dramatic Art* (2nd edn) (London: Routledge).

Kempe, A. and Ashwell, M. (2000) *Progression in Secondary Drama* (London: Heinemann).

Kohn, A. (1996) *Beyond Discipline: From Compliance to Community* (Alexandria, VA: Association for Supervision and Curriculum Development).

Maclure, J. S. (1973) *Educational Documents* (London: Methuen).

Martin-Smith, A. (1996) 'British Conceptions of Drama in Education', *NADIE Journal*, vol. 20, no.1, pp. 57–76.

Maynard, T. and Furlong, J. (1993) 'Learning to teach and models of mentoring', in D. McIntyre, H. Hagger and M. Wilkin (eds) *Mentoring: Perspectives on School-based Teacher Education*. London: Kogan Page,
pp. 94–9.

McIntyre, D. (1990) 'The Oxford Internship and the Cambridge Analytical Framework: Models of Partnership in Initial Teacher Training' in M. Booth, J. Furlong and M. Wilkin (eds) *Partnership in Initial Teacher Training* (London: Cassell), pp. 78–84.

McIntyre, D. and Hagger, H. (1993) 'Teachers' Expertise and Models of Mentoring' in D. McIntyre, H. Hagger and M. Wilkin (eds) *Mentoring: Perspectives on School-Based Teacher Education* (London: Kogan Page),
pp. 90–9.

Mulhern, F. (1981) *The Moment of Scrutiny* (London: Verso).

National Committee of Inquiry into Higher Education (1997) *Report 10: Teacher Education and Training: A Study* (The Sutherland Report) (London: HMSO).

National Drama (1998) *The National Drama Secondary Drama Teacher's Handbook* (London: National Drama).

Neelands, J. (1998) *Beginning Drama 11–14* (London: David Fulton).

Nicholson, H. (1995) 'Performative Acts: Drama, Education and Gender', *NADIE Journal*, vol. 19, no. 1, pp. 27–38.

Nicholson, H. and Taylor, R. (1998) 'The Choreography of Performance' in D. Hornbrook (ed.) *On the Subject of Drama* (London: Routledge), pp. 112–28.

Porter, L. (2000) *Behaviour in Schools* (Buckingham: Open University Press).

Postman, N. and Weingartner, C. (1971) *Teaching as a Subversive Activity* (London: Penguin).

Raffan, J. and Ruthven, K. (2000) 'Monitoring, Assessment, Recording, Reporting and Accountability' in J. Beck and M. Earl (eds) *Key Issues in Secondary Education* (London: Continuum), pp. 23–35.

Ruddock, J., Day, J. and Wallace, G. (1999) 'Students' Perspectives on School Improvement' in C. Day (1999) *Developing Teachers: The Challenges of Lifelong Learning* (London: Falmer Press), pp. 16–24.

Schon, D. (1983) *The Reflective Practitioner: How Professionals Think in Action* (New York: Basic Books).

Schon, D. (1987) *Educating the Reflective Practitioner: Towards a New Design for Teaching and Learning in the Professions* (New York: Basic Books).

School Teachers' Pay and Conditions Document 1997 in *The Law of Education 9th Edition* (2000) (London: Butterworths).

Scottish Office (1992) *National Guidelines: Expressive Arts 5–14* (Edinburgh: SOEID).

Scottish Office (1998) *Guidelines for Initial Teacher Education Courses* (Edinburgh: SOEID).

Scottish Office (1999) *SOEID Guidance on the Use of Information and Communications Technology (ICT) within Courses of Initial Teacher Training* (Edinburgh: SOEID).

Scottish Office Education Department (1991) *National Guidelines: English Language 5–14* (Edinburgh: SOEID)

Secondary Heads Association (1998) *Drama Sets You Free* (Bristol: SHA Publications).

Shulman, L. S. 'Those who Understand: Knowledge Growth in Teaching'. *Educational Researcher* **15** (4), 4–14, cited in L. Tickle (2000) *Teacher Induction: The Way Ahead* (Buckingham: Open University Press), p. 42.

Slade, P. (1954) *Child Drama* (London: London University Press).

Slade, P. (1958) *An Introduction to Child Drama* (London: University of London Press).

Stoppard, T. (1967) *Rosencrantz and Guildenstern Are Dead* (London: Faber and Faber).

Taylor, P. (ed.) (1996) *Researching Drama and Arts Education* (London: Falmer Press).

Teacher Training Agency (1999) *Supporting Induction for Newly Qualified Teachers: Overview* (London: HMSO).

Tickle, L. (2000) *Teacher Induction: The Way Ahead* (Buckingham: Open University Press).

Tully, J. (1995) *Strange Multiplicity: Constitutionalism in an Age of Diversity* (Cambridge: Cambridge University Press).

Vygotsky, L. (1962) *Thought and Language* (Cambridge, MA: MIT Press).

Wagner, B. J. (1979) *Dorothy Heathcote: Drama as a Learning Medium* (London: Hutchinson).

Warner, L. and Parr, A. (2000) 'Cross Gender Drama', *Drama*, vol. 7, no. 2, pp. 35–40.

Way, B. (1967) *Development Through Drama* (London: Longman).

Williams, R. (1961) *The Long Revolution* (Harmondsworth: Penguin).

Wooding, B. (2000) 'Authoring our Identities' in H. Nicholson (ed.) *Teaching Drama 11–18* (London: Continuum), pp. 89–100.

226

Further Reading

Drama in the primary school

Ackroyd, J. (2000) *Literacy Alive!* (London: Hodder & Stoughton).

Clipson-Boyles, S. (1998) *Drama in Primary English Teaching* (London: David Fulton).

Davies, G. (1995) *The Primary Performance Handbook* (East Grinstead: Ward Lock).

DES (1990) *The Teaching and Learning of Drama* (London: HMSO).

Kempe, A. and Lockwood, M. (2000) *Drama In and Out of the Literacy Hour* (Reading: RALIC).

Kitson, N. and Spiby, I. (1995) *Primary Drama Handbook* (London: Watts Books).

Kitson, N., and Spiby, I. (1997) *Drama 7–11* (London: Routledge).

QCA (1999) *Teaching Speaking and Listening in Key Stages 1 and 2* (London: QCA).

Winston, J. and Tandy, M. (2nd edn) *Beginning Drama 4–11* (London: David Fulton).

Woolland, B. (1993) *The Teaching of Drama in the Primary School* (Harlow: Longmans)

Practical secondary handbooks

Bennathan, J. (2000) *Developing Drama Skills 11–14* (Oxford: Heinemann).

Boal, A. (1992) *Games for Actors and Non-actors* (London: Routledge).

Cooper, S. and Mackey, S. (2000) *Theatre Studies* (2nd edn) (Cheltenham: Stanley Thornes).

Gibson, R. (1998) *Teaching Shakespeare* (Cambridge: CUP).

Kempe, A. (1997) *The GCSE Drama Coursebook* (2nd edn) (Cheltenham: Stanley Thornes).

Kempe, A. and Warner, L. (1997) *Starting with Scripts* (Cheltenham: Stanley Thornes).

Lambert, A. and O'Neill, C. (1982) *Drama Structures* (London: Hutchinson).

Mackey, S. (ed.) (1997) *Practical Theatre* (Cheltenham: Stanley Thornes).

O'Toole, J. and Haseman, B. (1986) *Dramawise* (Oxford: Heinemann).

Theory and practice of drama education

Arts Council of Great Britain (1992) *Drama in Schools* (London: ACGB).

Bolton, G. (1992) *New Perspective on Classroom Drama* (Hemel Hempstead: Simon & Schuster).

Bolton, G. (1998) *Acting in Classroom Drama* (Stoke on Trent: Trentham Books).

Burgess, R. and Gaudry, P. (1985) *Time for Drama* (Buckingham: OUP).

Fleming, M. (1994) *Starting Drama Teaching* (London: David Fulton).

Fleming, M. (1997) *The Art of Drama Teaching* (London: David Fulton).

Hornbrook, D. (1990) *Education in Drama* (London: Falmer Press).

Hornbrook, D. (1997) *Education and Dramatic Art* (2nd edn) (London: Routledge).

Hornbrook, D. (ed.) (1998) *On the Subject of Drama* (London: Routledge).

Kempe, A. and Ashwell, M. (2000) *Progression in Secondary Drama* (Oxford: Heinemann).

Kempe, A. (ed.) (1996) *Drama Education and Special Needs* (Cheltenham: Stanley Thornes).

Leach, S. (1992) *Shakespeare in the Classroom* (Buckingham: OUP).

Neelands, J. (1998) *Beginning Drama 11–14* (London: David Fulton).

Nicholson, H. (ed.) (2000) *Teaching Drama 11–18* (London: Continuum).

OFSTED (1998) *The Arts Inspected* (Oxford: Heinemann).

O'Neill, C. (1995) *Drama Worlds* (Portsmouth, NH: Heinemann).

O'Toole, J. (1992) *The Process of Drama* (London: Routledge).

Owens, A. and Barber, K. (1997) *Dramaworks* (Carlisle: Carel Press).

QCA (2000) *Language for Learning in Key Stage 3* (London: QCA).

Reynolds, P. (1991) *Teaching Shakespeare* (Buckingham: OUP).

Somers, J. (1994) *Drama in the Curriculum* (London: Cassell).

Taylor, P. (1996) *Researching Drama and Arts Education* (London: Falmer Press).

Winston, J. (1998) *Drama, Narrative and Moral Education* (London: Falmer Press).

Teacher education

Beck, J. and Earl, M. (2000) *Key Issues in Secondary Education* (London: Cassell).

Brook, V. and Sikes, P. (1997) *The Good Mentor Guide* (Buckingham: OUP).

Cooper, P. and McIntyre, D. (1996) *Effective Teaching and Learning* (Buckingham: OUP).

Day, C. (1999) *Developing Teachers* (London: Falmer Press).

Fish, D. (1995) *Quality Mentoring for Student Teachers* (London: David Fulton).

Furlong, J. Barton, L. Miles, S. Whiting, C. and Whitty, G. (2000) *Teacher Education in Transition* (Buckingham: OUP).

Goodwyn, A. (1997) *Developing English Teachers* (Buckingham: OUP).

Hagger, H. Burn, K. and McIntyre, D. (1993) *The School Mentor Handbook: Essential Skills and Strategies for Working with Student Teachers* (London: Kogan Page).

Hargreaves, D. H. (1982) *The Challenge for the Comprehensive School* (London: Routledge).

Porter, L. (2000) *Behaviour in Schools* (Buckingham: OUP).

Tickle, L. (2000) *Teacher Induction: The Way Ahead* (Buckingham: OUP).

Tomlinson, P. (1995) *Understanding Mentoring* (Buckingham: OUP).

Index

230